POPE PIUS XII LIB., ST. JOSEPH COLLEGE

3 2528 01312 0581

Y0-EEA-836

9780876304051

Child Abuse
and Neglect:
What Happens Eventually?

Child Abuse and Neglect:
What Happens Eventually?

By

Kim Oates, M.D.

*Douglas Burrows Professor of Pediatrics and Child Health,
The University of Sydney; Chairman, Division of Medicine,
The Children's Hospital, Camperdown, Australia*

BRUNNER/MAZEL Publishers • New York

Library of Congress Cataloging-in-Publication Data

Oates, Kim.
　　Child abuse and neglect.

　　Includes bibliographies and index.
　　1. Child abuse—Longitudinal studies.　2. Abused
children—Longitudinal studies.　3. Failure to thrive
syndrome—Longitudinal studies.　I. Title.
[DNLM: 1. Child Abuse.　WA 320 O11c]
RC569.5.C55O38　　1985　　616.85′82　　85-19023
ISBN 0-87630-405-6

Copyright © 1986 by Kim Oates

Published by
BRUNNER/MAZEL, INC.
19 Union Square
New York, New York 10003

All rights reserved. No part of this book may be reproduced by any process whatsoever
without the written permission of the copyright owner.

MANUFACTURED IN THE UNITED STATES OF AMERICA

To Sarah, Peter, Matthew, and Robyn

Foreword

In the 23 years since child abuse and neglect has become a major focus of medical and social concern, a vast literature has accumulated describing, from almost every point of view, the abuse itself and its short-term effects. Yet, there have been printed remarkably few longitudinal studies, efforts to learn in detail and with objective evidence what actually happens over time to children who have been subjected to deviant or inadequate parenting. We know there are rare reservoirs of such knowledge; a few pioneers like Dr. Brandt Steele have had personal experience of the reactions of those young, abused children of 23 years ago who have since become parents. But few centers of study in this field have yet been financially able to plan a longitudinal study, using prospective methods and a moderately stable population that could give us adequate information about which families are especially vulnerable, how families and individuals respond to different treatment modes, and which forms of prevention and treatment are effective over a full generation.

Dr. Kim Oates' book, *Child Abuse and Neglect: What Happens Eventually*, represents a most important step in making such objective information available. It demonstrates what most of those working with dysfunctional families whose children are abused or neglected suspect—that the effects of abuse and neglect outlive the immediate traumatic situation and may well handicap the child throughout his or her life. The persistence of difficulty (especially in certain cognitive deficits), lack of trust and low self-esteem, and continuing behavior problems seem to represent an unbroken line of pathological or inadequate development. Prospective studies might eliminate the possibility that these difficulties were present before abuse occurred. If the studies involved adequate serial evaluations of parent-child interactions, they might show that the effects of inadequate parenting were already demonstrable in a child well endowed at birth before

viii CHILD ABUSE AND NEGLECT

the overt signs of abuse and neglect were clear enough to warrant intervention.

Child Abuse and Neglect: What Happens Eventually is much more than the meticulous description and discussion of the author's own research and clinical experience. It includes a careful analytic review of the pertinent literature concerning physical abuse and failure to thrive, which endows Dr. Oates' conclusions and recommendations for future work with considerable authority.

Dr. Oates' demonstration of the persistence of symptoms unchanged during the years emphasizes the need for treatment for the abused or neglected children and their families that will go beyond the immediate medical attention. Treatment is needed for the children to improve their development and relationship difficulties and for the parents to help them provide for the children's future needs.

A very distressing aspect of working with abused and neglected children and their families is the tendency for all nations to turn away from the full significance of this problem and to provide only a very small portion of the legislation and financial resources needed to address adequately these children's needs. If one believes that any society's cultural values and the health and welfare of the next generation are in large degree entrusted to the individual family group that nurtures the child, it would seem not only logical, but necessary, to support and safeguard that family. Rather than allowing the family to become a mode of transmission of society's ills from one generation to the next, we need to help that family become the means of ensuring physical and mental health for each generation.

Dr. Oates' study and others like it are necessary to provide the hard facts upon which future programs must depend. To quote one of his conclusions, "Innovative programs need to be tried, but those having new ideas will have to have the courage to evaluate them" in order to prove their effectiveness. We need to provide our governments with facts about the protection of our children that are clear, directive, compelling—enough to establish their priority.

Ruth S. Kempe, M.D.
The C. Henry Kempe National Center
for the Prevention and Treatment of
Child Abuse and Neglect
Denver, Colorado

Preface

Child physical abuse and nonorganic failure to thrive are outward signs of problems within a family. That the phenomenon is repeated from one generation to the next is well-known. This suggests that the children who have been exposed to these conditions need considerable help so that they can develop into more effective parents than their own parents have been and thus prevent the cycle from continuing.

This book is divided into two main parts. The first part critically reviews the literature on abused children and those who have suffered from nonorganic failure to thrive. Particular emphasis in this section is placed on studies that have used comparison groups and on studies that have looked at the development of these children. The second part of the book gives information about the outcome of a group of children with nonorganic failure to thrive admitted to hospital over 12 years previously and a group of physically abused children first seen more than five years ago. Special attention is paid to the similarities and differences between the parents and children in these two related, but somewhat different conditions. The outcome in many of these children is not good, emphasizing the need for a long-term, child-oriented commitment to these cases. While the seriousness and extent of sexual abuse in the community are recognized, that problem is not discussed in this book as none of the original group of children studied was known to have been sexually abused.

A note should be made about the use of the pronouns "she" and "he." Where the text refers to children, the convention of using the pronoun "he" in a general sense has been followed. In the text there is also considerable mention of mothers, but little mention of fathers.

This is not to suggest in any way that only mothers are responsible for child abuse and neglect. These are family problems, and the father, either as perpetrator or contributor to a situation that leads to abuse and neglect, is also involved. However, there is a paucity of research data available on the fathers, so much of the literature quoted refers to mothers.

I am grateful to a number of people who have shown considerable interest and support over the years. To John Yu, General Superintendent of The Children's Hospital, Camperdown, who first suggested I look at the problem of nonorganic failure to thrive 15 years ago, I am particularly grateful. The section of the book describing the study of abused and neglected children would not have been possible without the enthusiasm and hard work of Douglas Forrest, Research Assistant, who helped to trace and locate the families as well as assist in the analysis of the data, and of Anthony Peacock, who performed the psychological tests. Helen Barrett, whose ordinary secretarial duties are more than most mortals can cope with and who patiently typed the text, deserves special thanks.

I am indebted to the publishers of the following journals for permission to reproduce some tables and data in this book: *Archives of Diseases in Childhood,* 59: 147–150 1984; *American Journal of Diseases of Children,* 138: 764–766 1984; *Developmental Medicine and Child Neurology,* 26: 649–656 1984; *Pediatrics,* 75: 36–40 1985; *Child Abuse and Neglect,* 8: 439–445 1984; *Clinical Pediatrics,* 24: 9–13 1985; and *Australian Paediatric Journal,* 2: 185–186 1984.

While the outlook for many abused children is not good, it is important to remember that a proportion do have positive outcomes. This suggests that, as well as focusing more on long-term programs with a commitment to help these children develop skills to cope more effectively, some future research should also be directed to study those factors that have led to some children doing well in spite of adverse circumstances.

September 1985

Kim Oates
The Children's Hospital
Camperdown, Sydney
Australia

Contents

Foreword by Dr. Ruth Kempe vii

Preface ix

1. Growth Failure and Emotional Deprivation 3

2. Family Studies in Nonorganic Failure to Thrive 20

3. Treatment and Outcome in Nonorganic Failure to Thrive ... 31

4. The Problem of Child Abuse 41

5. The Causes of Child Abuse 68

6. Prediction, Prevention, and Treatment of Child Abuse 89

7. The Development of Abused Children 99

8. A Study of Children Following Child Abuse and
   Nonorganic Failure to Thrive 106

9. Interviews with Parents and Children 127

10. Psychological Testing of Parents and Children Following
    Child Abuse and Nonorganic Failure to Thrive 158

11. Discussion and Implications of Findings 179

Index 203

List of Figures

CHAPTER 8

Figure 8.1   Research design 108

Figure 8.2   Comparison of reviewed abused children with those lost to follow-up 117

Figure 8.3   Comparison of reviewed failure-to-thrive children with those lost to follow-up 118

CHAPTER 9

Figure 9.1   Major diagnostic findings in 56 abused children previously reviewed and in 39 of those children seen in the present review 128

Figure 9.2   Comparison of failure-to-thrive families found and lost to follow-up 130

Figure 9.3   Problems in abuse and failure-to-thrive families 135

Figure 9.4   Comparison of abuse and failure-to-thrive groups on mothers' experiences during pregnancy, birth, and the child's first five years 142

Figure 9.5   Parents' realistic job expectations and parent ambitions for their children as shown by social class of occupation chosen 145

Figure 9.6   Height age and weight age of children who failed to thrive 152

xiv CHILD ABUSE AND NEGLECT

CHAPTER 10

Figure 10.1   Mean sten scores and standard deviations for six abuse-group and six comparison fathers on 16PF test 161

Figure 10.2   Results of Rutter Children's Behavior Questionnaire completed by teachers of abused and comparison children 174

Figure 10.3   Results of Rutter Children's Behavior Questionnaire completed by mothers of abused and comparison children 175

Figure 10.4   Results of Rutter Children's Behavior Questionnaire completed by teachers and mothers of children who failed to thrive 176

Child Abuse
and Neglect:
What Happens Eventually?

1

Growth Failure and Emotional Deprivation

WHAT IS NONORGANIC FAILURE TO THRIVE?

Failure to thrive is not a medical diagnosis. It is a descriptive term that is used to describe an infant who shows a decline from a previously established growth pattern. The term is often reserved for infants whose failure to gain weight, when plotted on standard growth charts, places them below the third percentile for age. Linear growth may also be affected, although usually to a lesser extent, and there may be evidence of delay in psychomotor development. When investigation of these children fails to reveal an organic cause for the growth disorder and when the history is suggestive of emotional or nutritional deprivation, or both, the condition is termed nonorganic failure to thrive. The implication is that the child's social, emotional, or nutritional environment is disturbed to the point where it interferes with normal growth and development.

There is no generally accepted definition of nonorganic failure to thrive. This is because many regard it as a diagnosis of exclusion and because there is not a generally accepted agreement about its actual cause. Some authors, in review articles of nonorganic failure to thrive, have chosen not to define the condition at all (1, 2). One of the earliest and most concise definitions of nonorganic failure to thrive was given by Togut and colleagues in 1969: "The presence of growth

3

4 CHILD ABUSE AND NEGLECT

retardation, with or without associated developmental deficit and the absence of organic disorders sufficient to account for these deviations" (3, p. 601). English (4) defined nonorganic failure to thrive as a condition in which the child's social or emotional environment is disturbed to the point where it interferes with normal growth and development. This definition emphasizes the psychosocial rather than the nutritional aspect. Ruth Kempe from Denver (5) defines failure to thrive as describing a child who has at some time during the first three years of life suffered a marked retardation or cessation of growth. She adds the important point that undoubtedly the most important cause is a lack of nurturing. A more suitable definition may be where growth progress fails to keep up with a previously established growth pattern and which responds to a combination of providing an adequate caloric intake as well as providing for the child's emotional needs (6). While acknowledging the emotional deprivation commonly associated with the condition, this definition also emphasizes the need for an adequate caloric intake.

The American Psychiatric Association has designated nonorganic failure to thrive as a reactive attachment disorder of infancy so as to emphasize the maternal-infant bonding aspect of the disorder. The Association's diagnostic criteria for the disorder include weight loss or failure to gain appropriate amounts of weight for age unexplainable by any physical disorder, the diagnosis being confirmed if the clinical picture is reversed shortly after the institution of adequate caretaking (7).

HISTORICAL ASPECTS

Growth failure was first noted to be associated with emotional deprivation in children living in institutions. Death rates in these institutions were high. The severity of this problem was brought to the attention of pediatricians by Henry Chapin, who in 1915 reported on 11 infant asylums (as institutions for the care of infants were then called) in different centers in the United States. The death rate in children under two years of age living in these homes was 42% (8). Chapin called the problem "the cachexia of hospitalization." In his enlightened report he postulated that this problem resulted from a

GROWTH FAILURE AND EMOTIONAL DEPRIVATION

combination of a poor physical environment coupled with a lack of individual care and nurturing in the institution (9).

Chapin was interested in alternative methods of caring for foundling infants. He contrasted the mortality in institutions with the results of the Speedwell Society. This organization took infants from institutions and fostered them with carefully selected private families where the foster mother would be instructed in feeding and caring for the baby. Chapin reported that the mortality rate among these infants was much lower than those kept in institutions, stating that "a majority of them can be saved if a fairly good individual environment can be secured and careful oversight of the feeding maintained" (10, p. 492).

Probably Chapin's most important observation, which attracted little attention, was that in some cases the condition of these infants was due to a problem in parenting. He was even aware that fathers played an important role in this area: "It may be said that the fault really lies in deficient and inefficient fathers and mothers and much of the trouble is undoubtedly here" (10, p. 491).

Chapin's concern for infants in institutions did not attract a great deal of attention. It was not until 1945 that interest in this problem was rekindled with the observations of Spitz, who reported anaclitic depression, malnutrition, and growth failure in infants under one year of age kept in foundling homes (11). Spitz did not believe that nutritional deprivation was an important factor but suggested that lack of emotional stimulation was the main reason for the depression and growth failure.

The characteristic behavior of hospitalized infants who were emotionally deprived was graphically described by Bakwin in 1949.

> The hospitalized infant is thin and pale, but the pallor is not always associated with a reduction in hemoglobin. The facial expression is unhappy and gives an impression of misery. Muscle tone is poor and it is possible to extend the legs fully at the knees, contrasting in this way with normal young infants. There is no alteration in deep reflexes. The infant shows no interest in his environment, lying quietly in bed, rarely crying and moving very little. Such movements as he makes are slow and deliber-

ate, unlike the quick movements one expects at this age. (12, pp. 512–513)

Bakwin noted the important role of the mother in preventing this disorder, recommending that it was vital for the mother to stay with her baby a much as possible whenever the baby was due for a prolonged period of hospitalization. While the dangers to infants of being in institutions and hospitals were starting to be recognized, Coleman and Provence, in an important observation in 1957, showed that the clinical syndrome of growth failure secondary to emotional deprivation could also occur in children living in their own homes (13). In Melbourne, Williams (14) was among the first to recognize that inadequate care in the family and inadequate nutrition were major factors in growth failure in infancy. He noted that adverse social circumstances and emotional deprivation were often found in these families and that at times differences in the temperament of the infant could add to the problem. He emphasized the importance of the history, including a history of the pregnancy and labor, and of observing the interaction between the mother and her infant. He also noted that only simple laboratory tests were necessary in most cases. The important influence of parental behavior on the child's growth now came to be more widely appreciated with reports by Elmer (15) and Patton and Gardner (16) of series of children with failure to thrive that emphasized the role of the mother.

INCIDENCE

The proportion of cases of failure to thrive that are regarded as nonorganic varies in different series of children. Shaheen's group (17) reviewed the records of 5,488 children admitted to the Philadelphia Children's Hospital over a 12-month period in 1963–64. Two hundred and eighty-seven, or 5%, of these children were below the third percentile for weight on admission. No organic cause could be found for the growth failure in 44 of these children—an incidence of 15%. This was the second largest group among the various diseases or bodily systems found responsible for growth failure. The authors suggested that the size of this nonorganic group may have been an

GROWTH FAILURE AND EMOTIONAL DEPRIVATION

underestimate. Glaser and colleagues (18), reporting from the Children's Hospital Medical Center (Boston) in 1968, found that 50 out of 153 cases of failure to thrive (35%) were nonorganic, while Hannaway (19) reported that of 100 cases of failure to thrive seen at the Boston Floating Hospital, 51 were nonorganic. English (4) reviewed the case notes of 9,605 children admitted to the New York Hospital and found that of 91 children admitted with failure to thrive, 29 (an incidence of 32%) were nonorganic. A review of 171 cases of failure to thrive admitted to the Colorado General Hospital between June 1976 and December 1978 found that 30% were considered nonorganic, while in another 28% the condition was thought to be due to a combination of organic and nonorganic factors (5). In a review of 185 children with failure to thrive, Sills found 58% had a nonorganic cause, with the cause unknown in a further 24% (20).

There are difficulties with the interpretation of these incidence figures. Not all of the studies have defined failure to thrive, and where definitions have been made they are not consistent across the various studies. The diagnosis of failure to thrive may have been made because of positive evidence of emotional or nutritional deprivation or simply because of failure to find an adequate organic cause. Whether a child's admission to hospital with a growth problem is labeled failure to thrive may depend on the clinical acumen of the pediatrician who recommends the child for admission and on the way the diagnosis is eventually coded in the medical record. If the cause for the child's poor weight gain is obvious, then the child is likely to be admitted to hospital with a definitive diagnosis, whereas the general term of failure to thrive is likely to be used initially if a variety of investigations are needed to elucidate the problem.

CLINICAL FEATURES

There is no test or clinical feature that reliably distinguishes infants with nonorganic failure to thrive from those who are eventually found to have an underlying organic cause. One approach is to make the diagnosis only after exhaustively excluding all possible causes for the child's growth failure. However, because emotional or environmental disorders are such a common cause of failure to thrive (5,

18–20), rather than do a large amount of investigations in a shotgun manner to search for an obscure diagnosis, the physician should consider nonorganic causes in parallel with his search for a hidden organic cause.

The history is the single most important part of the assessment. It is not uncommon for the mother to complain that the child is a fussy eater, that he is lethargic and falls asleep during meals, and that he vomits small amounts. Further history often reveals a lack of any specific pointer to an organic cause but may reveal that the mother is young and inexperienced, that there is little emotional support within the family, and that there is poverty and a chaotic family lifestyle. In taking the developmental history, one often finds that the mother has little awareness of the child's abilities and, indeed, little awareness that there is a problem (21).

Physical examination shows few signs apart from the evidence of growth failure. In addition to loss of fat, muscle wasting is common and is best noted in the large muscle groups. The gluteal muscles, because of their large size, are easy to detect as being wasted, with loose folds of skin being visible at the buttocks. This is best demonstrated when the legs are extended at the hip. Muscle wasting is also obvious at the inner aspect of the thighs where loose skin folds may be seen. Children with advanced failure to thrive may look at first sight as if they have enlarged heads because their other bodily proportions are small in relation to their head size. Developmental assessment shows that the children are often delayed in all milestones: social ability and gross and fine motor functions, as well as language development. McCarthy noted that the children often have cold hands and feet and that they may be indiscriminate in seeking affection (22). Others have noted that the behavior of these infants may give a clue to the diagnosis. Leonard, Rhymes, and Solnit reported that some infants with nonorganic failure to thrive, particularly the younger ones, show "watchfulness, minimal smiling, decreased vocalization and lack of cuddliness" (23, p. 603). Bullard and co-workers commented on the absence of physical findings but noted the presence of apprehensive, apathetic, and withdrawn behavior, as well as the presence of delays in fine and gross motor development (24). Five of the 50 children reviewed by these authors had healed or

GROWTH FAILURE AND EMOTIONAL DEPRIVATION

healing fractures discovered on X ray and 85% had retarded bone age. The high incidence of healed or healing fractures in these children, although not commented upon by Bullard's group, is evidence of the now established link between some cases of nonorganic failure to thrive and child abuse (25, 26).

Krieger and Sargent (27) reported that 10 of 19 infants suffering from growth failure and sensory deprivation showed an abnormal persistence of infantile posture when they were supine, being held, or standing. These infants held the elbow joint flexed 90 degrees or more, the humerus abducted and rotated outward, and the hands pronated and positioned at a variable distance from the side of the head. They suggested that this posture may have diagnostic significance in infants over five months of age. When these infants are lifted by placing the hands underneath the armpits to hold them in the standing position, they are often reluctant to bear weight on their legs; instead, they tend to flex their legs at the knees and hips. This posture is even found between six and nine months of age when infants normally enjoy being held in the standing position, bear most of their weight, and often bounce joyfully on their extended legs.

In an attempt to produce a tool that would assist in the diagnosis of nonorganic failure to thrive, Rosenn and co-workers developed a one-to-seven-point approach-withdrawal scale to quantify social interaction between examiner and infant (28). They compared three matched groups of infants aged between six and 16 months. One group of 10 infants had organic failure to thrive; another group of eight had nonorganic failure to thrive; and the third group of seven had normal growth and were in hospital for other reasons. Although the sample size was small, this was a well-defined study, with the researchers who were chosen to evaluate the infants' behavior not being aware of which group the infants belonged to. It was found that the scale regularly distinguished infants with nonorganic failure to thrive from those with organic disease and also from healthy infants. The infants with nonorganic failure to thrive preferred distant social encounters and inanimate objects, while infants with organic failure to thrive and the medically ill group responded to close, personal interaction such as touching and holding. Whether these findings can be replicated by others and whether the scale can be a useful diagnostic tool remain to be seen. It confirms the clinical impression that many infants with nonorganic failure to thrive are "vigilant towards people at a distance and increasingly distressed the closer someone comes" (28, p. 703) and that they dislike being touched and held.

The infant's growth pattern may help in reaching the diagnosis, although the features are not diagnostic. Previous weights, if available, should be plotted to show the curve of the child's growth pattern. The infant's weight is the parameter that deviates most from normal. If linear growth is also affected, this suggests that the condition has been present for some time. It is unusual for head circumference to be affected except in longstanding cases. The usual pattern to be found when percentiles are plotted is for the head circumference to be normal and for the weight to be reduced out of proportion to any reduction there may be in length. Extensive and expensive laboratory investigations to exclude any possible organic cause are likely to distract from the main cause of the problem within the family and to delay recovery.

Several authors have listed the basic investigations required to exclude the more common organic conditions and have emphasized that a careful history from the parents and observation of the infant are likely to assist in reaching a diagnosis of nonorganic failure to thrive (4, 29–31). Sills studied the degree of usefulness of laboratory investigations in nonorganic failure to thrive (20). He reviewed 185 children admitted to hospital with failure to thrive and found that a total of 2,067 laboratory tests had been performed on these children. Only 36 of these tests (1.4%) were of positive diagnostic assistance. No laboratory or radiological study was of positive value in the absence of a specific indication from history and physical examination that the investigation should be performed. Eighteen percent of the children in this group had proven organic causes for the growth failure and in every instance the specific diagnosis was strongly suggested by the history and physical examination, which then led to confirmatory laboratory investigations.

Children with nonorganic failure to thrive often make a rapid weight gain when admitted to hospital. Although this suggests a nonorganic cause, it has been shown that some infants do not make this

GROWTH FAILURE AND EMOTIONAL DEPRIVATION

rapid weight gain until the second or third week of hospital...
(32). In Glaser's series (18), slightly more than one-third of infants
with nonorganic failure to thrive actually lost weight during hospitalization. Thus, the diagnosis of nonorganic failure to thrive is not one
arrived at merely by the exclusion of organic disease. It is a clinical
diagnosis, based on the history (particularly the social history), physical features, behavior, and development of the child.

DEPRIVATION DWARFISM

Although deprivation dwarfism and nonorganic failure to thrive
are often discussed together, children with deprivation dwarfism
seem to constitute a distinct subgroup. Whereas in failure to thrive it
is the marked weight loss that is the striking feature, in deprivation
dwarfism it is the short stature that first brings the child to attention.
McCarthy (33) noted that although these children are dwarfed, they
do not present a picture of malnutrition.

Table 1 summarizes seven studies of deprivation dwarfism. Although in some of the reported cases the children were underweight
for their height, this was not a striking feature in any of the cases.
The reported ages of children with deprivation dwarfism have ranged
from two to 15 years. This is quite a different range from that seen in
nonorganic failure to thrive where the condition usually presents in
children under two years. The behavior of children with deprivation
dwarfism is also quite different. They are reported to steal and hoard
food, to gorge themselves, to eat large amounts of unusual foods,
such as condiments, and to eat from garbage cans (34, 35).

The first evidence that growth hormone abnormality may be responsible for the short stature found in these children came from
Talbot and co-workers in 1947 (36). These researchers studied 28
children with growth failure and found that the majority of these
children had an inadequate caloric intake and that there were also
psychosocial disturbances present in many of the families. They postulated that the children may be secreting abnormally low amounts
of pituitary growth hormone and suggested that relative hypopituitarism might be a method of adapting to malnutrition. Supportive evi-

Table 1

Documented Characteristics of
Deprivation Dwarfism

Author	Year	Number of Cases	Age (years)	Growth Hormone			Growth Improves as Environment Improves	Weight in Relation to Height Growth Hormone
				Measured	Low	Responds to Improved Environment		
Silver & Finkelstein (44)	1967	5	4–16	no			yes	low
Powell et al. (34, 37)	1967	13	3.3–11.5	yes	6 out of 8	6 out of 6	yes	"thin, not malnourished"
Reinhardt & Drash (45)	1969	1	6	no			yes	low
Apley et al. (38)	1971	9	2–15	yes	1 out of 9	—	—	"weight corresponded to height"
Krieger & Mellinger (43)	1971	7	3.4–10.1	yes	5 out of 7	3 out of 5	yes	low
Castells et al. (39)	1971	1	15	yes	yes	no	no	normal
Hopwood & Becker (35)	1975	35	2–14	yes	14 out of 28	—	yes	half "mildly underweight for height"

GROWTH FAILURE AND EMOTIONAL DEPRIVATION

dence for this hypothesis came in 1967 when Powell's group from the Johns Hopkins Hospital described 13 children with emotional deprivation and growth retardation, six of whom showed laboratory evidence of hypopituitarism (34, 37). When these children were removed from their emotionally disturbed environments, they grew rapidly. Concomitant with this, release of growth hormone returned to normal. These authors postulated that emotional deprivation may affect the hypothalamic-pituitary axis to inhibit growth hormone secretion. However, other studies have not been able to regularly replicate these results. Growth hormone seems to be affected in some infants with deprivation dwarfism but not in others. Apley and colleagues (38) reported nine cases of dwarfism where psychosocial factors were implicated, noting that growth hormone levels were normal in eight of these children. Hopwood and Becker (35) showed a decrease in pituitary function in 14 of 28 children who had a diagnosis of deprivation dwarfism. In most of these children there was catching up when the environment improved; however, three of the older children were thought to have developed permanent hypopituitarism. This inability to revert to normal pituitary function is of concern and has been confirmed by Castells (39), who reported a case of hypopituitarism thought to be secondary to maternal deprivation but which was not corrected after the child was placed in a satisfactory environment. It should be noted that there are some methodological difficulties in comparing these studies, as during the nine years encompassed by these reports of pituitary function, growth hormone assay techniques have improved greatly in terms of increased specificity.

The reason for low levels of growth hormone is not clear. (Harris (40) has suggested the following mechanisms:

1) The growth hormone inhibiting factor (somatostatin) may be present in excess, the growth hormone deficiency being secondary to a large amount of inhibitory factor.
2) The problem may be one of control of the release of growth hormone rather than one of production.
3) These children, who have been reported to have sleep distur-

14 CHILD ABUSE AND NEGLECT

bances, may spend a decreased amount of time in those sleep stages during which growth hormone is released.

All of these suggestions are speculative. In particular the third explanation begs the question why so many other children with sleep disturbances have normal growth patterns if sleep disturbance interferes with growth.

It is also possible that endocrine factors other than growth hormone are involved and that somatomedins, the growth hormone-dependent substances that stimulate growth tissue may also directly play a part. Somatomedins have not been measured in children with deprivation dwarfism but a deficiency in somatomedins may explain reported cases in growth failure secondary to emotional deprivation that failed to respond to growth hormone treatment (41, 42). It may also explain the work of Krieger and Mellinger (43) who demonstrated that some children with growth failure and deprivation dwarfism had increased growth hormone levels.

The concept of functional pituitary insufficiency may only be of academic interest, as it is clear from studies of these children that when the environment improves, there is usually an improvement in growth and development (34, 35, 37, 43, 44, 45). However, whether it is due to an improvement in the emotional environment or an improvement in caloric intake is controversial.

DEPRIVATION OF CALORIES OR AFFECTION?

There are two schools of thought to explain the growth pattern in failure to thrive. One school suggests that the problem is mainly due to psychological factors, particularly maternal deprivation, and that the children fail to grow despite an adequate caloric intake. The other school of thought suggests that the major cause of growth failure is a lack of calories.

In Spitz's report on growth failure and deprivation (11), it was claimed that the child failed to grow "despite food." However, an analysis of the amount of food actually consumed by these children was not carried out. Spitz inferred that given sufficient emotional stimulation, these children would grow. What is usually not pointed

GROWTH FAILURE AND EMOTIONAL DEPRIVATION

out when this work is discussed is that in Spitz's study of 123 infants separated from their mothers between six and eight months of age, only 19 of these infants experienced severe reactions and growth disturbance following the separation (46).

The concept of emotional deprivation being a major factor was strengthened by a report from Elsie Widowson (47) in 1951. She studied the growth of children in two orphanages in postwar Germany in 1948. The children in one orphanage had a harsh and unsympathetic house mother. These children did not grow as rapidly as those in the other nearby orphanage who had a more caring house mother, even though the official food rations received by children in both orphanages were identical. There was one group of children living with the harsh house mother who did make rapid gains in height and weight. It was found that these children were favorites of the house mother and regularly received praise. It was not possible to estimate the amount of food actually eaten by the children in these orphanages and it may be that the children in the care of the harsh house mother actually ate less because of the unhappiness of their situation, while her favorites may have been given extra tidbits. The children in this study had an average age of eight years eight months. This is an age when maternal deprivation would be expected to have far less effect than it would have in infants.

The importance of undereating in nonorganic failure to thrive was demonstrated in a well-designed study by Whitten and co-workers in 1969 (48). These researchers investigated 13 infants with nonorganic failure to thrive who were between three and 24 months of age. They simulated inadequate mothering by keeping the children for two weeks in a windowless room in hospital. During this two-week period the children received minimal handling and attention but were offered a generous diet. Despite the emotional and sensory deprivation, all but two of these children had an accelerated weight gain when provided with a generous food intake. Six of these infants were then subjected to a high level of mothering and sensory stimulation in the form of fondling, social contact, and physical handling for a further two weeks. During this period of high stimulation they were offered the same quantity of calories as when they had been understimulated in hospital. These infants showed a similar weight gain when highly stimulated to that when understimulated, suggesting that the weight gains were not dependent upon the level of stimulation or mothering. The authors then investigated three other infants who had nonorganic failure to thrive, seeing them in their own homes. Adequate calories were supplied by a daily visitor who brought the children food and observed it being eaten. These infants had an accelerated weight gain during this experimental period. The mothers admitted that the infants ate more food during this time even though the diets had been duplicates of what the mothers claimed they had fed to their infants. The authors accumulated evidence that the dietary histories that the mothers had given were grossly inaccurate. As a result of these studies it was argued that if children are given enough food, they will grow and that the problem of growth failure in maternal deprivation is due to inadequate caloric intake rather than to some psychological cause. It would be difficult to draw sweeping generalizations from this study because of the relatively short two-week periods of observation used and it would certainly be impossible, for ethical reasons, for the study to be repeated.

Whitten et al.'s study was criticized by Thompson and Blizzard (49) on the grounds that endocrine function was not studied, that the children were very underweight in relation to their height, and that Whitten's group was made up of children under two years of age. What Thompson and Blizzard did not appreciate was that Whitten was not studying the smaller, distinct subgroup of deprivation dwarfism but had concentrated his attention on the much larger group of younger children who failed to thrive without organic cause and whose weight loss was the major clinical sign.

Rutter, in two thoughtful reviews of the literature on maternal deprivation (50, 51) has noted that the earlier concept of maternal deprivation is far too simple and that factors within the child and outside the family, as well as the relationships that the child is able to develop with other people, are all important for the child's growth and emotional development. Rutter also makes the important point that for some reason certain children are still able to do well despite deprivation and disadvantage. Certainly, nonorganic failure to thrive is not due solely to a lack of calories or of stimulation. It is likely that both of these factors are involved in varying combinations and that

GROWTH FAILURE AND EMOTIONAL DEPRIVATION

other factors, such as characteristics of the parents, characteristics of the child, and interactions between the parents and child, are also involved.

REFERENCES

1. Goldbloom, R.B. (1982). Failure to thrive. *Pediatric Clinics of North America, 29,* 151–166.
2. Berwick, D.M. (1980). Non-organic failure to thrive. *Pediatrics in Review, 1,* 265–270.
3. Togut, M.R., Allen, J.E., & Lelchuck, L. (1969). A psychological exploration of the non-organic failure to thrive syndrome. *Developmental Medicine and Child Neurology, 11,* 601–607.
4. English, P.C. (1978). Failure to thrive without organic reason. *Pediatric Annals, 7,* 774–781.
5. Kempe, R.S., Cutler, C., & Dean, J. (1980). The infant with failure to thrive. In C.H. Kempe, & R.E. Helfer, (Eds.), *The battered child* (3rd ed.) Chicago: The University of Chicago Press.
6. Oates, R.K. (1984). Nonorganic failure to thrive. *Australian Paediatric Journal, 20,* 95–100.
7. American Psychiatric Association. (1980). *Diagnostic and statistical manual of mental disorders* (3rd ed.). Washington, DC: Author.
8. Chapin, H.D. (1915), A plea for accurate statistics in infants' institutions. *Archives of Pediatrics, 32,* 724–726.
9. Chapin, H.D. (1915). Are institutions for infants necessary? *Journal of the American Medical Association, 64,* 1–3.
10. Chapin, H.D. (1908). A plan of dealing with atrophic infants and children. *Archives of Pediatrics. 25,* 491–496.
11. Spitz, R. (1945). Hospitalism, an inquiry into the genesis of psychiatric conditions in early childhood. *Psychoanalytic Study of the Child, 1,* 53–74.
12. Bakwin, H. (1949). Emotional deprivation in infants. *Journal of Pediatrics, 35,* 512–521.
13. Coleman, R.W., & Provence, S. (1957). Environmental retardation (hospitalism) in infants living in families. *Pediatrics, 19,* 285–292.
14. Williams, H.E. (1959). Failure to thrive in infancy. *Medical Journal of Australia, 2,* 345–349.
15. Elmer, E. (1960). Failure to thrive, role of the mother. *Pediatrics, 25,* 717–725.
16. Patton, R.G., & Gardner, L.I. (1962). Influence of family environment on growth: The syndrome of "maternal deprivation." *Pediatrics, 30,* 957–962.
17. Shaheen, E., Alexander, D., Truskowsky, M., & Barbero, G.J. (1968). Failure to thrive: A retrospective profile. *Clinical Pediatrics, 7,* 255–261.
18. Glaser, H.H., Heagarty, M.C., Bullard, D.M., & Pivchik, E.C. (1968). Physical and psychological development of children with early failure to thrive. *Journal of Pediatrics, 73,* 690–698.
19. Hannaway, P. (1970). Failure to thrive, a study of 100 infants and children. *Clinical Pediatrics, 9,* 96–99.

20. Sills, R.H. (1978). Failure to thrive, the role of clinical and laboratory evaluation. *American Journal of Diseases of Children, 132,* 967–969.
21. Ayoub, C., & Milner, J. (1984). Non-organic failure to thrive: Parental awareness, failure to thrive type, prognosis and subsequent neglect. Abstract no. 377, Fifth International Congress on Child Abuse and Neglect, Montreal.
22. McCarthy, D. (1977). Deprivation dwarfism viewed as a form of child abuse. In A.W. Franklin (Ed.), *The challenge of child abuse.* London: Academic Press.
23. Leonard, M.F., Rhymes, J.P., & Solnit, A.J. (1966). Failure to thrive in infants, a family problem. *American Journal of Diseases of Children, 111,* 600–612.
24. Bullard, D.M., Glaser, H.H., Heagarty, M.C., & Pivchick, E.C. (1967). Failure to thrive in the neglected child. *American Journal of Orthopsychiatry, 37,* 680–690.
25. Koel, B.S. (1969). Failure to thrive and fatal injury as a continuum. *American Journal of Diseases of Children, 118,* 565–567.
26. Oates, R.K. (1982). Failure to thrive—Part of the spectrum. In R.K. Oates (Ed.), *Child abuse: A community concern.* Sydney: Butterworths.
27. Krieger, I., & Sargent, D.A. (1967). A postural sign in the sensory deprivation syndrome in infants. *Journal of Pediatrics, 70,* 332–339.
28. Rosenn, D.W., Loeb, L.S., & Jura, M.B. (1980). Differentiation of organic from non-organic failure to thrive syndrome in infancy. *Pediatrics, 66,* 698–704.
29. Illingworth, R.S. (1963). The child who will not thrive. *British Journal of Clinical Practice, 17,* 291–296.
30. Kohler, E.E., & Good, T.A. (1969). The infant who fails to thrive. *Hospital Practice, 2,* 54–61.
31. Oates, R.K. (1977). The child who fails to thrive. *Medical Journal of Australia, 1,* 300–302.
32. Oates, R.K., & Yu, J.S. (1971). Children with non-organic failure to thrive—A community problem. *Medical Journal of Australia, 2,* 199–203.
33. McCarthy, D. (1974). Physical effects and symptoms of the cycle of rejection. *Proceedings of the Royal Society of Medicine, 67,* 1057–1061.
34. Powell, G.F., Brasel, J.A., & Blizzard, R.M. (1967). Emotional deprivation and growth retardation simulating idiopathic hypopituitarism I: Clinical evaluation of the syndrome. *New England Journal of Medicine, 276,* 1271–1278.
35. Hopwood, N.J., & Becker, D.J. (1979). Psychosocial dwarfism: Detection, evaluation and management. *Child Abuse and Neglect, 3,* 439–447.
36. Talbot, N.B., Sobel, E.H., & Burke, B.S. (1947). Dwarfism in children: Its possible relation to emotional, nutritional and endocrine disturbances. *New England Journal of Medicine, 236,* 783–793.
37. Powell, G.F., Brasel, J.A., Raiti, S., & Blizzard, R.M. (1967). Emotional deprivation and growth retardation simulating idiopathic hypopituitarism II: Endocrinologic evaluation of the syndrome. *New England Journal of Medicine, 276,* 1279–1283.
38. Apley, J., Davies, J., Davis, D.R., & Silk, B. (1971). Dwarfism without apparent physical cause. *Proceedings of the Royal Society of Medicine, 64,* 135–138.
39. Castells, S., Reddy, C., & Choo, S. (1975). Permanent panhypopituitarism associated with maternal deprivation. *American Journal of Diseases of Children, 129,* 128–130.
40. Harris, J.C. (1982). Non-organic failure to thrive syndromes: Reactive attachment disorder of infancy and psychosocial dwarfism of early childhood. In P.J. Ac-

GROWTH FAILURE AND EMOTIONAL DEPRIVATION

cardo (Ed.), *Failure to thrive in infancy and childhood.* Baltimore: University Park Press.

41. Frasier, S.D., & Rallison, M.L. (1972). Growth retardation and emotional deprivation: Relative resistance to treatment with human growth hormone, *Journal of Pediatrics, 80,* 603–609.

42. Tanner, J.H. (1973). Resistance to exogenous human growth hormone in psychosocial short stature (emotional deprivation). *Journal of Pediatrics, 82,* 171–175.

43. Krieger, I., & Mellinger, R.C. (1971). Pituitary function in the deprivation syndrome. *Journal of Pediatrics, 79,* 216–225.

44. Silver, H.K., & Finkelstein, M. (1967). Deprivation dwarfism. *Journal of Pediatrics, 70,* 317–324.

45. Reinhardt, J.B., & Drash, A.L. (1969). Psychosocial dwarfism: Environmentally induced recovery. *Psychosomatic Medicine, 31,* 165–172.

46. McConaghy, N. (1979). Maternal deprivation: Can its ghost be laid? *Australian and New Zealand Journal of Psychiatry, 13,* 209–217.

47. Widowson, E.M. (1951). Mental contentment and physical growth. *Lancet, 1,* 1316–1318.

48. Whitten, C.F., Pettit, M.G., & Fischoff, J. (1969). Evidence that growth failure from maternal deprivation is secondary to undereating. *Journal of the American Medical Association, 209,* 1675–1682.

49. Thompson, R.G., & Blizzard, R.M. (1970). Growth failure, deprivation and undereating. *Journal of the American Medical Association, 211,* 1379.

50. Rutter, M. (1972). *Maternal deprivation reassessed.* Harmondsworth, England: Penguin Books.

51. Rutter, M. (1979). Maternal deprivation 1972–1978: New findings, new concepts, new approaches. *Child Development, 50,* 283–305.

2

Family Studies in Nonorganic Failure to Thrive

CHARACTERISTICS OF THE PARENTS

There are a number of problems in the methodology of many of the studies of parents whose children have failed to thrive: Most of the studies are descriptive; comparison groups have not been used; the concept of nonorganic failure to thrive has not always been clearly defined; and some of the information about the parents is anecdotal rather than based on measurements.

Because nonorganic failure to thrive is usually described in families from lower socioeconomic groups, it is important that studies should have a comparison group, matched for socioeconomic status, so that factors that are due to social class are not mistakenly attributed to the syndrome of nonorganic failure to thrive. What would be particularly useful in helping the understanding of this condition would be for an observational cohort study to be conducted. Two groups of infants free of the condition would be assembled, one group having a risk factor thought to be associated with the condition, but not the other group. Both groups would then be observed over time, preferably for at least two years, to determine the occurrence of failure to thrive. If the incidence of failure to thrive was

FAMILY STUDIES IN NONORGANIC FAILURE TO THRIVE

significantly higher in the group with the risk factor, then this factor would be suspected of being a causative element in the condition. Because of the large sample size that would be required to include some cases of nonorganic failure to thrive and because of the problems and expense of observing large groups over time, it is unlikely that this sort of study will ever be done. Most of the information has to come from descriptive studies, which may be misleading, and from case-control studies. While in some ways less effective than the cohort study, the case-control study does have the advantage of being cheaper, less difficult to perform, and controlling for several variables.

The earlier papers describing characteristics of parents of infants with nonorganic failure to thrive had a common theme. Leonard's group (1) found multiple problems in every family. They noted the presence of poverty, overcrowding, unemployment, illegitimacy, and seriously disturbed marital relationships. The mothers were reported to be lonely and isolated and the fathers were often absent, uninvolved in family life, and unsupportive. Similar family problems were noted by others (2–4). Hopwood and Becker (5) found a high incidence of family separation, unemployment, financial difficulties, and poor communication between the parents. Maternal depression and suicide attempts have been described (6) and in a psychological study of the mothers by Togut and colleagues (7) there was found to be a common theme of profound emotional and physical deprivation in the mothers' own early childhood. These authors described the mothers as having little to spare from their own meager stores of affection to pass on to their offspring. Nearly all of the families described came from lower socioeconomic groups. None of the studies just referred to used comparison groups, so it is not possible to evaluate the effect of social class on this condition.

That the condition is not entirely due to social class factors is demonstrated by studies that show that it can also occur in stable, intact families with favorable economic circumstances (8–10). Glaser's group, in a review of 50 cases of nonorganic failure to thrive (9), found that most were members of intact, relatively stable families with steady incomes.

Two case-control studies have looked at the characteristics of these parents. Hess and colleagues (11) compared the intelligence quotients of three groups, each including eight mothers. In the first group their children had nonorganic failure to thrive; the second group of mothers had infants who had failure to thrive for organic reasons; and the third group comprised mothers whose children were growing normally. These researchers showed that the mothers from the nonorganic group had a lower IQ on the vocabulary test of the Stanford-Binet intelligence scale. In this study the organic and the nonorganic failure-to-thrive groups were clearly defined and the three groups were matched for socioeconomic status. However, this study should be interpreted with caution as the numbers were small (eight in each group) and the study was not "blind," since the observers knew to which groups the mothers belonged. It would have been interesting to have had the mothers tested on measures of intelligence other than verbal abilities because, if these mothers are like their children (6), it may be that the greatest discrepancy in intelligence lies in the area of verbal ability.

Another case-control study is from Pollitt's group (12). These investigators strictly defined nonorganic failure to thrive and compared 19 preschool infants who had nonorganic failure to thrive with a comparison group matched for age, sex, and race. The groups were not matched for socioeconomic status. No significant differences were found between the two groups in marital history, family structure, or household crowding. There was no difference in the number of psychiatric disorders reported in the mothers of the two groups. However, it was found that the mothers in the study group were more likely to express annoyance with their children and to slap them. They were less likely to praise, kiss, or caress them. Studies such as this one need to be repeated, preferably with matching for socioeconomic status, to determine which of the characteristics of these mothers seem to contribute directly to the infants' growth failure.

FAMILY PROFILES

Recently, attempts have been made to distinguish different family profiles within the nonorganic failure-to-thrive syndrome. Jacobs and Kent (13) suggest that the mothers fall into three groups: a group

FAMILY STUDIES IN NONORGANIC FAILURE TO THRIVE

deficient in basic mothercraft skills; a group who have these skills but who are passive, with low affect, and who are overwhelmed by family problems so that they cannot respond to their infants' needs; and a third group with a significant psychological disorder with or without drug and alcohol abuse. Jacobs and Kent suggested this classification would be helpful in planning treatment programs. A different classification has been described by Evans and co-workers (14). They described three distinct groups and relate these groups to different forms of treatment. In the first group the mothers were young, immature, and depressed but were responsive to supportive treatment and counseling. The second group consisted of deprived mothers who were in poor health, had a chaotic lifestyle, related very poorly to the social worker involved, and needed a great deal of structural support. The third group displayed extreme anger and hostility both to their children and to staff who tried to work with them. Any form of treatment or follow-up was reported to be extremely difficult in this group.

Kempe and colleagues also described three different groups of mothers (15). The first was a group of mothers who had been temporarily overwhelmed by a rapid series of events which had undermined their basically good capacity to be a mother. These mothers responded well to support. The second group were immature, chronically deprived, and depressed. They were impulsive in their behavior, leading to difficulty in coping with their community's social systems, with relationships, and with the stresses of poverty. In the third group the mothers had a negative perception of their babies. The baby was seen not as just another burden but as a bad or defective child who deliberately misbehaved so as to cause the mother problems. These families were reported to often have evidence of other antisocial and aggressive behavior. These three profiles are summarized in Table 1.

In each of the profiles, treatment becomes progressively more difficult from the first through to the third group. Although these authors have made somewhat different classifications, the important message is that parents of children with failure to thrive are not a homogeneous group. It is essential that the individual problems of the family are assessed before starting a treatment program, since

Table 1
Attempts to Describe Characteristic Profiles of Mothers of Children with Nonorganic Failure to Thrive

	Evans et al. (14)	Jacobs & Kent (13)	Kempe et al. (15)
GROUP I	young, immature, depressed	deficient in basic mothercraft skills	basically capable, temporarily overwhelmed
GROUP II	poor health, chaotic lifestyle, need structural support	passive, low affect, overwhelmed	immature, chronically deprived and depressed
GROUP III	extreme anger and hostility	significant psychological disorder	antisocial, aggressive, sees baby as bad

different forms of treatment are indicated for different family characteristics.

After reviewing the family and social environments of 44 infants with nonorganic failure to thrive, Gagan, Cupoli, and Watkins (16) reported that the mothers are themselves usually deprived of social supports. They point out that the concept of maternal deprivation is misleading because it suggests that the mother is at fault. They emphasize that the mother herself is often deprived of the social supports needed for childrearing and that the concept of parental deprivation provides a more accurate description.

In an attempt to predict nonorganic failure to thrive, Fanaroff's groups reported that in a follow-up study of premature babies, those who developed nonorganic failure to thrive were more likely to be the ones whose mothers had visited them infrequently in the newborn nursery (17). They suggested that this was a simple way of predicting infants at risk for failure to thrive. However, this would seem to be a distinct subgroup as the majority of infants with failure to thrive are of normal gestation and birth weight.

It is important to stress that nonorganic failure to thrive should not be regarded as being solely due to parental and particularly maternal factors. Problems in mother-infant interaction to which the child contributes may also be important factors.

FAMILY STUDIES IN NONORGANIC FAILURE TO THRIVE

CHARACTERISTICS OF THE CHILDREN

It is becoming increasingly apparent that babies are born with differing temperaments and that these differences can be detected at birth (18, 19). The feeding behavior of babies with nonorganic failure to thrive is often reported as being difficult from the earliest weeks of life. These babies have been described as refusing the nipple, falling asleep or crying during feeding, having poor appetites, positing and vomiting frequently, and fighting against the person who feeds them (9, 20, 21). It is likely that an infant with this type of temperament, born to a mother with the characteristics already described and who therefore does not have the nurturing skills to overcome these feeding difficulties, will be at increased risk of failing to thrive.

There have been several reports of distinct personality and behavior patterns in these infants. Mention has already been made in the previous chapter of Rosenn et al.'s study (22), which showed that these infants preferred distant social encounters and inanimate objects to close personal interaction, such as being touched and held. In the absence of any neurological abnormalities, hypotonia has been described when these children are held and cuddled (23). Some researchers have noted apprehensive, frightened, apathetic, and withdrawn behavior (2), while others have observed that when admitted to hospital these infants are irritable, are difficult to hold and cuddle, and rarely smile or vocalize (14). Leonard and colleagues reported that in infants with nonorganic failure to thrive between four and 10 months of age, there was a delay in the establishment of specific, strong attachment to their parents and that the infants did not show anxiety with strangers or displeasure at being left by their parents (1).

Glaser and colleagues' uncontrolled study of 50 children with the condition reported no evidence of psychiatric disorders in the children but noted that seven had mild behavior disorders (9). A review of nonorganic failure to thrive at the Children's Hospital in Sydney (3), which was the beginning of the long-term follow-up to be described later in this book, found that eight of 11 children old enough to be tested had abnormal personalities on the Rutter scale (24) and that 11 of their 29 siblings also had abnormal personality scores. There have been other studies that have looked at the behavior and development of siblings of infants with nonorganic failure to thrive, but the evidence is conflicting. In 1969 Elmer's group reported growth failure in other children in the same family, as well as an increased incidence of physical disease and developmental retardation in the siblings (8). Similar observations were made by Shaheen's group the year before (10). Other authors (1, 3) have noted normal growth and health in the siblings, although they may be more likely to have behavior problems (3). No specific studies have been made of the fathers in these families, although they are usually described as being absent or else passive and of little help (1, 3, 7, 16, 25). Generally, when the fathers are present, they are seen as sharing the same deprived background and the same difficulties in coping as their partners.

As in those papers reporting on the characteristics of the parents, the literature describing the characteristics of the children contains

Table 2
Studies of Nonorganic Failure to Thrive Where a Comparison Group Has Been Used

Criteria	Pollitt & Eichler (21)	Gordon & Jameson (29)	Mitchell et al. (26)
Number of subjects	19	12	30
Type of study	case-control	case-control	cohort/case-control
Failure to thrive defined	yes	no	yes
Comparison group adequately matched	not for socio-economic status	yes	yes
Standardized test	no	yes	yes and interview
Observer blind	no	no	for psychological test
Appropriate statistical analysis	yes	yes	yes

FAMILY STUDIES IN NONORGANIC FAILURE TO THRIVE

very few studies in which a comparison group was used. Methodological problems may arise in case-control studies. Details of the approach used in three studies of nonorganic failure to thrive in which a comparison group was used to look at the children are shown in Table 2. The study by Mitchell's group (26) meets the methodological criteria adapted from Leventhal (27, 28), which are listed in Table 2. Pollitt and Eichler's study (21) failed to match for socioeconomic status, did not use a standardized test that could be repeated by others, and the observers were not "blind." The study by Gordon and Jameson (29) did not adequately define failure to thrive and the observers were not "blind." The clinical details from these three studies are summarized in Table 3.

Gordon and Jameson's study of 12 infants aged between 12 and 19 months concentrated on maternal attachment (29). Although they

Table 3

Main Features of Studies of Nonorganic Failure-to-Thrive Children Where a Comparison Group Was Used

Criteria	Pollitt & Eichler (21)	Gordon & Jameson (29)	Mitchell et al. (26)
No. of subjects	19	12	30
Ages	1–5 years	12–19 months	2–5 years
Increased neonatal illness	—	—	yes
Maternal attachment	—	poor	—
Feeding problems	yes	—	—
Lower caloric intake	yes	—	—
Overall increased behavior disorders	yes	—	no
More family problems	no	—	yes

reported that infants with nonorganic failure to thrive were less securely attached to their mothers than control infants, their results did not reach statistical significance at the 0.05 level. Pollitt and Eichler studied 19 preschool children (21). They found that the study group had more feeding difficulties as infants, that their daily caloric intake was lower than that of controls, but that there were no significant differences between the two groups in their sleeping, elimination, autoerotic, and self-harming behaviors. However, they did note that when all the disturbances were added together, the failure to thrive children had a significantly greater number of behavior abnormalities than the control group.

In a more recent study by Mitchell's group (26), a cohort of 312 children between two and five years of age was collected. Clinic records showed that 30 children from this group fitted the investigators' criteria for failure to thrive without an organic cause. They then matched these children with a control group of 30. These researchers found that minor neonatal problems were more significant in the study group but that there was no increased incidence of prematurity or problems during the pregnancy and birth. The study group had significantly more family problems but there was no increased incidence of behavior problems in the children and no increase in suspected or known physical abuse.

The results of these last two studies are at variance with some of the earlier, descriptive studies, which showed marked family pathology and disturbances in the children. Clearly, further control studies are required to clarify these differing results. Well-designed studies are also required to review the long-term outcome in these children and to evaluate the effectiveness of treatment.

REFERENCES

1. Leonard, M.F., Rhymes, J.P., & Solnit, A.J. (1966). Failure to thrive in infants, a family problem. *American Journal of Diseases of Children, 111,* 600–612.
2. Bullard, D.M., Glaser, H.H., Heagarty, M.C., & Pivchik, E.C. (1967). Failure to thrive in the neglected child. *American Journal of Orthopsychiatry, 37,* 680–690.
3. Oates, R.K., & Yu, J.S. (1971). Children with non-organic failure to thrive—A community problem. *Medical Journal of Australia, 2,* 199–203.

FAMILY STUDIES IN NONORGANIC FAILURE TO THRIVE

4. Kerr, M.A.D., Bogues, J.L., & Kerr, D.S. (1978). Psychosocial functioning of mothers of malnourished children. *Pediatrics, 62,* 778–784.
5. Hopwood, N.J., & Becker, D.J. (1979). Psychosocial dwarfism: Detection, evaluation and management. *Child Abuse and Neglect, 3,* 439–447.
6. Hufton, I.W., & Oates, R.K. (1977). Non-organic failure to thrive: A long-term follow-up. *Pediatrics, 57,* 73–77.
7. Togut, M.R., Allen, J.E., & Lelchuck, L. (1969). A psychological exploration of the non-organic failure to thrive syndrome. *Developmental Medicine and Child Neurology, 11,* 601–607.
8. Elmer, E., Gregg, G., & Ellison, P. (1969). Late results of the failure to thrive syndrome. *Clinical Pediatrics, 8,* 584–588.
9. Glaser, H.H., Heagarty, M.C., Bullard, D.M., & Pivchik, E.C. (1968). Physical and psychological development of children with early failure to thrive. *Journal of Pediatrics, 73,* 690–698.
10. Shaheen, E., Alexander, D., Truskwosky, M., & Barbero, G.J. (1968). Failure to thrive, a retrospective profile. *Clinical Pediatrics. 7,* 255–261.
11. Hess, A.K., Hess, K.A., & Hard, H.E. (1977). Intellectual characteristics of mothers of failure to thrive syndrome children. *Child Care, Health and Development, 3,* 377–387.
12. Pollitt, E., Eichler, A., & Chan, C.R. (1975). Psychosocial development and behavior of mothers of failure to thrive children. *American Journal of Orthopsychiatry, 45,* 525–537.
13. Jacobs, R.A., & Kent, J.T. (1977). Psychosocial profiles of families of failure to thrive infants—A preliminary report. *Child Abuse and Neglect, 1,* 469–477.
14. Evans, S.L., Reinhart, J.B., & Succop, R.A. (1972). Failure to thrive. A study of 45 children and their families. *Journal of the American Academy of Child Psychiatry, 11,* 440–457.
15. Kempe, R.S., Cutler, C., & Dean, J. (1980). The infant with failure to thrive. In C.H. Kempe & R.E. Helfer, (Eds.), *The battered child* (3rd ed.). Chicago: The University of Chicago Press.
16. Gagan, R.J., Cupoli, M., & Watkins, A.H. (1984). The families of children who fail to thrive. Preliminary investigations of parental deprivation among organic and non-organic cases. *Child Abuse and Neglect, 8,* 93–103.
17. Fanaroff, A.A., Kennell, J.H., & Klaus, M.H. (1972). Follow-up of low birth-weight infants—The predictive value of maternal visiting patterns. *Pediatrics, 49,* 287–290.
18. Thomas, A. (1968). *Temperamental and behavioral disorders in childhood.* New York: New York University Press.
19. Brazelton, T.B. (1973). Neonatal Behavioural Assessment Scale. *Clinics in developmental medicine No. 50.* London: William Heinemann Medical Books.
20. Freud, A. (1946). The psychoanalytic study of infantile feeding disturbances. *Psychoanalytic Study of the Child, 2,* 119–132.
21. Pollitt, E., & Eichler, A. (1975). Behavioral disturbances amongst failure to thrive children. *American Journal of Diseases of Children, 130,* 24–29.
22. Rosenn, D.W., Loeb, L.S., & Jura, M.B. (1980). Differentiation of organic from non-organic failure to thrive syndrome in infancy. *Pediatrics, 66,* 698–704.
23. Buda, F.B., Rothney, W.B., & Rahe, E.F. (1972). Hypotonia and the maternal-child relationship. *American Journal of Diseases of Children, 124,* 906–907.

24. Rutter, M. (1967). A child's behavior questionnaire for completion by teachers. *Journal of Child Psychology and Psychiatry, 8*, 1–11.
25. Coleman, R.W., & Provence, S. (1957). Environmental retardation (hospitalism) in infants living in families. *Pediatrics, 19*, 285–292.
26. Mitchell, W.G., Gorrell, R.W., & Greenberg, R.A. (1980). Failure to thrive: A study in a primary care setting, epidemiology and follow-up. *Pediatrics, 65*, 971–977.
27. Leventhal, J.M. (1981). Risk factors for child abuse: Methodologic standards in case-control studies. *Pediatrics, 68*, 684–690.
28. Leventhal, J.M. (1982). Research strategies and methodologic standards in studies of risk factors for child abuse. *Child Abuse and Neglect, 6*, 113–123.
29. Gordon, A.H., & Jameson, J.C. (1979). Infant-mother attachment in patients with non-organic failure to thrive syndrome. *Journal of the American Academy of Child Psychiatry, 18*, 251–259.

3

Treatment and Outcome in Nonorganic Failure to Thrive

TREATMENT

The earlier treatment approach of excluding organic disease, keeping the child in hospital until a good weight gain has been achieved, and then discharging the child to the same situation is of short-term benefit unless the home environment can also be improved. This was recognized by Powell's group (1) from the Johns Hopkins Hospital which noted that improvement of the environment was extremely difficult and recommended removal of the child from home.

It is relatively simple, in a hospital situation, to take these children from their parents, to provide care for them by other females who are efficient and competent, and to bring their nutritional status up to normal. However, this is a demonstration to the mother that others have been able to succeed where she has failed and is likely to reinforce her feelings of inadequacy. Recognition that nonorganic failure to thrive is often a problem in the interaction between mother and child (2–4) has led to a treatment approach at the Children's Hospital in Sydney in which the mother is involved in the care of her child right from the moment of admission to hospital. She is encouraged to live in the hospital and to be involved in the care and feeding of her child; she receives support from nursing and social work staff in learning to relate to her child. Emphasis is placed on praising her for her efforts and for giving her the credit for the progress the child makes. Wherever possible this warm, supportive relationship is continued when the child returns home either by home visiting by hospital staff or usually by use of community resources (5). As these parents have difficulty in keeping appointments (6), community resources should be utilized to cooperate with the hospital in providing the aftercare that is usually essential for the child's continued well-being.

Throughout, the emphasis should be on supporting the mother and child together. This has been recognized by other researchers who have realized the importance of working closely with the family. Leonard, Rhymes, and Solnit (7) emphasize the importance of warm, encouraging, nonjudgmental support of the mother so as to help her understand her baby's needs and to respond to them appropriately. Barbero and Shaheen (8) suggested that from the outset the parents should be encouraged to become active members of the hospital care team.

Unfortunately, in practice hospital wards often do not provide the sort of clinical climate in which mothers can be actively involved in the care of their children. Frequent shift changes make it difficult for the mothers to have consistent ward staff members to whom they can relate, and some of the more junior members of the hospital team may not have the skills necessary to work comfortably with these parents.

An assessment of the mother's personality and capabilities is required when making a treatment plan. A character disorder was the main feature in 10 out of 12 mothers studied by Fischoff, Whitten, and Pettit (9). They pointed out that while a problem-solving approach is appropriate for treating a psychoneurotic problem, where the mother has the capacity for introspection, a mother with a character disorder has a limited ability to perceive and assess the environment and needs of her child. Her patterns of thought are literal and concrete and therefore the emphasis on treatment should be on providing basic help in all phases of her life with practical help in feeding, childrearing, and other general aspects of child care. Other

TREATMENT IN NONORGANIC FAILURE TO THRIVE

researchers (10) have also emphasized this practical approach, with some progress being made in classifying maternal characteristics as a way of developing appropriate treament programs (11–13).

Ayoub and colleagues (14) in a review of 100 cases stressed the importance of helping the mother develop a positive relationship with the infant and of working to increase her confidence in her own mothering ability. Part of their program involved teaching the mothers to play with their infants. They report that the mothers fall into the three groups previously described by Jacobs and Kent (12) and report that mothers in the first two groups—"those deficient in basic mothercraft skills and those overwhelmed by family problems"—respond to their treatment program. However, the response to the program is poor from those in the third group who are characterized by significant psychological disorder.

Because of the magnitude of the problem and because it is likely that there will never be enough professionally trained workers to meet the needs of these families, the Denver group (13) has used the volunteer lay health visitor to provide practical help and friendship for these mothers. However, in a recent report (4) that studied 50 children with nonorganic failure to thrive, 25 of whom had lay health visitor support provided for their families, it was found that this form of intervention had no measurable effect on the children's weight, development, or interaction patterns. This paper emphasized the severity of the condition in some cases and the need for more intensive intervention in cases where the mother-child relationship was severely disturbed.

SUBSEQUENT GROWTH

In 1962 Patton and Gardner reported that these children may be limited in their ability to regain a normal growth pattern (15). However, their series contained only six cases and their follow-up was reported at less than one year. A study of 40 children followed at a mean of three years five months found that 14 were still below the third percentile for weight and 13 remained below the third percentile for height (16). Elmer's group, in a review of 15 children between three and 11 years after hospital admission, showed that eight were still below the third percentile in both height and weight (17). Chase and Martin (18), reporting on 19 children seen at a mean of three years six months after presentation, found that 13 were still below the third percentile for weight and 10 were below the third percentile for height.

The importance of frequent, supportive follow-up was emphasized by Ayoub, Pfeiffer, and Leichtman (14), who reported that 35 out of 40 children who received intensive follow-up were thriving. However, the average period of follow-up was only 14 months. Mitchell's group was able to follow only 12 of a cohort of 30 children with nonorganic failure to thrive (19). They showed that over 80% regained normal weight and over 90% regained normal height over a one-year period. Much of the value of this study is lost because of the high proportion of children from the original group who were not reviewed.

When catch-up growth is assessed, the physical features of the parents, which have some influence on the child's size (20), are usually not taken into account. However, these factors were considered in a follow-up study (5) that was the prelude to the study to be described in more detail later in this book. This research showed that in a review of 21 children seen at an average of six years four months after presentation, five children were below the 10th percentile for weight and only one child was below the 10th percentile for height when corrected for midparent height, this being the average of the mothers' and fathers' height. The studies of catch-up growth are summarized in Table 1.

It is clear from these six studies of subsequent growth that catch-up is common in these children. Prader, Tanner, and Von Harnack (21) have reported that catch-up growth following starvation or severe illness can often restore the situation to normal in prepubertal children. As children who have had nonorganic failure to thrive become older, they are less dependent on an adult to feed them and can usually fend for themselves. This is likely to be the explanation for growth improvement in most cases. It has also been shown that when the environment suddenly improves, catch-up growth is more likely to occur. Patton and Gardner (15) noted that an improvement in growth correlated with an improvement in the environment, while Ayoub, Pfeiffer, and Leichtman (14) reported that 91% of their pa-

TREATMENT IN NONORGANIC FAILURE TO THRIVE

Table 1
Catch-up Growth Following Nonorganic Failure to Thrive

Author	Number of Cases	Length of Follow-up	Weight Above 3rd Percentile	Height Above 3rd Percentile
Glaser et al. (16) (1968)	40	3 yrs 5 mths	65%	68%
Elmer et al. (17) (1969)	15	3–11 yrs	47%	47%
Chase & Martin (18) (1970)	10	3 yrs 6 mths	32%	47%
Hufton & Oates (5) (1977)	21	6 yrs 4 mths	76%	95%
Ayoub, Pfeiffer, & Leichtman (14) (1979)	35	14 mths	80%	—
Mitchell et al. (19) (1980)	12	1–4 yrs	86%	97%

tients placed in foster care had catch-up growth. Even more important than the way it may affect growth is the way in which an adverse environment may have long-term effects on the child's intellectual and emotional development.

INTELLECTUAL DEVELOPMENT

There is some evidence that severe and prolonged malnutrition during the first years of life may lead to a decrease in intellectual functioning (22–25). However, a recent study, which followed severely malnourished children for 20 years and compared them with a matched control group, found that although the study group was significantly lower in intelligence than the control group, the study group had integrated effectively into the community and their own children were not experiencing the deprivation they had suffered during their own childhoods (26).

It is difficult to draw parallels between these kinds of studies, which are usually of severely malnourished children, and studies of children with nonorganic failure to thrive where the degree of malnutrition is usually not so severe. What is probably more important is the fact that the child's development is most likely to be impaired if he remains in an unstimulating and unsupportive environment. The importance of a good environment was shown by Winick's group (27), which found that malnourished Korean children adopted in middle-class American homes at an average age of 18 months had intelligence quotients within the normal range when tested six to 11 years later. However, the results for these children were significantly lower than those for a group of Korean children adopted at the same time who had not been malnourished.

Richardson (28) demonstrated the importance of environmental factors when he showed that malnourished children with a favorable social background had an average IQ only two points lower than those who had not been malnourished, while malnourished children from an unfavourable background had an average IQ nine points lower than controls. In Glaser's study (16) of 40 infants followed at a mean interval of three years five months, 15% of the children were of borderline or retarded intelligence and 37% of the school-age children had significant difficulties in school. The review of 15 children by Elmer and colleagues (17) found six to be mildly mentally retarded and four others to be moderately retarded. Common findings were slow speech development and difficulty in conceptual thinking. A review of longer duration supported these findings when it was found that 14 of 21 children, seen six years after admission to hospital, had a reading age one or two years below their chronological age (5). Ten of the children were described by their teachers as functioning below average. These studies all suffer from lack of a control group.

In a follow-up study that did use a well-matched comparison group, Mitchell and co-workers (19), using the McCarthy Scales of Children's Abilities, did not find any significant difference between the children who had suffered from nonorganic failure to thrive and the comparison group. The discrepancy between this study and the earlier descriptive studies may lie in the way the authors chose their subjects. The group they studied was selected from health clinic records. Families who had not registered at the clinic within six months of their child's birth or who had made fewer than three visits to the clinic were excluded from the study. It is likely that this selection process inadvertently excluded those families in which the worst cases of nonorganic failure to thrive are most likely to occur. It is the mothers who are overwhelmed, depressed, or antisocial who are least likely to attend health clinics. If this is so, the cases of nonorganic failure to thrive that the researchers did detect are likely to be the ones with the best prognosis.

The Denver group (4) followed 25 children for six months, comparing them with a group of normal controls. After six months, more than half of the children were delayed on the Bayley Scales of Infant Development, while the majority of controls were developing normally. Another question that has not been answered from the available follow-up studies is whether some of these children may have been intellectually handicapped from the start and whether this problem contributed to the earlier feeding difficulties and problems in the maternal-child relationship.

EMOTIONAL DEVELOPMENT

Follow-up studies have suggested that children with nonorganic failure to thrive have difficulties in their emotional development. Glaser and colleagues (16) found 28% to have psychological or behavioral problems. Elmer, Gregg, and Ellison (17) found that 47% of their group developed behavioral disturbances. On a personality questionnaire completed by the child's school teachers (29), 10 of 21 children who had nonorganic failure to thrive six years previously had abnormal personality profiles (5). When the mothers of children in this study completed the same personality score for their own child, 16 of the 18 mothers who participated gave answers that scored their children as abnormal, suggesting that these mothers perceive their children as being abnormal more often than others do.

A drawback to these three studies is the lack of a control group, although in one of the studies, where the behavior of the siblings was compared with that of the index children, the siblings had significantly fewer behavior disorders (5).

38 CHILD ABUSE AND NEGLECT

Mitchell's study, which did use a comparison group (19), did not find any significant differences in the parents' reports of behavior problems. However, in addition to the potential bias in selection of subjects for this study which has already been noted, only 12 of the 30 children initially seen with failure to thrive were able to be reviewed. Only 19 were sought for follow-up and, of these, seven were either living interstate, refused to cooperate, or could not be found. The known characteristics of the parents of these families (including high mobility) suggest that it is in the group that could not be reviewed where the greatest discrepancy might have been found. The main studies of the intellectual and emotional sequelae of nonorganic failure to thrive are summarized in Table 2.

Although most of the data show the intellectual and emotional development of children with nonorganic failure to thrive to be gloomy, it is important to look at the other side of the picture. While

Table 2
Studies of Intellectual and Emotional Sequelae of Nonorganic Failure to Thrive

Author	Number of Cases	Average Age at Review	Mean Interval to Review (Months)	Intellectual Status	Psychological Status
Glaser et al. (16) (1968)	40	4 yrs 6 mths	41	15% retarded 37% of school age having problems at school	28% behavior or psychological problems
Elmer et al. (17) (1969)	15	3 yrs 3 mths– 11 yrs 7 mths	57	67% mildly or moderately retarded	47% behavioral disturbances
Hufton & Oates (5) (1977)	21	7 yrs 10 mths	76	67% delayed reading age 48% below average on teacher ratings	48% abnormal on teacher rating scale
Mitchell et al. (19) (1980)	12	3–6 yrs	12–48	no different than controls	3% behavior problems no different than controls

TREATMENT IN NONORGANIC FAILURE TO THRIVE

studies report abnormalities in intellect and personality development in approximately 15% to 65% of children, this leaves 35% to 85% of children who do not have any detectable adverse sequelae. This supports Rutter's assertion (30) that many children are particularly resilient and do well despite adverse social circumstances. However, there is no room for complacency. To prevent adverse sequelae in many of these children, long-term management aimed at supporting the mother and also at providing specific management for the child is indicated.

REFERENCES

1. Powell, G.F., Brasel, J.A., & Blizzard, R.M. (1967). Emotional deprivation and growth retardation simulating idiopathic hypopituitarism I: Clinical evaluation of the syndrome. *New England Journal of Medicine, 276,* 1271–1278.
2. Haynes, C.F., Cutler, C., Gray, J., O'Keefe, K., & Kempe, R.S. (1983). Nonorganic failure to thrive: Decisions for placement and videotaped evaluations. *Child Abuse and Neglect, 7,* 309–319.
3. Dietrich, K.N., Starr, R.H., & Weisfeld, G.E. (1983). Infant maltreatment: Caretaker-infant interaction and developmental consequences at different levels of parenting failure. *Pediatrics, 72,* 532–540.
4. Haynes, C.F., Cutler, C., Gray, J., & Kempe, R.S. (1984). Hospitalized cases of nonorganic failure to thrive: The scope of the problem and short-term lay health visitor intervention. *Child Abuse and Neglect, 8,* 229–242.
5. Hufton, I.W., & Oates, R.K. (1977). Non-organic failure to thrive: A long-term follow-up. *Pediatrics, 57,* 73–77.
6. Oates, R.K., & Yu, J.S. (1971). Children with nonorganic failure to thrive—A community problem. *Medical Journal of Australia, 2,* 199–203.
7. Leonard, M.F., Rhymes, J.P., & Solnit, A.J. (1966). Failure to thrive in infants, a family problem. *American Journal of Diseases of Children, 111,* 600–612.
8. Barbero, G.J. & Shaheen, E. (1967). Environmental failure to thrive: A clinical view. *Journal of Pediatrics, 71,* 639–644.
9. Fischoff, J., Whitten, C.F., & Pettit, M.G. (1971). A psychiatric study of mothers of infants with growth failure secondary to maternal deprivation. *Journal of Pediatrics, 79,* 209–215.
10. Kerr, M.A.D., Bogues, J.L., & Kerr, D.S. (1978). Psychosocial functioning of mothers of malnourished children. *Pediatrics, 62,* 778–784.
11. Evans, S.L., Reinhart, J.B., & Succop, R.A. (1972). Failure to thrive. A study of 45 children and their families. *Journal of American Academy of Child Psychiatry, 11,* 440–457.
12. Jacobs, R.A., & Kent, J.T. (1977). Psychosocial profiles of families of failure to thrive infants—Preliminary report. *Child Abuse and Neglect, 1,* 469–477.
13. Kempe, R.S., Cutler, C., & Dean, J. (1980). The infant with failure to thrive. In

40 CHILD ABUSE AND NEGLECT

C.H. Kempe & R.E. Helfer (Eds.), *The battered child* (3rd ed.). Chicago: The University of Chicago Press.

14. Ayoub, C., Pfeiffer, D., & Leichtman, L. (1979). Treatment of infants with nonorganic failure to thrive. *Child Abuse and Neglect, 3,* 937–941.

15. Patton, R.G., & Gardner, L.I. (1962). Influence of family environment on growth: The syndrome of "maternal deprivation." *Pediatrics, 30,* 957–962.

16. Glaser, H.H., Heagarty, M.C., Bullard, D.M., & Pivchik, E.C. (1968). Physical and psychological development of children with early failure to thrive. *Journal of Pediatrics, 73,* 690–698.

17. Elmer, E., Gregg, G. & Ellison, P. (1969). Late results of the failure to thrive syndrome. *Clinical Pediatrics, 8,* 584–588.

18. Chase, H.P., & Martin, H. (1970). Undernutrition and child development. *New England Journal of Medicine, 282,* 933–939.

19. Mitchell, W.G., Gorrell, R.W., & Greenberg, R.A. (1980). Failure to thrive: A study in a primary care setting, epidemiology and follow-up. *Pediatrics, 65,* 971–977.

20. Tanner, J.M., Goldstein, N., & Whitehouse, R.H. (1970). Standards for children's height at ages 2–9 years allowing for height of parents. *Archives of Disease in Childhood, 45,* 755–759.

21. Prader, A., Tanner, J.M., & Von Harnack, G.A. (1963). Catch-up growth following illness or starvation. *Journal of Pediatrics, 62,* 646–659.

22. Cabak, V., & Najdanvic, R. (1965). Effect of undernutrition in early life on physical and mental development. *Archives of Disease in Childhood, 40,* 532–534.

23. Cravioto, J., De Licardie, E.R., & Birch, H.G. (1966). Nutrition, growth and neurointegrative development: An experimental and ecologic study. *Pediatrics, 38,* 319–372.

24. Hertzig, M., Birch, H.G., Richardson, S.A., & Tizard, J. (1972). Intellectual levels of school children severely malnourished during the first two years of life. *Pediatrics, 49,* 814–824.

25. Stoch, M.B., & Smyth, P.M. (1976). Fifteen-year developmental study of effects of severe undernutrition during infancy on subsequent physical growth and intellectual functioning. *Archives in Disease of Childhood, 51,* 327–336.

26. Stoch, M.B., Smyth, P.M., Moodie, A.D., & Bradshaw, D. (1982). Psychosocial outcome and C.T. findings after gross undernourishment during infancy: A 20-year developmental study. *Developmental Medicine and Child Neurology, 24,* 419–436.

27. Winick, M., Meyer, K.K., & Harris, R.C. (1975). Malnutrition and environmental enrichment by early adoption. *Science, 190,* 1173–1175.

28. Richardson, S.A. (1976). The relation of severe malnutrition in infancy to the intelligence of school children with differing life histories. *Pediatric Research, 10,* 57–61.

29. Rutter, M. (1967). A child's behavior questionnaire for completion by teachers: Preliminary findings. *Journal of Child Psychology and Psychiatry, 8,* 1–11.

30. Rutter, M. (1980). The long-term effects of early experiences. *Developmental Medicine and Child Neurology, 22,* 800–815.

4

The Problem of
Child Abuse

HISTORICAL ASPECTS

It has been suggested that the history of child abuse can be grouped into four periods (1). In the first period prior to 1946 child abuse was professionally unrecognized. This long period was followed by the early scientific phase when a number of hitherto unidentified syndromes of broken bones, bleeding, and bruising were reported in journal articles between 1946 and 1962. However, the significance of these unusual injuries was rarely appreciated. The third period started in 1962 when the classic paper by Henry Kempe's group (2) ushered in a period of professional awareness and concern. The fourth period dates from the mid-1970s where emphasis has been placed on protection and therapy, with child abuse legislation being widely introduced and many techniques aimed at detection, prevention, and treatment coming into use.

Despite this progress, child abuse remains a major problem. Further efforts have to be made before a fifth phase, encompassing the widespread prevention of child abuse, can be said to have occurred.

Although not widely recognized by the medical profession until the late 1960s and early 1970s, the abuse of children has been a feature of society for many centuries. Many cultures used infanticide as an accepted method of family planning and for the disposal of weak, premature, or deformed infants (3). At times, children were killed for superstitious reasons. It was believed that slain infants would benefit the sterile woman, kill disease, and confer health, vigor, and youthfulness. To ensure durability of important buildings, children were sometimes buried under the foundations (4).

During the English industrial revolution in the mid-18th century, children from poor families provided industry with a cheap workforce. Children from five years of age worked in factories for up to 14 hours each day and often suffered additional cruel treatment during this time. A movement for child labor reform, begun by Robert Owen and aided by Sir Robert Peel, led to the English parliament passing the first Factory Act in 1802. However, this Act applied only to poor children who had been separated from their parents. While it protected this group of children from being forced to work long hours in factories in appalling conditions, the Act did not apply to children still living with their parents. Because parents were entitled to their children's earnings, they could put their children out to work in factories and collect their children's wages without any fear of the Factory Act, as it did not apply to their children.

Although illegal, there were many cases of infanticide in England as late as the 19th century. Eighty percent of illegitimate children who were put out to nurse in London in the 19th century died. Apparently this often occurred because the wet nurses would kill the infants and continue to collect the nursing fee (5). A newborn child could be insured for about one pound sterling under a "burial club" insurance policy. If the child died, the parents were able to claim between three and five pounds from the insurance company. This led to infants being killed by their parents or being given to a third party to be killed so that the insurance could be collected (5).

In the late 19th century, moves to protect children's rights occurred in the United States and in England. Fontana (6) tells the story of eight-year-old Mary-Ellen Wilson, a girl in New York who was regularly beaten by her legal guardian. Attempts to convince local authorities to take action to protect Mary-Ellen failed as there was no law to prevent parents or guardians from chastizing their children, no matter how cruelly. An approach was then made to the New York Society for the Prevention of Cruelty to Animals, which promptly

THE PROBLEM OF CHILD ABUSE

took action on the grounds that Mary-Ellen was a member of the animal kingdom and her case could therefore be heard under the laws against animal cruelty. Mary-Ellen was placed in the care of Mrs. Wheeler, a voluntary church worker who had made the approach to the New York Society, and the guardian was sentenced to one year in prison. As a direct result of this incident, the Society for the Prevention of Cruelty to Children was founded in New York City in 1871, the founders being Henry Bergh, the President of the New York Society for the Prevention of Cruelty to Animals, and Ellridge Gerry, the Society's legal advisor. In 1881 a Liverpool banker, T.F. Agnew, visited the premises of the New York Society and was so impressed that on his return to Liverpool he established England's first Society for the Prevention of Cruelty to Children in 1883 (7).

The medical features of child abuse were first described by Ambrose Tardieu, a specialist in forensic medicine working in Paris in 1860. He published a medicolegal study on 32 children who had been battered to death (8); his description clearly stated the demographic, social, psychiatric, and medical features that eventually came to be recognized as the battered child syndrome.

The members of the Royal Society of Medicine in London were not aware that the syndrome of child abuse was being described to them at one of their meetings in 1888. At that meeting, Samuel West, a founder of the Hospital for Sick Children in London, described a child aged five weeks who presented with an unexplained swelling of the arm (9). There had been similar lesions, which he presumed to be periosteal, in an arm and a leg on previous occasions. Other infants in the family had been similarly affected and bruising had been noticed. West could not rule out a greenstick fracture but was of the opinion that this was an unusual case of early rickets. In the ensuing discussion, West's diagnosis was disputed, although none of the physicians at the meeting suggested that maltreatment might be the explanation.

The eminent radiologist, John Caffey, reported a new syndrome in 1946. He described six children with subdural hematomas who also had multiple long-bone fractures (10). Other injuries, including bruising and retinal hemorrhages, were noted. He reported that some of these children were undernourished and developmentally delayed but that there was no evidence of any underlying skeletal disease. Caffey concluded that the fractures were of traumatic origin but was unable to obtain a history of trauma from the parents, although he felt negligence may have been a factor. Although it is easy to see in retrospect that Caffey erred on the side of believing the parents' stories, this was an important paper as it focused attention on these "unexplained" injuries.

In 1953 Astley (11), an English orthopedic surgeon, described six children with normal bone structure who had multiple metaphyseal fractures. Some of these children were also noted to have bruising, retinal detachment, and bilateral black eyes. The parents were described as normal, sensible individuals who gave no history of trauma. Despite the associated soft-tissue injuries, Astley did not speculate on the cause of these features but labeled the findings as a new condition, "metaphyseal fragility of bones." Silverman (12), in the same year, provided the answer in a much more perceptive paper. He described three children with unusual fractures involving the metaphyseal region and wrote that an adequate history of trauma for fractures of this nature could be elicited by careful questioning of the parents.

An important contribution to understanding the causes of these injuries was made by Woolley and Evans (13) in 1955. They reviewed earlier radiological studies and emphasized the traumatic nature of these findings, pointing out that the environments of these infants were often hazardous and undesirable.

The landmark paper from Kempe and colleagues (2) in 1962 ushered in the period of awareness of child abuse. These authors coined the term *the battered child syndrome* to direct attention to the seriousness of the problem. Kempe's group concluded that physical abuse was a significant cause of death and injury among children and suggested that psychiatric factors were likely to be of importance in understanding the disorder. Since then the extent of child abuse has been much more widely recognized and an extensive literature has developed. There now exists an International Society for the Prevention of Child Abuse and Neglect, formed in 1976, which publishes a quarterly journal, *Child Abuse and Neglect.*

THE PROBLEM OF CHILD ABUSE

PROBLEMS OF DEFINITION

The term *the battered child* suggests that the subject is a clear-cut clinical entity which only needs to be recognized to be defined. This is far from the truth. Child abuse is an extremely complex phenomenon ranging from fatal assault to deprivation of food or affection (14) and also includes the various forms of sexual abuse. Besharov (15) points out that no one definition has achieved wide acceptance and that there are almost as many definitions as there are research projects. This makes it extremely difficult to compare the results of different researchers, as some do not define their criteria of child abuse at all, while others use such varied criteria that the studies lack comparability.

It is also sometimes difficult to draw the line between acceptable punishment and physical abuse. The Newsons showed that in Nottingham, England, 62% of children at one year of age and 97% of children at four years of age were subject to physical modes of correction and that in 8% of these children physical correction occurred daily (16). While not necessarily desirable, this incidence of physical punishment suggests that it was acceptable in that community. Although different communities and societies differ in their attitudes toward children, Korbin (17) has made an important point: While at one level childrearing practices that are acceptable in one cultural group may be unacceptable in another, at a second level there are more extreme instances of behavior toward children that are recognized as abusive and unacceptable by all cultures.

Straus (18) In his survey of child abuse, used a definition that excluded the "normal" violence of family life, such as pushing, slapping, and throwing things, but included acts that put the child at risk of serious injury, such as kicking, biting, punching, hitting with an object, or using a knife or gun. However, if one simply looks at the physical injuries, the problem in the family may be missed altogether. Physical injuries often depend on the circumstances surrounding the violent act. For example, a child may be pushed roughly to the ground by his father. He first lands against a soft armchair and then falls to the carpeted floor. No injury is sustained. Exactly the same amount of force and aggression could be used where a different child is pushed; but in this case the child hits his head on a protruding cupboard, sustains a fracture, and then falls to a cement floor receiving further head injury. The latter case will present to a medical service and is likely to be diagnosed as child abuse. The other will not present at all. It is the *act* of violence on the part of the parent that is the constant feature rather than the visible injury (19).

Gil (20) tries to overcome the problem of being too specific by defining abuse as any force that compromises a child's capacity to achieve his physical and psychologic potential. While comprehensive and having enormous social implications, this definition is too broad to be very useful in research studies. Kempe and Helfer have defined the battered child as "any child who receives nonaccidental physical injury (or injuries) as a result of acts (or omissions) on the part of his parents or guardians" (21, p. xi). This is a useful definition. Although it does not include severe neglect, which may be at least as harmful, it does have the advantage of recognizing the vulnerability of the child and placing responsibility on the child's caretaker.

INCIDENCE

In 1971 Kempe (22) estimated that the incidence of child abuse in the United States was six cases per 1,000 live births. Because of the clinician's difficulty and reluctance in making the diagnosis, the actual incidence is probably much higher than that reported. In 1979, over 1.1 million children were reported to the authorities in the United States as suspected victims of child abuse or neglect (23). Increased recognition of the problem is shown by the fact that this figure is almost eight times the 150,000 cases reported in 1960 (24).

The incidence of reported cases in Australia and New Zealand is also increasing. A survey from New Zealand found an incidence of 2.6 cases per 10,000 children (25). These researchers pointed out that the actual incidence was probably much higher as their figures were based on cases that had been brought to the attention of the authorities. A South Australian survey found a similar incidence to the New Zealand estimate (26).

THE PROBLEM OF CHILD ABUSE

In New South Wales an amendment to the Child Welfare Act in 1977 made it mandatory for medical practitioners to notify cases of child abuse. In the first year after the amendment 887 cases were notified (27). In 1982 this number had increased to 2,900, an incidence of 23 cases per 10,000 children under 14 years (28). It is estimated that in 1985 the number of cases reported in New South Wales, a state with a population of 5.5 million, will have risen to over 10,000.

The interpretation of incidence data requires caution. One must consider whether the figure given is based on the actual reported incidence of child abuse to an official agency or whether the figure has been an estimate to include cases thought to occur that have not been reported. Varying definitions of child abuse used by different authorities compound the difficulties in the interpretation of the data. While most who have worked in the child abuse area would agree that many cases still go unreported, there is also a considerable amount of over-reporting. In the United States it was found that 60% of all reports are determined to be "unfounded" by the agencies that investigate them (29). Thus, there is a situation of simultaneous under-reporting of many real cases and over-reporting of cases where child abuse and neglect have not occurred. Besides being stressful to parents, this over-reporting places a heavy burden on the staff in child protection agencies whose limited resources may make it difficult for them to respond promptly and effectively when children really are in need of protection.

Besharov (15) has pointed out that figures for abuse in the United States have varied from Kempe and Helfer's (21) figure of 55,000 to 65,000 reported cases in 1972, based on an incidence of 250 to 300 cases per 1,000,000 population per year, to Gil's (30) estimate of 2,500,000 to 4,000,000 cases per year based on a definition of "some degree of physical injury." More recently Straus (31), using a national probability survey of American children aged between three and 17 years, estimated that approximately 6,500,000 children were abused each year. Straus makes the point that the most likely reason for his figure being so high is that his data were based on violent acts carried out *toward* children, rather than on injuries received.

Other methods of obtaining data on child abuse incidents can be from surveys within a defined community or by making estimates from the number of cases presenting to medical services. Using a strict definition of severe physical abuse, Baldwin and Oliver (32) carried out a retrospective and a prospective study in North-East Wiltshire, England. They found a rate of one case per 1,000 children in their prospective survey, a rate that was 2.6 times that found in their retrospective study.

Kempe and Helfer (21) estimated that 15% of children under five years of age who attend hospital casualty departments are likely to have inflicted injuries. Twenty-five percent of all fractures seen in the first two years of life at the University of Colorado Medical Center are estimated to be due to the battered child syndrome (22). Holter and Friedman (33) in New York found seven cases of child abuse in 69 children who attended the casualty department over a two-week period. Six months later they repeated the study with similar findings, detecting seven cases out of 87 casualty presentations. A study from the Royal Alexandra Hospital for Children in Sydney showed that 40% of children under five years of age presenting to the casualty department with injuries or burns had features strongly suggestive of child abuse (34).

Although family practitioners are in a unique position to detect child abuse and more importantly to detect those features and developing stresses in the family that may lead to abuse, the great majority of child abuse reports come from hospitals. A survey of a family practice containing 1,841 children in Oxford, England, found 12 cases of actual abuse during a three-year period and 30 children thought to be at risk (35). (This is probably a higher incidence than would normally be detected as this practice had a particular interest in child abuse.)

Although there is a lack of clarity about the definition of child abuse and its true incidence, the important conclusion that should be drawn from these studies is that child abuse is a relatively common problem. It is far more prevalent than many other diseases to which considerable pediatric time and resources are devoted; as such it is worthy of a greater share of resources, as well as further study, for appropriate treatment and prevention.

THE PROBLEM OF CHILD ABUSE

VIOLENCE IN SOCIETY

Violence in society, and in particular within families, is common. Brandon (36) has pointed out that statistically it is safer to be on the streets after dark with a stranger than to be at home in the bosom of one's family, for it is here that accidents, murder, and violence are likely to occur. Although considerable public interest has been focused on child abuse, there are less publicized episodes of violence in the home such as wife battering, violence by children, and "granny bashing" (37).

Straus (38) claims that human beings have an inherent capacity for violence. In a national sample of adults in the United States he showed that stressful life experiences were associated with assaults between husband and wife and that the number of violence incidents correlated with the amount of stress. However, he pointed out that stress by itself does not necessarily lead to violence. Men who have a supportive network rarely assault their wives as compared with men who are socially isolated and who have a high rate of assault. The most important implication for child abuse from this study is the finding that early experiences of violence carry over into adult behavior. This study suggests that physical punishment of children by parents trains them to respond to stress by violence.

Violence toward children in families is common. In 1978 Gelles (39) reported a survey done on a true cross-section of American families. He found that of 46,000,000 children in the United States aged between three and 17 years who were living with their parents in 1976, between one and 1.9 million were bitten, kicked, or punched by their parents. A gun or knife was used by 0.2% of the parents. Gelles makes the disturbing comment that the parents questioned in the survey may have admitted to these acts of violence because they felt they were *acceptable* ways of bringing up children.

Graham (40) has shown that in a survey of mothers interviewed one month after the birth of their child, 61% admitted that there had been times when they felt angry with their baby and 81% felt that the experience of having a young baby to cope with had made them more sympathetic to baby batterers. Frude and Goss (41) surveyed 111 Welsh mothers with children aged between one and four years and found that 26% had punished their children in ways they believed to be wrong. Fifty-seven percent admitted that on at least one occasion they had lost their tempers completely and had hit their child really hard, while 40% had entertained the fear that they might lose their tempers and seriously damage the child. Even though child abuse is widespread and even considering the frequency with which the mothers seem to become intensely angry with their babies, these findings indicate that the strategies of most mothers for self-control are effective.

Violence to children does not only occur in families. Abuse of children can also take place in schools, children's homes, children's courts, childcare centers, hospitals, and mental health establishments (42–46). The importance of extrafamilial violence was recognized by the Fourth International Congress on Child Abuse and Neglect in 1982. This conference took violence outside the family as its theme, with papers presented on violence occurring to children in foster homes, schools, hospitals, and other institutions (47).

From the medical and social work viewpoint child abuse is thought to be a result of family maladjustment and the failings of particular family members. This is in contrast to Gil's view (30). He contends that the common medical and social work assumption is false and that the fundamental problem is within a social structure that condones poverty and condones physical force in rearing children. He defines violence as "acts which obstruct the spontaneous unfolding of innate human potential, the inherent human drive toward development and self-actualization" (48, p. 384). Gil argues that personal violence is usually rooted in structural violence, which he defines as violence that occurs at institutional and societal levels (49). Views such as those of Gil and of the traditional medical and social work sector are complementary rather than in conflict. While it is important to recognize the need for major changes in society's values and attitudes to children, one should not lose sight of and abandon the valuable role played by the professional working with individual families.

The stresses of modern society and the problems of alcohol and drug addiction may also contribute to child abuse. It has been shown in a nationally representative sample of 1,146 parents in the United

THE PROBLEM OF CHILD ABUSE

States that stressful events have a direct correlation with the incidence of child abuse. The greater the number of stressful events in the parents' lives, the higher the incidence of child abuse. Parents who experienced the least stress had the lowest rate of child abuse (50). A study of the adequacy of childcare in families with alcohol or opiate addiction showed that in 41% of these families abuse or neglect of the child occurred (51).

CROSS-CULTURAL ASPECTS

Jill Korbin, an anthropologist who has studied childrearing and child abuse in different societies, has pointed out that the westerners' concept of childrearing is based on a narrow slice of humanity which hampers an understanding of childrearing in other cultures (52). With increasing migration resulting in many societies becoming multicultural, it is important for those working in the child abuse area to have an appreciation of childrearing patterns of other cultures. Consider the following case illustration documented by Korbin (53).

In London in 1974 an East African woman cut the faces of her two young sons with a razor blade and rubbed charcoal into the lacerations. The woman was arrested and tried for child abuse. During the proceedings it was found that she was a member of a tribe that traditionally practiced facial scarification. Her actions were an attempt to assert the cultural identity of her children since without such markings her boys would be unable to participate as adults in their own culture. Failure to scarify the children would have been neglectful or abusive within the cultural context of her tribe. Korbin points out that this sort of incident demonstrates the difficulty of comparing practices taken out of their cultural context. How would we explain to the East African community that the practice of scarification is abuse, while painful orthodontic work done on children in our own society is not only acceptable but also desirable (54)!

Even normal childrearing practices differ markedly between cultures. Middle-class Americans, British, and Australians believe that each child should have his own bed, if not his own room. In contrast, Hawaiian-American women are incredulous that middle-class Americans should put their infants into a separate bed or even a separate room. Their cultural belief is that such a practice is detrimental to child development and is potentially dangerous (52). A tribal group in New Guinea was appalled that the American anthropologist living in their midst allowed her newborn infant to cry without being immediately picked up. The American mother was adhering to her own cultural belief about parenting, while the New Guinea tribe was concerned that if the baby cried for too long its spirit would escape through the open fontanel and the child would then die (52).

Children are likely to experience difficulties in countries that are becoming westernized and adopting Western standards. The transition between the old and new culture may result in a breakdown of cultural standards without an adequate social support structure to replace them. This has been shown among the Samia of Kenya where, probably because of a strong clan and extended family structure, child abuse was rare. Now, due to increasing migration to the towns, socioeconomic change, and mixed marriages, the clan and family structure are being eroded and cases of child abuse are appearing (55). A similar problem has been reported amongst the Zulus (56) and in Nigeria (57), where child abuse has increased along with growing industrialization and a breakdown of the traditional extended family structure.

Some cultures are very reluctant to recognize child abuse. In Indonesia people who make complaints about child abuse are liable to be sued for invasion of a family's privacy and there are no laws that specifically protect children from cruelty (58). In a prospective study from the University Hospital of Kuala Lumpur, Malaysia, only 19 cases of child abuse could be found over two years. The authors of this study stated that the social and cultural constraints prevented adequate identification of the problem (59). Kempe (60), taking the historical view, pointed out that 30 years ago child abuse in the industrial world was thought to be uncommon and he suggested that the low incidence of child abuse and neglect from many other cultures may reflect the need for greater active public and professional concern about the condition.

Although it is difficult not to be greatly influenced by one's own cultural beliefs about what constitutes good and bad childrearing, some helpful guidelines for understanding childrearing practices

THE PROBLEM OF CHILD ABUSE

from other countries have been produced by Korbin. She suggests that in trying to decide whether a practice is harmful to the child one should consider the cultural acceptance of the act, the intent of the adult who performs it, the way the child perceives the incident, and what this means to the development of the child as a member of his culture (52).

CHILD ABUSE AND THE LAW

Following the publication of the paper by Kempe and colleagues in 1962 (2), intense interest in child abuse was aroused in the United States. This was followed by the introduction of state laws to make the reporting of child abuse mandatory. By 1973 every state had mandatory reporting laws (61–63). However, it soon became clear that merely the passage of a law was not enough and that community follow-up and support services were required to ensure that appropriate treatment was provided for reported cases (64). Few states made provision for extra services to treat these families. An exception was the state of Massachusetts where a committee was formed to make recommendations for providing services for families reported under child abuse legislation (65). In many cases legislation led to a dramatic increase in case reports but the services available to the families were quite inadequate to deal with this sudden increase (66, 67). Problems of fragmentation of services have occurred but although child protection programs still have grave weaknesses, there has been a steady increase in their scope and quality (29). Increased reporting and specialized child protection agencies have saved many thousands of children from danger and serious injury. New York State has had a reduction in child fatality due to abuse from 200 per year to less than 100 (68). In Denver, the number of hospitalized abused children who died from their injuries dropped from 20 per year to less than one per year in 1978 (69).

Although widely debated, compulsory notification has not been introduced in England. The extensive and highly regarded system of health visitors available in that country makes it likely that many actual and potential child abuse cases are detected at an early age.

In recent years Australia has moved toward compulsory notification. A review of Australian child abuse legislation by Fotheringham (70) in 1974 showed that only South Australia had compulsory notification legislation. In 1974 Tasmania formulated a statewide plan to coordinate the activities of persons or bodies involved in the care of child abuse victims and, after lengthy discussion on whether to introduce mandatory reporting laws, decided not to do this (71). Since the mid-1970s each of the Australian states has announced its policy on child abuse, created management structures for dealing with it, developed treatment programs, and devised legislation that has included a redefinition of child abuse (72). New South Wales, Queensland, South Australia, Tasmania, and the Northern Territory now have compulsory notification, although New South Wales is the only state that provides penalties for failure to notify (73).

Having cared for abused children both before and after the introduction of mandatory notification in New South Wales, the author is firmly in favor of mandatory notification, providing this notification is made to a state welfare department with the aim of protecting the child and helping the family rather than to the police where an investigative and punitive approach may be taken. Notification legislation has also meant that strong pressure has been put on governments to mobilize and provide support services to deal with notified cases. Although these services are far from adequate, without the impetus of notification legislation it is likely that services would have been minimal. From a practical point of view it often helps when seeing a case of child abuse to use the notification legislation to bring the issue into the open with the family. This gives the opportunity to stress the need felt by all parties, including the parents, to ensure that the child grows up well and happy, without any further injuries, and to provide some ongoing support for the parents.

CLINICAL FEATURES

The clinical features of child abuse were clearly documented in the classic study of Kempe's group in 1962 (2). They pointed out that the clinical spectrum ranged from children where the trauma was very mild to cases with florid evidence of injuries to the skeleton and soft

THE PROBLEM OF CHILD ABUSE

tissues. They described the children's health as often being below par and said that the children frequently showed evidence of neglect, including poor skin hygiene and multiple soft-tissue minor injuries. Subdural hematomas, with or without fractures of the skull, were a common finding. Fontana's (74) description was similar and also mentioned burns as a feature. Silverman (75) commented that bruises were often in different stages of development and recommended that observers should look for bruise patterns that may be consistent with human bite marks.

A history of repeated accidents in the past and of frequent visits to casualty departments, often at different hospitals, has been noted as a possible indication of child abuse. Sometimes these repeated visits for what seem to be trivial complaints are really cries for help from a stressed parent (76). Schmitt noted that while bruises, head injuries, burns, and fractures were common, poisons and lacerations were relatively uncommon (77). A report of 132 cases from Canada (78) showed that bruising was the most frequent manifestation, occurring in 41% of cases, and that fractures, usually involving the long bone, occurred in 38% of cases. A report from Sydney showed a similarly high incidence of bruises and fractures (79). A study of 146 fatal cases (80) showed that the most common injuries were multiple rib fractures and lacerations of the lungs, liver, spleen, mesentery, and pancreas, with accompanying hemothorax and hemoperitoneum.

Shaking Injuries

It has been pointed out that subdural hematomas can occur in the absence of any direct head injury (81–83). The damage to the brain and surrounding tissues occurs as a result of the repeated acceleration–deceleration and rotation forces produced when the child is shaken. It is likely that many of the so-called spontaneous subdural hematomas of infants described in earlier pediatric texts were actually occurring in abused children who had been violently shaken. Ingraham and Matson published a series of 98 cases of subdural hematoma of infancy in 1944 (84). In this beautifully written paper they discussed the clinical features and pathology of this condition,

56   CHILD ABUSE AND NEGLECT

emphasizing that the presentation is often subtle with no other evidence of injury or history of birth trauma in half of the cases. Although they noted that more than one-third of the infants in their series were in poor general condition, often malnourished, and from homes where the economic circumstances were poor, the climate in 1944 was not ripe for concluding that the parents may have produced the injuries in a proportion of these cases.

Eye Injuries

The suggestion that shaking can cause retinal hemorrhages was first made in 1967 (85). Idiopathic retinal hemorrhages occurred in 14% of newborns but this incidence dropped to 2.6% by the third to fifth day (86) so that it is unlikely that retinal hemorrhages seen after the first month of life would be idiopathic. The majority of retinal hemorrhages that follow child abuse are minimal and undergo complete resolution (87). However, in some cases the damage to the eyes may be more serious, leading to permanent visual handicap (87, 88). Mushin emphasizes that a complete ophthalmic examination should always be included as a part of the assessment of the abused child (86). Pale-centered retinal hemorrhages in the absence of systemic disease have been reported to be highly suggestive of child abuse (89).

Drowning

Drowning or attempted drowning is another form of abuse that may be particularly difficult to diagnose in infants as it leaves no specific sign. Pearn's group (90–92) emphasized that this diagnosis should be considered in the differential diagnosis of atypical immersion incident in infants.

Burns

Burns are a common manifestation of abuse. Smith and Hanson (93) reported serious burns or scalds in 20% of 124 battered children

THE PROBLEM OF CHILD ABUSE

studied in Birmingham, England, and drew attention to burns of the buttocks or perineum inflicted by placing the child on a hot metal surface such as a stove. Glove and stocking types of burns of the hands and feet are suspicious, suggesting that the child's limbs may have been held in hot water. Stone and co-workers (94) reported that 4.2% of 623 children admitted to a burn unit were intentionally burnt and that abuse was suspected in an additional 4% of the children. Burns and scalds seem to be more premeditated than injuries produced by sudden outbursts of violence, suggesting that a high proportion of psychopathic parents might be found in this group (95).

Unusual Injuries

A variety of more unusual injuries may occur. These include subgaleal hematomas caused by hair-pulling, genital injuries, tears to the floor of the mouth caused by trauma at feeding, traumatic cysts of the pancreas, and intramural hematoma of the bowel caused by blows to the abdomen and leading to symptoms and signs of intestinal obstruction (96). Cutaneous lesions may take the shape of a recognizable object such as the loop mark caused by a flexible object like a belt or electric cord (97). Diffuse or nonfocal neurological signs may also occur and should make one think of child abuse in a child who presents with unusual and unexplainable neurological features (98).

Poisoning and Factitious Illness

An unusual form of child abuse is that in which the child is deliberately poisoned by the parents, not with homicidal intent but to an extent that leads to prolonged hospitalization and extensive investigations to find the cause of the child's unusual symptoms. The poisoning often continues in the hospital environment when the mother visits the child. The mother, who is often described as pleasant and cooperative, encourages the medical team to try further investigative measures, while she is actually continuing to poison her child. In addition to poisoning, the parent may produce factitious illness in

58   CHILD ABUSE AND NEGLECT

her child by producing contaminated bodily excretions said to have come from the child or by inducing other symptoms such as high temperature or respiratory difficulties (99–102).

Radiology

Because the junction of the cartilage with the shaft of the long bone is one of the weakest areas in the growing child and because these areas are the most vulnerable to the torsion and tension forces that occur when the child is pulled or shaken, epiphyseal separations and metaphyseal fractures are the commonest lesions. Subperiosteal hemorrhages commonly occur, lifting the periosteum, which then lays down new bone in its new position. Spiral fractures, which are unusual in normal childhood accidents, occur as a result of twisting, shearing forces applied to long bones.

Sudden Infant Death Syndrome

It is probable that a small number of cases of sudden infant death syndrome are actually cases of child abuse (102, 103), although an epidemiological study published in 1977 did not support this hypothesis (104). This is a sensitive area as sudden infant death syndrome is common and good management dictates that a supportive, blamefree approach should be stressed with these parents. The situation is further clouded by social factors such as lower socioeconomic status, young parents, poor antenatal care, and illegitimacy, which have an increased incidence in both child abuse and the sudden infant death syndrome.

DIAGNOSIS AND CASE FINDING

A major difficulty in making the diagnosis of child abuse is likely to be the doctor's own denial that he is faced with this condition. Doctors are often poorly trained to deal with child abuse, are reluctant to become involved in court action, and may be uncomfortable in working cooperatively with other professionals (105). Doctors may

THE PROBLEM OF CHILD ABUSE

also feel uncomfortable when confronted with an abused child and his parents, and are likely to accept at face value a most unlikely explanation for the injury rather than to seek its real cause (106). Doctors who have worked with such families will understand the feelings of Sanders when he says that in his experience it is more difficult to tell the parents he is reporting them than it is for them to accept his action (106).

Silver and colleagues (107) reviewed 52 situations in which doctors had difficulty in establishing or making the diagnosis of child abuse and found that in each case the prime difficulty was the doctor's own subjective feelings or his misunderstanding of his role and responsibility under the child abuse reporting laws. In many cases the diagnosis is difficult. Gregg and Elmer (108) studied 146 accidents, 30 of which were due to abuse. They found it was difficult to separate the two groups on the history of the accident alone and stressed that assessment of the family, particularly its childcare practices, was the most useful differentiating factor. Widespread acceptance that child abuse does occur and the availability of experienced colleagues have lessened the problem, although the individual practitioner still needs to be aware of the unconscious tendency to overlook this diagnosis.

History and Physical Examination

Kempe (2), in contrast to Gregg and Elmer, pointed out that an important diagnostic clue was the discrepancy between the clinical findings and the history given by the parents. For example, abusive parents whose child has a severe head injury may say that it occurred when the child fell out of bed. However, in a study of 246 children under five years who fell out of bed, Helfer did not find any cases of severe head injury (109). This discrepancy between the explanation given and the features of the injuries offers the initial clue that the injury may not have been accidental. Bruising is often found in areas unlikely to be damaged in an accidental injury, and sometimes bruises carry the pattern of adult fingerprints where the child has been gripped around the arm or face. Of course, a certain amount of bruising, particularly on shins and knees, is normal in preschool chil-

60   CHILD ABUSE AND NEGLECT

dren (110). Roberton and colleagues (111) compared the pattern of bruising in 400 normal children with that found in 84 abused children and showed that the pattern varied considerably, with injuries to the face, head, and lumbar region being much more common in the abused group. The age of the bruise might suggest that it occurred at a different time to that given in the history, and data are available to assist in determining the age of bruises (112).

Assessment of the Family

There are many characteristics known to occur more commonly in parents who abuse their children and these will be discussed in a following chapter. Family assessment, which may take several interviews and require the assistance of other professionals, as well as often being necessary for the diagnosis, is essential for deciding upon the most appropriate treatment plan. An assessment of the children's behavior and development should also be made. Abused children may exhibit withdrawn, apathetic behavior and delay in their developmental milestones, particularly speech development.

Investigations

Coagulation studies may be required to exclude a bleeding disorder where there is marked bruising. Although bleeding disorders are only rarely misdiagnosed as child abuse, it is often wise to do coagulation studies in order to be able to refute in court the suggestion that the child has a coagulation disorder. Examination of urine for blood is also important when there has been an abdominal injury. A skeletal survey may indicate the typical skeletal injuries as described above and may also reveal old fractures at different stages of healing, suggesting multiple injuries in the past. Radionuclide bone scanning has been shown to be more sensitive than radiological studies in detecting early evidence of periosteal injury (113, 114). Ultrasound is useful for demonstrating duodenal hematomas and in the evaluation of pancreatic pseudocysts following pancreatic trauma (115). Patterns of radiological findings are useful in helping to differentiate acciden-

THE PROBLEM OF CHILD ABUSE

61

tal from nonaccidental injury. Skull fractures in abused children are more likely to be complex, multiple, or depressed with associated intracranial injuries (116), and rib fractures in abuse are likely to be multiple, of different ages, and to affect adjacent ribs (117).

Case Finding

Hospital-based staff play a particularly important role in the detection of child abuse, as cases usually present to these areas (33, 34) in contrast to general practice (118). It is uncertain whether this is because family doctors are not recognizing the condition or whether the families prefer the anonymity of a hospital. Although child abuse can occur in all socioeconomic classes (119), it seems to be far more common in the lower socioeconomic groups (30, 120) and these groups tend to use hospital casualty and outpatient services rather than privately based medicine.

It is incumbent on medical practitioners, especially those working in a hospital setting, to be aware of the various presentations of child abuse. Although the laboratory and radiological investigations may be of some value, the most important factor is the doctor's own clinical acumen. This is not to say that all medical practitioners should be experts in child abuse. Those who work with abused children and their families need to have special training in this area and to be able to work comfortably and on equal terms with other professional groups in providing child abuse services. While it is not reasonable to expect all medical practitioners to automatically be interested and competent in child abuse management, it is reasonable to expect them to be aware of the problem and to refer a suspected case to a colleague or other agency.

REFERENCES

1. Pearn, J.G. (1981). *Child abuse—An overview with priorities for the future.* Second Australasian Conference on Child Abuse, Queensland; Government Printer, pp. 534–558.
2. Kempe, C.H., Silverman, F.N., Steele, B.F., Droegmueller, W., & Silver, H.K. (1962). The battered child syndrome. *Journal of the American Medical Association, 181,* 17–24.

3. Bakan, D. (1971). *Slaughter of the Innocents: A study of the battered child phenomenon.* San Francisco: Jossey-Bass.
4. Radbill, S.X. (1974). A history of child abuse and infanticide. In R.E. Helfer & C.H. Kempe (Eds.), *The battered child* (2nd ed.). Chicago: University of Chicago Press.
5. Fraser, B.G. (1976). The child and his parents: A delicate balance of rights. In R.E. Helfer & C.H. Kempe (Eds.), *Child abuse and neglect: The family and the community.* Cambridge, MA: Ballinger.
6. Fontana, V.J. (1964). *The maltreated child: The maltreatment syndrome in children.* Springfield, IL: Charles C Thomas.
7. Allen, A., & Morton, A. (1961). *This is your child.* London: Routledge & Kegan Paul.
8. Tardieu, A. (1860). Etude medico-légale sur les services et mauvais traitements exercés sur des enfants. In S.M. Smith (Ed.), *The battered child syndrome.* London: Butterworths, 1975.
9. West, S. (1888). Acute periosteal swellings in several young infants of the same family, probably rickety in nature. *British Medical Journal, 1,* 856–857.
10. Caffey, J. (1946). Multiple fractures in the long bones of infants suffering from chronic subdural hematoma. *American Journal of Roentgenology, 56,* 163–173.
11. Astley, R. (1953). Multiple metaphyseal fractures in small children (metaphyseal fragility of bone). *British Journal of Radiology, 26,* 577–583.
12. Silverman, F.N. (1953). The Roentgen manifestations of unrecognized skeletal trauma in infants. *American Journal of Roentgenology, 69,* 413–427.
13. Woolley, P.V., & Evans, W.A. (1955). Significance of skeletal lesions in infants resembling those of traumatic origin. *Journal of the American Medical Association, 158,* 539–543.
14. Mitchell, R.G. (1975). The incidence and nature of child abuse. *Developmental Medicine and Child Neurology, 17,* 641–646.
15. Besharov, D.J. (1981). Toward better research on child abuse and neglect: Making definitional issues an explicit methodological concern. *Child Abuse and Neglect, 5,* 383–390.
16. Newson, J., & Newson, G. (1965). *Patterns of infant care in an urban community.* Harmondsworth, England: Penguin Books.
17. Korbin, J. (1982). What is acceptable and unacceptable child-rearing. In R.K. Oates (Ed.), *Child abuse—A community concern.* Sydney: Butterworths. (New York: Brunner/Mazel, 1984)
18. Straus, M.A. (1980). Stress and child abuse. In C.H. Kempe & R.E. Helfer (Eds.), *The battered child* (3rd ed.). Chicago: The University of Chicago Press.
19. Oates, R.K. (1982). Child abuse—A community concern. In R.K. Oates (Ed.), *Child abuse—A community concern.* Sydney: Butterworths. (New York: Brunner/Mazel, 1984)
20. Gil, D.G. (1975). Unravelling child abuse. *American Journal of Orthopsychiatry, 45,* 346–356.
21. Kempe, C.H., & Helfer, R.E. (1972). *Helping the battered child and his family.* Philadelphia: J.B. Lippincott.
22. Kempe, C.H. (1971). Pediatric implication of the battered baby syndrome. *Archives of Disease in Childhood, 46,* 28–37.

THE PROBLEM OF CHILD ABUSE

23. U.S. National Center on Child Abuse and Neglect (1981). National Study of the Incidence and Severity of Child Abuse and Neglect. Washington, D.C.: D.H.H.S., p. 11.
24. U.S. Children's Bureau (1966). Juvenile Court Statistics, U.S. Washington, D.C.: D.H.E.W., p. 13.
25. Ferguson, D.M., Fleming, J., & O'Neill, D.P. (1972). *Child abuse in New Zealand.* Wellington: Research Division, Department of Social Welfare, Government Printer.
26. Report of the Community Welfare Advisory Committee (1979). Inquiry into Nonaccidental Physical Injury to Children in South Australia. South Australian Department of Community Welfare. Catalogue #362-74.
27. Department of Youth and Community Services. Annual Report 1977-1978. Sydney: New South Wales Government Printer.
28. Australian Bureau of Statistics. 1981 Census Figures. Canberra: Australian Government Printer.
29. Besharov, D.J. (1983). Child protection: Past progress, present problems and future directions. *Family Law Quarterly, 17*(2), 151-172.
30. Gil, D.G. (1970). *Violence against children.* Cambridge, MA: Harvard University Press.
31. Straus, M.A. (1980). Stress and physical abuse. *Child Abuse and Neglect, 4,* 75-88.
32. Baldwin, J.A., & Oliver, J.E. (1975). Epidemiology and family characteristics of severely abused children. *British Journal of Preventive and Social Medicine, 29,* 205-221.
33. Holter, J.C., & Friedman, S.B. (1968). Child abuse: Early case finding in the emergency department. *Pediatrics, 42,* 128-138.
34. Springthorpe, B.J., Oates, R.K., & Hayes, S.C. (1977). Non-accidental childhood injury presenting at a hospital casualty department. *Medical Journal of Australia, 2,* 629-632.
35. Beswick, K., Lynch, M.A., & Roberts, J. (1976). Child abuse and general practice. *British Medical Journal, 2,* 800-802.
36. Brandon, S. (1976). Physical violence in the family: An overview. In M. Borland (Ed.), *Violence in the family.* Atlantic Highlands, N.J.: Humanities Press.
37. Freeman, M.D.A. (1979). *Violence in the home.* London: Saxon House.
38. Straus, M.A. (1980). Social stress and marital violence in a national sample of American families. *Annals of the New York Academy of Science, 347,* 229-250.
39. Gelles, R.J. (1978). Violence towards children in the United States. *American Journal of Orthopsychiatry, 48,* 580-592.
40. Graham, H. (1980). Mothers' accounts of anger and aggression towards their babies. In N. Frude (Ed.), *Psychological approaches to child abuse.* London: Batsford Academic Press.
41. Frude, N., & Goss, A. (1980). Maternal anger and the young child. In N. Frude (Ed.), *Psychological approaches to child abuse.* London: Batsford Academic Press.
42. Polier, J.W. (1979). Professional abuse of children. In D.G. Gil (Ed.), *Child abuse and violence.* New York: AMS Press.
43. Fisher, S.M. (1979). Life in a children's detention centre. In D.G. Gil (Ed.), *Child abuse and violence.* New York: AMS Press.

44. Royal Commission on Human Relationships (1977). Final Report, Vol. 2. Canberra: Australian Government Printing Service.
45. Duncan, C. (1979). They beat children don't they? In D.G. Gil (Ed.), *Child abuse and violence.* New York: AMS Press.
46. Rindfleish, N., & Rabb, J. (1984). How much of a problem is resident mistreatment in child welfare institutions? *Child Abuse and Neglect, 8,* 33–40.
47. Abstracts, Fourth International Congress on Child Abuse and Neglect, Paris (September 1982). Paris: International Children's Center.
48. Gil, D.G. (1979). Societal violence and violence in families. In D.G. Gil (Ed.), *Child abuse and violence.* New York: AMS Press.
49. Gil, D.G. (1978). Societal violence and violence in families. In D.G. Gil (Ed.), *Family violence, an international interdisciplinary study.* Toronto: Butterworths.
50. Straus, M.A., Gelles, R.J., & Steinmetz, S.K. (1980). *Behind closed doors: Violence in the American family.* New York: Doubleday.
51. Black, R., & Mayer, J. (1980). Parents with special problems: Alcoholism and opiate addiction. *Child Abuse and Neglect, 4,* 45–54.
52. Korbin, J. (1980). The cross-cultural context of child abuse and neglect. In C.H. Kempe & R.E. Helfer (Eds.), *The battered child* (3rd ed.). Chicago: The University of Chicago Press.
53. Korbin, J. (1977). Anthropological contributions to the study of child abuse. *Child Abuse and Neglect, 1,* 7–24.
54. Korbin, J. (1980). Cultural context of child abuse and neglect. *Child Abuse and Neglect, 4,* 3–13.
55. Fraser, G., & Kilbride, R.L. (1980). Child abuse and neglect—Rare, but perhaps increasing phenomena among the Samia of Kenya. *Child Abuse and Neglect, 4,* 226–232.
56. Leoning, W.E.K. (1981). Child abuse among the Zulus; a people in cultural transition. *Child Abuse and Neglect, 5,* 3–7.
57. Okeahialim, T.C. (1984). Child abuse in Nigeria. *Child Abuse and Neglect, 8,* 69–73.
58. Haditono, B.R. (1981). Prevention and treatment of child abuse and neglect among children under five years of age in Indonesia. *Child Abuse and Neglect, 5,* 97–101.
59. Nathan, L., & Hwang, W.T. (1981). Child abuse in an urban center in Malaysia, *Child Abuse and Neglect, 5,* 241–248.
60. Kempe, C.H. (1982). Cross-cultural perspectives in child abuse. *Pediatrics, 69,* 497–498.
61. Paulsen, M.G. (1974). The law and abused children. In R.E. Helfer & C.H. Kempe (Eds.), *The battered child* (2nd ed.). Chicago: The University of Chicago Press.
62. Fraser, B.G. (1974). A survey of child abuse legislation, 1973. In R.E. Helfer & C.H. Kempe (Eds.), *The battered child* (2nd ed.). Chicago: The University of Chicago Press.
63. Isaacs, J.L. (1973). The law and the abused and neglected child. *Pediatrics, 51,* 783–792.
64. Felder, S. (1971). A lawyer's view of child abuse. *Public Welfare, 29,* 181–188.
65. Newberger, E.H., Haas, G., & Mulford, R.M. (1973). Child abuse in Massachusetts. *Massachusetts Physician, 32,* 31–38.

THE PROBLEM OF CHILD ABUSE

66. Rosenfeld, A.A., & Newberger, E.H. (1977). Compassion vs. control. *Journal of the American Medical Association, 237*, 2086–2088.
67. Bergman, A.B. (1978). Abuse of the child abuse law. *Pediatrics, 62*, 266–267.
68. New York State Department of Social Services (1980). Child Protective Services in New York State, 1979 Annual Report. New York: New York State Department of Social Services.
69. Kempe, R.S., & Kempe, C.H. (1978). *Child abuse.* London: Fontana.
70. Fotheringham, B.J. (1974). Legislative aspects of the battered baby syndrome in the various states of Australia. *Medical Journal of Australia, 2*, 235–239.
71. Everett, M.G., Lewis, I.C., Moir, C.H., Smith, G.C., & Stranger, D.McK. (1973). The battered baby syndrome: The Tasmanian approach. *Medical Journal of Australia, 2*, 735–737.
72. Boss, P. (1981). Towards an understanding of child abuse: An overview of Australian Policy. Second Australasian Conference on Child Abuse, Conference Proceedings. Queensland: Government Printer.
73. Kirby, M.D. (1981). Child abuse: What can the law do? Second Australasian Conference on Child Abuse, Conference Proceedings. Queensland: Government Printer.
74. Fontana, V.J., Donovan, D., & Wong, R.J. (1963). The "maltreatment syndrome" in children. *New England Journal of Medicine, 269*, 1389–1394.
75. Silverman, F.N. (1972). Unrecognized trauma in infants: The battered child syndrome and the syndrome of Ambrose Tardieu. *Radiology, 104*, 337–352.
76. Oates, R.K. (1976). Child abuse—Recognition and management. *Bulletin of the Postgraduate Committee in Medicine,* University of Sydney, July, 120–125.
77. Schmitt, B.D. (1974). Battered child syndrome. In H.K. Silver & C.H. Kempe (Eds.), *Current pediatric diagnosis and treatment.* Los Altos, CA: Lange Medical Publications.
78. McRae, K.N., Ferguson, C.A., & Lederman, R.S. (1973). The battered child syndrome. *Canadian Medical Association Journal, 108*, 859–860.
79. Ryan, M.G., Davis, A.A., & Oates, R.K. (1977). One hundred and eighty-seven cases of child abuse and neglect. *Medical Journal of Australia, 2*, 623–628.
80. Adelson, L. (1961). Slaughter of the innocents: A study of forty-six homicides in which the victims were children. *New England Journal of Medicine, 264*, 1345–1349.
81. Guthkelch, A.N. (1971). Infantile subdural hematoma and its relationship to whiplash injuries. *British Medical Journal, 2*, 430–431.
82. Caffey, J. (1972). On the theory and practice of shaking infants. *American Journal of Diseases of Children, 124*, 161–169.
83. Caffey, J. (1974). The whiplash shaken infant syndrome. *Pediatrics, 54*, 396–403.
84. Ingraham, F.D., & Matson, D.D. (1944). Subdural hematoma in infancy. *Journal of Pediatrics, 24*, 1–37.
85. Gilkes, M.J., & Mann, T.P. (1967). Fundi of battered babies. *Lancet, 2*, 468–469.
86. Sezen, F. (1970). Retinal hemorrhages in newborn infants. *British Journal of Ophthalmology, 55*, 248–253.
87. Mushin, A.S. (1971). Ocular damage in the battered baby syndrome. *British Medical Journal, 3*, 402–404.

88. Harcourt, B., & Hopkins, D. (1971). Ophthalmic manifestations of the battered baby syndrome. *British Medical Journal, 3,* 398–401.
89. Carter, J.E., & McCormick, A.Q. (1983). Whiplash shaking syndrome: Retinal hemorrhages and computerized axial tomography of the brain. *Child Abuse and Neglect, 7,* 279–286.
90. Pearn, J., & Nixon, J. (1977). Attempted drowning as a form of non-accidental injury. *Australian Paediatric Journal, 13,* 110–113.
91. Pearn, J., & Nixon, J. (1977). Non-accidental immersion in the bath: Another extension to the syndrome of child abuse and neglect. *Child Abuse and Neglect, 1,* 445–448.
92. Pearn, J.H., Brown, J., Wong, R., & Bart, R. (1979). Bathtub drownings: Report of seven cases. *Pediatrics, 64,* 68–70.
93. Smith, S.M., & Hanson, R. (1974). One hundred and thirty-four battered children: A medical and psychological study. *British Medical Journal, 3,* 666–670.
94. Stone, N.N., Rinaldo, L., Humphrey, C.R., & Brown, R.K. (1970). Child abuse by burning. *Surgical Clinics of North America, 50,* 1419–1424.
95. Keen, J.G., Lendrum, J., & Wolman, B. (1975). Inflicted burns and scalds in children. *British Medical Journal, 4,* 268–269.
96. Kempe, C.H. (1975). Uncommon manifestations of the battered child syndrome. *American Journal of Diseases of Children, 129,* 1265–1266.
97. Ellerstein, N.S. (1979). The cutaneous manifestations of child abuse and neglect. *American Journal of Diseases of Children, 133,* 906–909.
98. Baron, M.A., Bejar, R.L., & Sheaff, P.J. (1970). Neurological manifestations of the battered child syndrome. *Pediatrics, 45,* 1003–1007.
99. Meadow, R. (1977). Munchausen syndrome by proxy: The hinterland of child abuse. *Lancet, 2,* 343–345.
100. Watson, J.B.G., Davis, J.M., & Hunter, J.L.P. (1979). Non-accidental poisoning in childhood. *Archives of Disease in Childhood, 54,* 143–144.
101. Schnaps, Y., Frond, M., Rand, Y., & Tirosh, M. (1981). The chemically abused child. *Pediatrics, 68,* 119–121.
102. Hick, J.F. (1973). Sudden infant death syndrome and child abuse. *Pediatrics, 52,* 147.
103. Berger, D. (1979). Child abuse simulating "near miss" sudden infant death syndrome. *Journal of Pediatrics, 95,* 554–556.
104. Kukull, W.A., & Peterson, D.R. (1977). Sudden infant death and infanticide. *American Journal of Epidemiology, 106,* 485–493.
105. Oates, R.K. (1979). Battered children and their families. *New Doctor, 14,* 15–18.
106. Sanders, R.W. (1972). Resistance to dealing with parents of battered children. *Pediatrics, 50,* 853–857.
107. Silver, C.B., Dubbin, C.C., & Lourie, R.S. (1969). Child abuse syndrome: The "grey areas" in establishing a diagnosis. *Pediatrics, 44,* 594–600.
108. Gregg, G.S., & Elmer, E. (1969). Infant injuries: Accident or abuse? *Pediatrics, 44,* 434–439.
109. Helfer, R.E., Slovis, T.L., & Black, B.S. (1977). Injuries resulting when small children fall out of bed. *Pediatrics, 60,* 533–535.
110. Keen, J.H. (1981). Normal bruises in preschool children. *Archives of Disease in Childhood, 56,* 75.

THE PROBLEM OF CHILD ABUSE

111. Roberton, D.M., Barbor, P., & Hull, D. (1982). Unusual injury? Recent injury in normal children and children with suspected non-accidental injury. *British Medical Journal, 285,* 1399–1401.
112. Wilson, E.F. (1977). Estimation of the age of cutaneous contusions in child abuse. *Pediatrics, 60,* 750–752.
113. Haas, G.M., Ortiz, V.N., Sfakianakis, G.N., & Mose, T.S. (1980). The value of radionuclide bone scanning in the early recognition of deliberate child abuse. *Journal of Trauma, 20,* 873–875.
114. Jandes, P.K. (1984). Comparison of radiography and radionuclide bone scanning in the detection of child abuse. *Pediatrics, 73,* 166–168.
115. Wilkinson, R.H. (1982). Imaging of the abused child. In E.H. Newberger (Ed.), *Child abuse.* Boston: Little, Brown.
116. Hobbs, C.J. (1984). Skull fracture and the diagnosis of child abuse. *Archives of Disease in Childhood, 59,* 246–252.
117. Feldman, K.W., & Brewer, D.K. (1984). Child abuse, cardiopulmonary resuscitation and rib fractures. *Pediatrics, 73,* 339–342.
118. Fontana, V. (1966). Recognition of maltreatment and prevention of the battered child syndrome. *Pediatrics, 38,* 1078.
119. Steele, B.F., & Pollock, C.B. (1974). A psychiatric study of parents who abuse infants and small children. In R.E. Helfer & C.H. Kempe (Eds.), *The battered child* (2nd ed.). Chicago: The University of Chicago Press.
120. Pelton, L.H. (1978). Child abuse and neglect: The myth of classlessness. *American Journal of Orthopsychiatry, 48,* 608–617.

5

The Causes of Child Abuse

CHARACTERISTICS OF THE PARENTS

Much has been written about the social and psychological characteristics of the abusing parents. However, while these descriptions enhance the understanding of the individual parent, more recent studies, using comparison groups, have shown that some of the characteristics thought to be typical of abusive parents also occur in families where abuse has not occurred. In the following pages the descriptive data on parental characteristics and the more important studies that have tried to control for confounding variables will be reviewed.

Parental Background

The way in which the parents were treated in their own childhood is said to color their own childrearing practices. Steele (1) reported that if parents have a history of significant deprivation and neglect, with or without abuse, in their own earliest years, this is of crucial importance. He emphasized that this factor stood out more than any other factor, such as the socioeconomic situation, living conditions, race, education, psychiatric state, cultural milieu, or family structure. Feshback (2) also argues that there is a positive relationship between

THE CAUSES OF CHILD ABUSE

the degree of parental punitiveness and the development of agressive behavior in children when they become adults. Solomon (3) reported that between 30% and 50% of abusing parents claimed to have been abused in their own childhood. An English study found that 31% of 85 abusive mothers reported being victims of child abuse (4).

Kadushin and Martin (5) found that 30% of the parents they studied characterized their relationship with their own parents as primarily negative. A national study from the United States based on 13,000 cases found that 20.1% of parents gave a history of abuse in their own childhood (6). It is important to realize from these figures that although many abusive parents were abused in their own childhood, the majority were not abused and did not find their own childhood experiences particularly poor.

Parental Age

Earlier descriptive studies, such as that of Skinner and Castle (7), suggested that abusive parents tended to be younger than average. Sills and colleagues (8) reported that abusive mothers in the Central Liverpool area of England were younger than the national average, but failed to take into account social class, which by itself may have accounted for the more youthful pregnancy in these mothers who were all from a lower socioeconomic group.

Seven studies (9–15) used a comparison group when looking at maternal age. Three of these studies (9–11) showed a significant difference in age groups of the mothers, the abusive mothers being shown to be younger than the control mothers. However, in these three studies the comparison group had not been matched for social class. This contrasts with the four studies that showed no difference in maternal age and in which the comparison group was matched for social class. This suggests that the association between young mothers and child abuse may be confounded by the association of each of these variables with social class, thus demonstrating how important it is to control for such factors to avoid drawing false conclusions. These seven studies are summarized in Table 1.

Table 1
Age of Abusive Mothers Compared with Controls

Author	Number of Cases	Comparison Group Matched for Social Class	Abusive Mothers Younger than Comparison Mothers
Smith et al. (9) (1974)	134	no*	yes
Lynch & Roberts (10) (1977)	50	no	yes
Lauer et al. (11) (1974)	130	no	yes
Elmer (12) (1977)	17	yes	no
Robertson & Juntz (13) (1979)	49	yes	no
Earp & Ory (14) (1980)	50	yes	no
Kinard & Klerman (15) (1980)	30	yes	no

*Age of mothers was compared with Registrar General's population data

Social Class

Child abuse has been said to occur predominantly in the lower socioeconomic groups (16). Nixon and co-workers (17), in an analysis of violent forms of death, showed that all of the children who died from child abuse in Queensland came from the lower socioeconomic groups. However, Steele and Pollock (18) have pointed out that abuse can occur in all social classes. There is likely to be a bias toward detecting child abuse cases in the lower socioeconomic groups and underdiagnosing it in the higher social classes with which the professional working in this area is more likely to identify.

Criminal Background

Frequently, a criminal record has been noted in the fathers of abused children (7, 19). Smith (19), in a comparison study, found that

THE CAUSES OF CHILD ABUSE

29% of the fathers had a criminal record. In contrast, Steele and Pollock (18) in a study of 50 families from all socioeconomic groups found no association with criminal tendencies. It is possible that social class may be the variable common to both of these factors.

Health of the Parents

A high incidence of ill health was reported in a group of abusive mothers from Oxford, England, studied by Lynch (20). This, as well as an increase in ill health in other family members, was confirmed in the study of 56 abusive families and a comparison group from Sydney (21). It has even been suggested but not proven, that premenstrual irritability may be a factor that precipitates the abusive incident (22).

Self-esteem

Four studies have compared the self-esteem of abusive mothers with that of a control group (23–26). However, these studies give conflicting results. Rosen and Stein (23), Evans (24), and Anderson and Lauderdale (25) all show that self-esteem is lower in abusive mothers. Nonetheless, the studies of Rosen and Stein and of Anderson and Lauderdale were not well controlled for other factors that may be related to self-esteem. Rosen and Stein used other mothers attending the ambulatory clinic as their controls with no matching criteria. Anderson and Lauderdale used the test norms of the self-esteem scale; these provided a nonspecific rather than a specific comparison group, which would have been more valid. The study of self-esteem by Shorkey was the best controlled, matching 14 abusive mothers and 14 controls for number of children, age of children, and age, education level, and income of the parents. This study showed no significant differences in self-esteem between the study and control mothers, although unfortunately the numbers in each group were small. A further difficulty in comparing results of self-esteem studies is that a different measure of self-concept was used in each study. If low self-esteem is a feature of abusive mothers (and this is

Table 2
Self-esteem in Abusive Mothers

Author	Rosen & Stein (23)	Evans (24)	Anderson & Lauderdale (25)	Shorkey (26)
Sample size	30	20	111	14
Controls well-matched	no	yes	no	yes
Self-esteem low	yes	yes	yes	no
Self-esteem scale used	Weedman's Self-Concept Scale	California Test of Personality	Tennessee Self-Concept Scale	Rosenberg Self-Esteem Scale

certainly the clinical impression one obtains), then treatment programs should include practical measures to build up self-concept. The four studies of self-esteem in abusive mothers are summarized in Table 2.

Psychiatric Disorders

The role of psychiatric disorders in the parents is not clear. In their study of 50 families Steele and Pollock (18) reported that significant psychiatric factors were present in only 10% of the families. This is in contrast to Hyman's (27) survey of 72 families in the southeast of England, which showed that 40 (56%) of the mothers had been treated for psychological disorder, the national normal expectation being 20%.

Baldwin and Oliver conducted an epidemiological study in northeast Wiltshire, England, and found 38 cases of child abuse. They reported that 58% of the parents had received psychological treatment, with 34% having been psychiatric inpatients. The criteria for inclusion in this study were very strict: Only severely injured children were accepted. Sampling techniques such as this may explain some of the conflicting results of these studies, with more likelihood of psychiatric disorders being found at the extreme end of the syndrome. Two studies that looked at this question and that used control groups gave differing results. Smith and colleagues (19) reported that

THE CAUSES OF CHILD ABUSE

of 214 abusive parents seen in Birmingham, England, 48% of the mothers were neurotic and more than half of the fathers were psychopaths. Although this study used a comparison group, the observers were not "blind" as to which parents were in the study or comparison groups. This leaves the study open to the possibility that observer bias influenced the observed results. In contrast with these results, a controlled study by Green and colleagues (29), in which two psychiatrists blindly assessed 20 abusing, 20 neglectful, and 20 control mothers using standardized interviews, found no increase in psychopathology in the abusive parents.

Ability to Relate to Others

Abusive mothers are reported to have few relationships outside the home and are likely to discourage outside involvement on the part of their children. They are said to have a lifelong history of avoiding activities that would bring them into contact with other adults (30). Role reversal, in which the abusive parent turns to the child for love and affection, has been described as a common feature (31).

The quality of the relationship between the mother and child has been observed in four well-matched control studies. Melnick and Hurley (32) showed that abusive mothers are much less able to empathize with their children compared with control mothers. Similar findings were described by Burgess and Conger (33), who showed that compared with controls, abusing parents had lower rates of interaction with their children and were more likely to emphasize the negative aspects of their relationships with the children. Frodi and Lamb (34) studied the way abusive parents respond to videotapes of crying infants and showed that compared with controls, the abusive group reported more aversion and less sympathy in response to infant crying. Mothers who had neglected their children were studied by Aragona and Eyberg (35), who found that these mothers were more negative than controls toward their children during child-directed play. These findings point out that it is the *quality* of the relationship between the parent and the child that is probably the

Table 3
Controlled Studies of How Abusive and Neglectful Mothers React to Their Children

Author	Sample size	Observation	Finding
Melnick & Hurley (32) (1969)	10	Thematic Apperception Test (T.A.T.)	inability to empathize with their child's needs
Burgess & Conger (33) (1978)	17	observation of family at home	less interaction with children than controls
Frodi & Lamb (34) (1980)	14	reaction to videotapes of infants crying	more aversion and less sympathy than controls
Aragona & Eyberg (35) (1981)	9	observation and behavior inventory	negative toward their child during play

most important factor in determining whether child abuse will occur. The four studies of reactions between abusive parents and their children are summarized in Table 3.

There are little data, apart from some descriptive information noted above, on the characteristics of the fathers in abusive families. This suggests that the focus in child abuse research should be less exclusively on the mothers so that the role of the father in abusive families can be more clearly defined.

Intelligence

Steele and Pollock's 1974 study (18) found that the majority of abusive parents were within the normal intellectual range. Studies since then that have specifically looked at the intelligence level of the parents have shown conflicting results. In Smith et al.'s study (19) almost half of the mothers were of borderline or subnormal intelligence when tested with the short form of the Wechsler Adult Intelligence Scale (WAIS). Baldwin and Oliver (28) found that 30% of the 65 mothers they studied were of borderline intelligence or moder-

THE CAUSES OF CHILD ABUSE

ately mentally subnormal. It is difficult to interpret this finding as their paper does not give information about whether formal psychological assessment was done or whether the designated level of intelligence was a clinical judgment. Baldwin and Oliver's study had very strict criteria for admission, with only severe forms of abuse being included. It is possible that this might have biased the result toward detecting more parents at the lower end of the intellectual range. In a study of 41 parents tested with the WAIS, Hyman (36) found no statistical difference in intelligence compared with the general population. It is possible that the differences between this study and Smith's may be due to the sampling of Hyman's group coming from a cross-section of the community and Smith's coming from a hospital casualty population.

Personality Tests

Study of the personality of abusive parents using Cattell's 16 Personality Factor test shows that compared with controls, abusive mothers have a high incidence of immature impetuosity and that the fathers have a high incidence of intraversion (36–38). Paulson's group from the University of California at Los Angeles has used the Minnesota Multiphasic Personality Inventory (MMPI) to study abusive parents (39–41). They claim that the MMPI shows a characteristic profile, which distinguishes abusive from nonabusive parents. However, there is considerable overlap between the results of the study group and the control group; complex statistical analysis is required to differentiate the groups, making this test of little use in clinical practice.

Smith and colleagues (42) performed EEG studies on 35 abusive parents. Eight had an abnormal tracing, all of whom were found to be psychopaths and of low intelligence. Smith et al. suggest that parents with these characteristics may be a separate subgroup. This study has not been repeated and one wonders just how useful this information would be. A study employing the Michigan Screening Profile of Parenting did not find significant differences between abusers and nonabusers in their expectations for their children (43). It would be simplistic to assume that there is a single psychological test

CHILD ABUSE AND NEGLECT

that could be used or created to diagnose abusive parents. The parents' personality is just one factor in a complex syndrome.

The widely varying personality characteristics, personality traits, and psychiatric symptoms that have been described in parents who physically abuse their children and the lack of these same features in many other abusive parents suggest that a specific abusive personality does not exist. The personality features of these parents, which are also seen in some successful parents, do not seem to be sufficient to cause child abuse by themselves. There must be other factors that also contribute. These include the parents' own support network, the characteristics of the child, and the quality of the relationship between the parent and the child.

PROBLEMS IN MATERNAL-INFANT ATTACHMENT

In recent years an awareness has developed of the importance of the neonatal period for the development of attachment between the mother and her newborn infant. Klaus et al. (45) and Kennell et al. (46) have shown that a lack of contact in the first few hours after birth can have adverse effects on mothering which may persist for some months. However, the importance of these observations for long-term attachment is far less certain.

Whiten reported that the effects of neonatal separation on maternal behavior were fairly transitory (47). Evidence that the majority of adopted children do well in their adoptive families suggests that bonding is not an all-or-nothing phenomenon occurring in the first few hours after birth. This is supported by the report of Robson and Kumar (48). These researchers, writing in the *British Journal of Psychiatry*, reported that in two groups of primiparous mothers, 25% recall that the predominant emotional reaction on holding their babies for the first time was one of indifference. A survey (49) of 97 mothers in Oxford, England, who had normal deliveries were asked the question, "When did you feel love for your baby?" Sixty-five percent reported this feeling during pregnancy or at birth, but 27% did not experience this until some time in the first week after birth, while 8% took more than one week.

THE CAUSES OF CHILD ABUSE

Prematurity and Low Birthweight

Descriptive studies have suggested that a history of prematurity and low birthweight is frequently found in abused children. In 1967 Elmer and Gregg (50) studied a sample of 22 abused children from the Chicago area and found a 30% incidence of prematurity (50). In contrast, when comparison groups have been used and when the data from these studies are critically reviewed, the relationship between prematurity and child abuse becomes less obvious. This is shown in the following six studies.

Klein and Stern (51) reviewed 51 battered children seen at the Montreal Children's Hospital and found that 23% were of low birthweight compared with a rate of 7%–8% for Quebec. However, the use of a regional population statistic for comparison can lead to potential bias. The group in the general population may differ substantially from the case group with respect to variables such as socioeconomic status and maternal age and may lead to an overestimation of prematurity as a risk factor for child abuse. A similar question is raised about the study of Hunter's group (52). These workers followed up 225 premature and sick newborns discharged from a regional and newborn intensive care unit and found a 3.9% incidence of maltreatment in the first year. This was compared with a statewide incidence of 0.5% for reported cases of abuse. Since this group of premature and sick newborns was carefully followed for child abuse and neglect, it is likely that the increased surveillance will have detected some cases that may not have been reported to the authorities in the usual way. A small follow-up study by Jeffcoate et al. (53) from St. George's Hospital, London, found that child abuse occurred in the first year of life in two out of 17 premature infants compared with no cases occurring in 17 full-term infants. However, the comparison group was not matched for social class, being selected as the next full-term, normal birthweight child born in the hospital. Although these authors noted an increase in abuse in the premature infants, their results were not statistically significant.

In a similar study Collingwood and Alberman (54) followed 32 mothers of premature children and 32 matched mothers of full-term children. They found that six of the mothers of premature children demonstrated negative behavior or attitudes toward their children and that one had physically abused her child. None of the comparison mothers demonstrated negative attitudes or abuse. Although these differences were significant, when an analysis of the factors associated with the adverse relationship (including length of neonatal separation, illegitimacy, unplanned pregnancy, child's behavior and family lifestyle) was made, no connection was found between the disturbed mother-child relationship and the length of neonatal separation.

The siblings of abused children were used as controls by Cater and Easton (55) in an attempt to see if there was a relationshp between abuse and prematurity. They examined 80 abused children and looked at the incidence of prematurity in these children compared with that in their nonabused sibling controls. These researchers were unable to demonstrate a relationship between prematurity and abuse; they concluded that other stress factors found in the families

Table 4
Relationship of Neonatal Separation to Later Physical Abuse

Author	Sample Size	Type of Study	Type of Comparison Group	Abuse Related to Neonatal Separation
Lynch & Roberts (10) (1977)	50	case-control	nonspecific	yes
Klein & Stern (51) (1971)	51	cohort	nonspecific	yes
Hunter et al. (52) (1978)	225	cohort	nonspecific	yes
Jeffcoate et al. (53) (1979)	17	cohort	nonspecific	yes*
Collingwood & Alberman (54) (1979)	32	cohort	specific	no
Cater & Easton (55) (1980)	80	case-control	specific	no
* result did not reach significance at 0.05 level				

THE CAUSES OF CHILD ABUSE

had predisposed toward abuse. These findings contrast with those of Lynch and Roberts (10) who did demonstrate a relationship between neonatal separation and abuse. However, the control group used (the next child born in the hospital) was not specific and so was a less satisfactory control group than that used by Cater and Easton. These six studies are summarized in Table 4. It can be seen that while four of the six studies purport to show a relationship between neonatal separation and child abuse, the comparison group was not specific in these studies. When a better matched comparison group was used, as in the other two studies, the relationship between prematurity, the consequent separation of mother and infant, and child abuse is not evident.

In an analysis of 18 studies of the relationship between prematurity or low birthweight and child abuse, Leventhal (56) found that while 11 of the studies showed that neonatal separation was more common in abused children than in controls, those studies that met rigorous methodological standards did not show this association. The relationship between neonatal separation and child abuse is clearly not as straightforward as had originally been thought.

Early and Extended Contact

Following the work of Klaus and colleagues (44–46), there has been considerable speculation on the importance of early contact between the mother and her newborn infant. This contact is said to be important for maternal-infant attachment and is thus seen as a precursor of optimal maternal behavior. If this is true, the implication is that early mother-infant contact may be able to prevent some cases of child abuse. However, although early contact does seem to have some positive short-term effects, positive long-term effects have not been demonstrated (57). Some recent, well-designed studies have started to clarify these issues. O'Connor and colleagues (58), in a randomized controlled trial, assigned 301 low-income mother-infant pairs to rooming-in or to routine nursery contact. They found that at follow-up at a mean age of 17 months, two of the rooming-in and 10 of the contact children had experienced parenting inadequacy including abuse. They concluded that rooming-in correlated with a reduced

80   CHILD ABUSE AND NEGLECT

incidence of parenting inadequacy. These findings contrasted with a prospective study by Egeland and Vaughan (59), which failed to show any relationship between limited contact with the newborn at birth and later disorders of mothering among a high-risk group of mothers. An important contribution to understanding the significance of early contact has been made by Siegel's group in North Carolina (60). In a randomized controlled trial, these researchers studied the effect of early neonatal contact on later maternal attachment. They showed that at four months of age there were significant differences in mother-child interaction between those who had early neonatal contact compared with those who did not. However, the most important finding of this study was that only 2%–3% of the variance could be explained by this intervention compared with 10%–20% due to background variables such as the mothers' economic status, race, housing, parity, and age. This evidence suggests that while early mother-infant contact has some importance for childrearing, there are other more diffuse factors, which are of greater importance.

Clearly this is a complex area. It is important to be aware of the danger of finding a relatively high proportion of premature births in a sample of abused children and of concluding that prematurity or bonding failure causes child abuse. Hindsight often suggests a cause, but the inferred relationship may be misleading. Prospective studies are more likely to reveal the true situation, although, as with Siegel et al.'s study, they are likely to show that the answer is far from simple.

CHARACTERISTICS OF ABUSED CHILDREN

Features at the Time of Diagnosis

Galdston (61) described the abused infant as apathetic and withdrawn following the injury and as clinging indiscriminately to strangers in the recovery phase. This apathetic behavior combined with visual alertness has been graphically described as "frozen watchfulness" (62). Green (63) found that the children have an impaired self-concept, a failure to develop basic trust, and overall impairment of ego functioning. However, Green used a biased sample: a group of

THE CAUSES OF CHILD ABUSE

81

children selected for referral to a child psychiatrist because of personality problems. Yates (64) has described a subgroup of abused children belonging to middle-class families who appear superficially well adjusted but who are aloof, fear becoming dependent, and are unable to form meaningful relationships. Bishop and Moore (65) have described 11 different categories of behavior ranging from children who are withdrawn and deprived to those who are hyperactive and destructive.

In order to try to make some sense of the wide range of behavior seen in abused children, McRae and Longstaffe (66) from the Winnipeg Children's Hospital have described a behavioral classification that can be used as a guide to management. They described four major behavioral categories:

1) Behavior seen as the child's attempt to cope with a hostile environment.
2) Behavior primarily related to emotional abuse in association with physical assault.
3) Normal behavior and development in spite of abuse.
4) Behavior colored by the massive nature of the injuries.

These authors believe that such a classification is of practical use in understanding the child's needs and in providing him with a specific treatment program.

For too long the specific needs of the child have been overlooked when treatment programs aimed largely at child protection have been provided. Once protected, the child needs an individually tailored program if emotional development is to progress satisfactorily. Looking at a child's particular behavior, and basing management on the child's needs, is an important step in this direction.

The Child as Perceived by the Parents

Abusive parents may perceive the child as being different from birth. In a series of 30 abused children compared with their non-abused siblings, Lynch (67) found that many parents claimed that their abused child was different and more difficult to rear than their other children. Herrenkohl and Herrenkohl (68) studied the parental attitudes of 295 abused children, using 284 of their siblings as controls. They found that compared with their siblings the abused children were seen more negatively by their parents and were described by them in derogatory terms.

Physical Handicap and Health

Some authors have reported a higher incidence of congenital abnormalities or chronic illness in abused children (69–71). This finding has not been confirmed in most other series. However, it would not be surprising if in families with a predisposition to child abuse, the additional stresses caused by having a handicapped child were enough to tip the balance and result in abuse in some cases. An increased occurrence of abuse in twins has also been noted (72, 73). Groothuis (74) found a higher incidence of physical abuse in families with twins than in an appropriately matched group of singleton families, and because twin births have a higher incidence of prematurity and complications that may have accounted for this finding, he performed a regression analysis on the data. This showed that, of these variables, twin status was the most predictive factor of child abuse.

Behavior of Abused Children

Green (75) has reported that the aggressive behavior of abused children may be turned inward, resulting in increased nail biting, hair pulling, and suicidal attempts. He suggests that the abused child's sense of worthlessness and self-hatred as a result of parental rejection is the basis of this self-destructive behavior. These are unusual features in abused children.

Three well-controlled studies have looked at the subsequent behavior of abused children. Reidy (76) compared 20 abused children with 20 nonabused children and found that the abused children were more aggressive in free play, fantasy play, and psychological testing. Reidy claims this is evidence for the theory that children exposed to aggressive parental models will demonstrate aggressive characteris-

THE CAUSES OF CHILD ABUSE

tics in situations outside the home. George and Main (77) demonstrated that in a preschool situation 10 abused children, who were matched with a control group from families experiencing stress, more often assaulted other children at the preschool, were verbally aggressive to the preschool staff, and were less likely to approach staff in response to friendly overtures. Although Jacobson and Straker (78) found that abused children were not more hostile than a control group of children, they were found to be less socially interactive. These three studies are summarized in Table 5. Unfortunately, none of these studies provided information about the interval between the detection of abuse in the children and the assessment of their behavior, nor do they say whether the children have been in therapeutic treatment programs. This would have been useful information as it is difficult to know whether the described behaviors are a result of the physical abuse or of remaining in a disturbed environment, and whether the behavior may have been modified by any intervention given.

Table 5
Comparison Studies Showing the Behavior of Abused Children

Criteria	Reidy (76) 1977	George & Main (77) 1979	Jacobson & Straker (78) 1982
Sample size	20	10	19
Age of children	average 6½ years	1–3 years	5–10 years
Specific control group	yes	yes	yes
Observation used	T.A.T., free play, & observations at school	behavior in daycare setting	videotape of free play
Observers blind	not mentioned	no	yes
Appropriate statistical analysis	yes	yes	yes
Abused children compared with controls	more aggressive	more aggressive, wary of adults	less socially interactive

Contribution of the Child

To simply look at the child as a passive recipient of abuse ignores the importance of the interaction between the parent and the child and the likelihood that some children, by their behavior, may precipitate an abusive incident in a predisposed parent. This has been suggested by Martin (79), who believes that in a situation where the parents have the potential for abuse, some aspect of the child, such as delayed development or provocative behavior may be enough to precipitate an abusive incident. Gaensbauer and Sands (80) observed 48 abused and neglected children with their caretakers in a structured laboratory setting. They found that compared with normal children, the abused and neglected group related to their caretakers in a variety of ways, which caused feelings of inadequacy in the mothers about not being able to meet their child's needs and also caused feelings of rage in the mothers about their child's demanding behavior. In a review of the literature on the role of the child in abuse, Freidrich and Boriskin (81) point out that the view that child abuse is exclusively a function of parental defect is simplistic. Particular types of children produce particular parental stress reactions, some of which might precipitate abuse. These include infant temperament, mental retardation, and physical handicaps. Other children have personality characteristics, such as unusual and constant crying patterns which influence the parents' reaction to them (82).

The wide range of behavior seen in abused children suggests that there is no such thing as a typical abused child. In addition to the way parents perceive undesirable features in these children, the child's own behavior may contribute to precipitation of the abuse. What is disturbing from these studies is that the aggressive and withdrawn behavior shown by abused children is likely to have serious implications for the way they develop relationships in adult life.

REFERENCES

1. Steele, B.F. (1976). Violence within the family. In R.E. Helfer & C.H. Kempe, (Eds.), *Child abuse and neglect—The family and the community.* Cambridge, MA: Ballinger.

THE CAUSES OF CHILD ABUSE

2. Feshback, N.D. (1973). The effects of violence in childhood. *Journal of Clinical Psychology, 2,* 284–293.
3. Solomon, T. (1973). History and demography of child abuse. *Pediatrics, 51,* 773–776.
4. Court, J. (1974). Characteristics of parents and children. In J. Carter (Ed.), *The maltreated child.* London: Priory Press.
5. Kadushin, A., & Martin, J.A. (1981). *Child abuse: An interactional event.* New York: Columbia University Press.
6. Annual Statistical Report: National analysis of official child neglect and abuse reporting. American Humane Association, 1979. Denver, Colorado.
7. Skinner, A.E., & Castle, R.L. (1969). *Seventy-eight battered children—A retrospective study.* National Society for the Prevention of Cruelty to Children, London.
8. Sills, J., Thomas L., & Rosenbloom, L. (1977). Non-accidental injury: A two-year study in Central Liverpool. *Developmental Medicine and Child Neurology, 19,* 26–33.
9. Smith, S.M., Hanson, R., & Noble, S. (1974). Social aspects of the battered baby syndrome. *British Journal of Psychiatry, 125,* 568–582.
10. Lynch, M., & Roberts, J. (1977). Predicting child abuse: Signs of bonding failure in the maternity hospital. *British Medical Journal, 1,* 624–626.
11. Lauer, B., Broeck, E.T., & Grossman, M. (1974). Battered child syndrome: Review of 130 patients with controls. *Pediatrics, 54,* 67–70.
12. Elmer, E. (1977). *Fragile families, troubled children.* Pittsburgh, PA: University of Pittsburgh Press.
13. Robertson, B.A., & Juntz, J.M. (1979). Characteristics of the families of abused children. *Child Abuse and Neglect, 3,* 857–862.
14. Earp, J.A. & Ory, M.G. (1980). The influence of early parenting on child maltreatment. *Child Abuse and Neglect, 4,* 237–245.
15. Kinard, E.M., & Klerman, L.V. (1980). Teenage parenting and child abuse: Are they related? *American Journal of Orthopsychiatry, 5,* 481–503.
16. Gil, D.G. (1970). *Violence against children.* Cambridge, MA: Harvard University Press.
17. Nixon, J., Pearn, J., Wilkey, I., & Petrie, G. (1981). Social class and violent child death: Analysis of fatal non-accidental injury, murder and fatal child neglect. *Child Abuse and Neglect, 5,* 111–116.
18. Steele, B.F., & Pollock, C.B. (1974). A psychiatric study of parents who abuse infants and small children. In R.E. Helfer & C.H. Kempe, (Eds.), *The battered child* (2nd ed.). Chicago: The University of Chicago Press.
19. Smith, S.M., Hanson, R., & Noble, S. (1973). Parents of battered children: A controlled study. *British Medical Journal, 4,* 388–391.
20. Lynch, M.A. (1975). Ill health and child abuse. *Lancet, 2,* 317–319.
21. Oates, R.K., Davis, A.A., & Ryan, M.G. (1980). Predictive factors for child abuse. *Australian Paediatric Journal, 16,* 239–243.
22. Dalton, K. (1975). Paramenstrual baby battering. *British Medical Journal, 2,* 279.
23. Rosen, B., & Stein, M.T. (1980). Women who abuse their children. *American Journal of Diseases of Children, 134,* 947–950.
24. Evans, A.L. (1980). Personality characteristics and disciplinary attitudes of child-abusing mothers. *Child Abuse and Neglect, 4,* 179–187.

25. Anderson, S.C., & Lauderdale, M.L. (1982). Characteristics of abusive parents: A look at self-esteem. *Child Abuse and Neglect, 6,* 285–293.
26. Shorkey, C.T. (1980). Sense of personal worth, self-esteem and anomia of child-abusing mothers and controls. *Journal of Clinical Psychology, 36,* 817–820
27. Hyman, L.A. (1978), Non-accidental injury. *Health Visitor, 51,* 168–174.
28. Baldwin, J.A., & Oliver, J.E. (1975). Epidemiology and family characteristics of severely abused children. *British Journal of Preventive and Social Medicine, 29,* 205–221.
29. Green, A.H., Liang, V., Gaines, R., & Sultan, S. (1980). Psychopathological assessment of child-abusing, neglecting and normal mothers. *Journal of Nervous and Mental Diseases, 168,* 356–360.
30. Garbarino, J., & Stocking, H.S. (1980). *Protecting children from abuse and neglect.* San Francisco: Jossey-Bass.
31. Morris, M., & Gould, R. (1963). Role reversal: A necessary concept in dealing with the battered-child syndrome. *American Journal of Orthopsychiatry, 33,* 298–299.
32. Melnick, B., & Hurley, J.R. (1969). Distinctive personality attributes of child-abusing mothers. *Journal of Consulting Clinical Psychology, 33,* 746–749.
33. Burgess, R.L., & Conger, R.D. (1978). Family interaction in abusive, neglectful and normal families. *Child Development, 49,* 163–173.
34. Frodi, A.M., & Lamb, M.E. (1980). Child abusers' responses to infant cries and smiles. *Child Development, 51,* 238–241.
35. Aragona, J.A., & Eyberg, S.M. (1981). Neglected children: Mother's report of child behavior problems and observed verbal behavior. *Child Development, 52,* 596–602.
36. Hyman, C.A. (1977). A report on the psychological test results of battering parents. *British Journal of Social and Clinical Psychology, 16,* 221–224.
37. Hyman, C.A., & Mitchell, R. (1975). A psychological study of child battering. *Health Visitor, 48,* 294–296.
38. N.S.P.C.C. Battered Child Research Team (1976). *At risk.* London: Routledge & Kegan Paul.
39. Paulson, M.J., Afifi, A.A., Thomason, M.L., & Chaleff, A. (1974). The MMPI: A descriptive measure of psychopathology in abusive parents. *Journal of Clinical Psychology, 30,* 387–390.
40. Paulson, M.J., Afifi, A.A., Chaleff, A., Liu, V.Y., & Thomason, M.L. (1975). A discriminative function procedure for identifying abusive parents. *Suicide, 5,* 104–113.
41. Paulson, M.J., Schwemer, G.T., & Bendel, R.B. (1976). Clinical application of the Pd, Ma and (OH) experiental MMPI scales to further understanding of abusive parents. *Journal of Clinical Psychology, 32,* 558–564.
42. Smith, S.M., Honigsberger, J., & Smith, C.A. (1977). E.E.G. and personality factors in baby batterers. *British Medical Journal, 2,* 20–22.
43. Gaines, R. (1978). Etiological factors in child maltreatment: A multivariate study of abusing, neglecting and normal mothers. *Journal of Abnormal Psychology, 87,* 531–540.
44. Klaus, M.H., & Kennell, J.H. (1976). *Maternal-infant bonding.* St. Louis, MO: C.V. Mosby Co.

THE CAUSES OF CHILD ABUSE

45. Klaus, M.H., Jerauld, R., & Kreger, N. (1972). Maternal attachment—Importance of the first postpartum days. *New England Journal of Medicine, 286,* 460–463.
46. Kennell, J.H., Jerauld, R., Wolfe, H., Chester, D., Kreger, N.C., McAlpine, W., Steffa, M., & Klaus, M.H. (1974). Maternal behavior one year after early and extended post partum contact. *Developmental Medicine and Child Neurology, 16,* 172–179.
47. Whiten, A. (1977). Assessing the effects of perinatal events on the success of mother-infant relationship. In N.R. Schaffer (Ed.), *Studies in mother-infant interaction.* London: Academic Press.
48. Robson, K.M., & Kumar, R. (1980). Delayed onset of maternal affection after childbirth. *British Journal of Psychiatry. 135,* 347–353.
49. MacFarlane, D.M., & Garrow, D.H. (1978). The relationship between mother and neonate. In S. Kitzinger & J.A. Davis (Eds.), *The place of birth.* Oxford: Oxford University Press.
50. Elmer, E., & Gregg, G. (1967). Developmental characteristics of abused children. *Pediatrics, 40,* 596–602.
51. Klein, M., & Stern, L. (1971). Low birthweight and the battered child syndrome. *American Journal of Diseases of Children, 122,* 15–18.
52. Hunter, R.S., Kilstrom, A.C., Kraybill, E., & Loda, F. (1978). Antecedents of child abuse and neglect in intensive care unit. *Pediatrics, 61,* 629–635.
53. Jeffcoate, J.A., Humphrey, M.E., & Lloyd, J.K. (1979). Disturbance in parent-child relationship following preterm delivery. *Developmental Medicine and Child Neurology, 21,* 344–352.
54. Collingwood, J., & Alberman, E. (1979). Separation at birth and mother-child relationship. *Developmental Medicine and Child Neurology, 21,* 608–618.
55. Cater, J.I., & Easton, P.M. (1980). Separation and other stresses in child abuse. *Lancet, 1,* 972–974.
56. Leventhal, J.M. (1982). Research strategies and methodologic standards in case-control studies. *Pediatrics, 68,* 684–690.
57. Lamb, M.E. (1982). Early contact and maternal-infant bonding: One decade later. *Pediatrics, 70,* 763–768.
58. O'Connor, S., Vietze, P.M., Sherrod, K.B., Sandler, H.M., & Altemeir, W.A. (1980). Reduced incidence of parenting inadequacy following rooming-in. *Pediatrics, 66,* 176–182.
59. Egeland, B., & Vaughan, B. (1981). Failure of "bond formation" as a cause of abuse, neglect and maltreatment. *American Journal of Orthopsychiatry, 51,* 78–84.
60. Siegel, E., Bauman, K.E., Schaefer, E.S., Sanders, M.M., & Ingram, D.D. (1980). Hospital and home support during infancy: Impact on maternal attachment, child abuse and neglect and health care utilization. *Pediatrics, 66,* 182–190.
61. Galdston, R. (1965). Observations on children who have been physically abused and their parents. *American Journal of Psychiatry, 122,* 440–443.
62. Ounsted, C.V., & Lindsay, J. (1974). Aspects of bonding failure. *Developmental Medicine and Child Neurology, 16,* 447–456.
63. Green, A.H. (1978). Psychopathology of abused children. *Journal of the American Academy of Child Psychiatry, 17,* 92–103.
64. Yates, A. (1981). Narcissistic traits in certain abused children. *American Journal of Orthopsychiatry, 51,* 55–62.

88   CHILD ABUSE AND NEGLECT

65. Bishop, F.I., & Moore, B.G. (1978). *Maltreating families.* Ministry of Health, Victoria, Australia.
66. McRae, K.N., & Longstaffe, S.E. (1982). The behaviour of battered children—An aid to diagnosis and management. In R.K. Oates (Ed.), *Child abuse—A community concern.* Sydney: Butterworths.
67. Lynch, M. (1976). Risk factors in the child: A study of abused children and their siblings. In H.P. Martin (Ed.), *The abused child.* Cambridge, MA: Ballinger.
68. Herrenkohl, E.C., & Herrenkohl, R.Y. (1979). A comparison of abused children and their non-abused siblings. *Journal of the American Academy of Child Psychiatry, 18,* 260–269.
69. Birrell, R.G., & Birrell, J.H.W. (1966). Re "maltreatment syndrome" in children. *Medical Journal of Australia, 2,*1134–1138.
70. Holman, R.R., & Kanwar, S. (1975). Early life of the battered child. *Archives of Disease in Childhood, 50,* 78–80.
71. Glaser, D., & Bentovim, A. (1979). Abuse and risk to handicapped and chronically ill children. *Child Abuse and Neglect, 3,* 565–575.
72. Soeffing, M. (1975). Abused children are exceptional children. *Exceptional Child, 42,* 126–133.
73. Nakou, S., Adam, H., Stathacopoulou, N., & Agathonos, H. (1982). Health status of abused and neglected children and their siblings. *Child Abuse and Neglect, 6,* 279–284.
74. Groothuis, J.R., Altemeier, W.A., Robarge, J.P., O'Connor, S., Sandler, H., Vietze, P., & Lustig, J.V. (1982). Increased child abuse in families with twins. *Pediatrics, 70,* 769–773.
75. Green, A.H. (1978). Self-destructive behavior in battered children. *American Journal of Psychiatry, 135,* 579–582.
76. Reidy, T.J. (1977). The aggressive characteristics of abused and neglected children. *Journal of Clinical Psychology, 33,* 1140–1145.
77. George, C., & Main, M. (1979). Social interactions of young, abused children: Approach avoidance and aggression. *Child Development, 50,* 306–318.
78. Jacobson, R.S., & Straker, G. (1982). Peer group interaction of physically abused children. *Child Abuse and Neglect, 6,* 321–327.
79. Martin, H.P. (1976). Which children get abused: High risk factors in the child. In H.P. Martin (Ed.), *The Abused Child.* Cambridge, MA: Ballinger.
80. Gaensbauer, T.J., & Sands, K. (1970). Distorted affective communications in abused/neglected infants and their potential impact on caretakers. *Journal of the American Academy of Child Psychiatry, 18,* 236–249.
81. Freidrich, W.N., & Boriskin, J.A. (1976). The roles of the child in abuse—A Review of the literature. *American Journal of Orthopsychiatry, 46,* 580–590.
82. Frodi, A.M. (1981). Contribution of infant characteristics to child abuse. *American Journal of Mental Deficiency, 85,* 341–349.

6

Prediction, Prevention, and Treatment of Child Abuse

PREDICTION AND PREVENTION

If families likely to abuse their children could be identified before, or just after, the children were born, it might be possible to prevent child abuse by offering supportive services to these families. This question can be studied either by looking back at the birth and neonatal histories of battered children to try to find the factors that may distinguish them, or by trying to identify at-risk families at the time of the child's birth and following them to look at the incidence of abuse compared with matched families thought not to be at risk of abuse.

Retrospective Studies

Lynch and colleagues (1) studied 29 abused children and compared factors at the time of the pregnancy and neonatal period with similar factors found in 55 controls. The control group was chosen by selecting every twentieth case referred to the hospital's maternity department in Oxford, England, over the same period. Unfortunately, the controls were not matched and the analysis of social class obtained

89

90 CHILD ABUSE AND NEGLECT

from data in the paper suggests that the higher social classes were overrepresented in the comparison group. These researchers found that the abused and nonabused groups were significantly different on three measures:

1) The abused children were more likely to have been separated at birth and placed in a special care nursery.
2) The families where abuse occurred were more likely to have had social problems noted at the time of birth which were "diffuse" rather than defined.
3) There was more likely to be concern over mothering recorded by hospital staff in the hospital records in those families where abuse later occurred.

If mothers with the above characteristics were studied prospectively, it is likely that there would be many more with these characteristics who did not abuse their children than those who did. Although some abusive mothers would be likely to be found within this group, analysis of the data provided in Lynch et al.'s paper suggests that approximately 30% of the abusive families in this study would not have been predicted in this way, these three factors having not been present. Nevertheless, this is a useful study as it shows that simple measures can detect a proportion of high-risk mothers and that it would seem realistic to offer extra help to these people.

The birth records of 80 abused children from Wales were compared with those of 80 nonabused children by Murphy and co-workers (2). Matching was done for sex and the day of birth. It was found that 11 factors were more common in the abused children. These were: young maternal age; marital instability; low social class; maternal smoking; late booking in to the maternity hospital; fewer antenatal attendances; less attendance at preparation for parenthood classes; prematurity; low birthweight, admission of the baby to a special-care baby unit; and a lower incidence of breast feeding after seven days. Many of these factors, such as prematurity, low birthweight and the need for a special-care baby unit, are closely interrelated. In addition, these factors are all nonspecific in that they occur in many instances where abuse does not, so that this sort of information is of little practical use in individual cases.

PREDICTION, PREVENTION, AND TREATMENT 91

Prospective Studies

A number of controlled prospective studies have looked at ways of predicting abuse and parenting disorders in the neonatal period. The excellent randomized controlled prospective studies of O'Connor et al. (3) and Siegel et al. (4) have already been discussed in the preceding chapter. Two other studies have looked at broader areas than child abuse. Egeland and Brunnquell (5) followed 275 mothers for 20 months after the births of their children and found that 26 of the children were not receiving adequate care. In contrast with 26 mothers providing good quality care, the less successful mothers were younger, less well educated, had more pregnancy and birth complications, and had less family support. Geddes's group from New Zealand (6) followed 200 mothers referred to the social work service during pregnancy. They found that of the 18% of mothers initially classified as being at high risk for having parenting problems, one-third had their babies placed in some form of foster care during the period of the study. This contrasted with only 3% of those mothers judged to be at low risk having their babies placed in care. The follow-up period of this study was short, between three and 12 months, and no information was given about whether any of the children were abused.

The best known study on prediction and intervention was reported by the Denver group in 1977 (7). By using a screening system consisting of parent interviews, labor and delivery observations, and nursery observations, a group of high-risk mothers was identified. Fifty high-risk mothers were randomly assigned to an intervention group and 50 others at high risk received routine care. A third group of 50 low-risk mothers were controls. Intervention consisted of single-physician health care, frequent telephone calls to the families, and weekly public health nurse visits. Approximately two years later 25 families from each of the three groups were chosen at random for evaluation. Five children from the high-risk nonintervention group had been admitted to hospital for serious injuries thought to be secondary to "abnormal parenting practices." There had been no such injuries in the high-risk group that received intervention or in the low-risk group.

Altemeier and colleagues (8) interviewed 1,400 expectant mothers and found 273 who were thought to be at high risk for parenting disorders. These mothers and 225 selected randomly from the remaining mothers were followed in a double-blind fashion for 12 months. Abuse, neglect, and failure to thrive were found to have occurred significantly more often in the high-risk families.

A predictive study of children presenting to an emergency room was done by Rosenberg and co-workers (9). These researchers randomly enrolled in the study 476 children under two years of age who presented to the emergency room. They assessed the attitudes of the parents and the appearance and condition of the child at the time of presentation. Children known to be already reported as abused were excluded. Hospital records of abuse and notifications to the Department of Social Service were reviewed 12 months later. Child abuse had occurred in 4.2% of the sample. It was found that the incidence of abuse was 30% in those cases in which there had been evidence of an abnormal parenting pattern and the child had been brought to the emergency room in an unkempt condition and with abnormal bruises, burns, or bites. These findings are not surprising, as the features that the authors found to correlate with later abuse would be considered by many to be already a form of abuse or at least warnings that these children may be at risk for abuse.

A recent paper (10) from the University of Bradford, England, showed that in a survey of 2,802 pregnancies 18% were thought to be at risk for later child abuse. The ability to predict the at-risk infants was shown by the fact that after 18 months two-thirds of the abused children from the total sample came from this group of 18% thought to be at risk. It is disturbing to note that supportive measures were not able to prevent the abuse.

It does appear that some predictive factors, while nonspecific, do detect a group within which a smaller group of abusive parents is likely to be contained. The study from Denver (7) is particularly important as it demonstrates that providing support not vastly different from that already available can reduce the incidence of abuse; however, the more recent study from the University of Bradford (10) shows that this cannot always be achieved.

Although predictive programs are valuable, some ethical concerns could arise. If a widespread screening of pregnant mothers for poten-

PREDICTION, PREVENTION, AND TREATMENT

tial child abuse were to occur, a large number of families would be stigmatized as potential child abusers. Daniel and colleagues (11) argue that because of the large number of false negatives in such screening programs, the social cost of this type of labeling is likely to make such an approach unacceptable.

TREATMENT

Although child abuse treatment programs have often been described, there is a scarcity of good papers that present the results. This is disturbing, suggesting that the outcomes may not be particularly good. A recently published collection of 43 major papers on child abuse (12) did not include any that described the results of treatment of either the parents or the children.

Schmitt and Beezley (13) have described four prerequisites for optimal long-term management.

1) A comprehensive diagnostic assessment of the family.
2) A multidisciplinary team to make decisions and to plan treatment.
3) The availability of diversified treatment options.
3) Periodic assessment of treatment plans.

Although a multidisciplinary team is required because of the complexity of the situation, it is important for the team to have some direction so that team members are clearly aware of their short- and long-term responsibilities to the families. Because the situation is complex, it is essential to have a treatment plan that is flexible, is reviewed periodically, and is realistic and practical. Multidisciplinary teams where each member feels that the responsibility for the family lies with another member of the team, or which produce an ideal but totally unrealistic treatment plan, do little for these children.

Treatment of the Parents

Bishop and Moore (14) argue that the majority of parents would benefit from psychiatric intervention. But treating the parent can be

94   CHILD ABUSE AND NEGLECT

hazardous. It has been reported that stressful psychotherapy sessions
for abusive parents are likely to precipitate future episodes of abuse
(15). Rosen and Stein (16) suggested that rather than psychotherapy
the parents require educative and supportive treatment aimed at en-
hancing their own self-esteem and lowering their unrealistic expectations for the child.

The Denver group (17) has described the advantages of nonprofes-
sional volunteers, who can give abusive parents some of the parenting they missed in their own childhood, thus preventing the parents
from depending on the child for their emotional needs. In the Denver
group's experience this form of treatment has been successful. Because child abuse is such a large problem in relation to the number of
professionally trained staff available, and because volunteers can often provide a type of caring that professionals cannot give, this
would seem to be a particularly valuable form of treatment. Parents
Anonymous, a self-help group for abusive parents, has flourished in
the United States (18) and appears to be effective, although it may be
that those who attend Parents Anonymous groups comprise a self-
selected group who would find help in any event.

The form of treatment offered to parents depends on the degree of
problem found in that parent. Treatment without a thorough initial
assessment is irresponsible and is not likely to succeed. While some
parents will respond to relatively simple, supportive measures, such
as lay therapy and Parents Anonymous, these measures are less
likely to work for a hard core of parents, variously estimated as
between 20%–40% of cases, who have serious personality disturbances (19). This group will require intense, skilled, and sustained
intervention; it is for this group that services that require very many
hours of work for each individual case, such as psychiatric intervention and long-term casework, should be reserved.

Treatment of the Child

In cases of severe family pathology the child may be removed
from the parents and placed in foster care. It would be naive to
believe that this solves the problem. A report from Arizona (20),
which reviewed over 5,000 children in foster care, showed that the

PREDICTION, PREVENTION, AND TREATMENT

risk of maltreatment at the hands of a foster parent was over three times greater than in a natural family. Bishop and Moore (14) found that 31% of 106 abusive mothers had spent part of their own childhood in an institution or in some form of care, indicating that such an environment is not conducive to developing good childrearing practices. Although only approximately 10% of abused children are placed in foster care (21), this is still a substantial number, bearing in mind the total number of cases. Being placed in foster care is a confusing and unsettling experience for the child. Children need, wherever possible, to be prepared for the separation and should have a specific treatment program provided for them during this period of fostering. Without this, the potential adverse emotional sequelae for the child may be even more harmful. In some cases short-term fostering or even long-term fostering with eventual return to the parents may be less in the child's interests than permanent placement in another family. Hensey and colleagues (22) showed that in a four-year follow-up of 50 abused children in Liverpool, England, those children for whom an early decision had been made to sever all family contacts fared significantly better than those who were returned to their parents.

As the majority of abused children remain in their homes, it is in this context that treatment should be planned. Kempe (23) has pointed out that treatment starts with a complete evaluation of the child's strengths and weaknesses. She notes that treatment of the infant involves working with the mother, that preschool children often respond to a therapeutic day care center, and that a more traditional psychotherapeutic approach may be suitable for the school-aged child. The value of therapeutic day care was shown by Carter (24), who interviewed a random sample of 29 parents whose children were receiving this treatment. The majority of parents reported that their child's behavior had become easier to manage and that they themselves had benefited from meeting other parents.

Joint Treatment Programs

Residential programs for the parent and child, such as the one at the Park Hospital, Oxford (25), and more recent programs at Booth

96 CHILD ABUSE AND NEGLECT

Beryl Court in Melbourne (26) and at Montrose in Sydney (27), appear to be successful, although these are expensive facilities which can only be available to a small number of carefully selected families. Perhaps more practical is the type of program that provides a therapeutic preschool environment for abused children in conjunction with a supportive program for the parents (28).

Morse and colleagues (29) have demonstrated the effectiveness of a family advocacy program where the emphasis is on direct provision of practical help for the parents rather than on trying to bring about change through counseling. This sort of program aims at improving the child's environment, making sure that the parents have access to community services, and helping the parents learn to control their environment as the advocate works with them to improve their social conditions.

Despite the large number of treatment programs available, there is a lack of well-documented studies of their effectiveness. It is unlikely that child abuse treatment programs will ever be able to be "packaged," as different approaches will be required for different families. What does seem to come out of the available studies is the need for treatment programs to include a practical component and for specific treatment to be available for the child. Treatment is a long-term commitment. Speight and co-workers (30), in a review of child abuse cases studied in Newcastle, England, pointed out how frequently follow-up arrangements broke down and emphasized the need for a long-term commitment to follow-up being made. The aim of this should be not only to prevent further physical abuse but also to improve the family environment in which the child develops.

REFERENCES

1. Lynch, M.A., Roberts, J., & Gordon, M. (1976). Child abuse: early warning in the maternity hospital. *Developmental Medicine and Child Neurology, 18,* 759–766.
2. Murphy, J.F., Jenkins, J., Newcombe, R.G., & Sibert, J.R. (1981). Objective birth data and the reduction of child abuse. *Archives of Diseases in Childhood, 56,* 295–297.
3. O'Connor, S., Vietze, P.M., Sherrod, K.B., Sandler, H.M., & Altemeier, W.A. (1980). Reduced incidence of parenting inadequacy following rooming-in. *Pediatrics, 66,* 176–182.

PREDICTION, PREVENTION, AND TREATMENT

4. Siegel, E., Bauman, K.E., Schaefer, E.S., Sanders, M.M., & Ingram, D.D. (1980). Hospital and home support during infancy: Impact on maternal attachment, child abuse and neglect and health care utilization. *Pediatrics, 66,* 183–190.
5. Egeland, B., & Brunnquell, D. (1979). An at-risk approach to the study of child abuse. *Journal of the American Academy of Child Psychiatry, 18,* 219–235.
6. Geddes, D.C., Monaghan, S.M., Muir, R.C., & Jones, C.J. (1979). Early prediction in the maternity hospital: The Queen Mary Child Care Unit. *Child Abuse and Neglect, 3,* 757–766.
7. Gray, J.D., Cutler, C.A., Dean, J.G., & Kempe, C.H. (1977). Prediction and prevention of child abuse and neglect. *Child Abuse and Neglect, 1,* 45–53.
8. Altemeier, W.A., Vietze, P.M., Sherrod, K.B., Sandler, H.M., Falsey, S., & O'Connor, S. (1979). Prediction of child maltreatment during pregnancy. *Journal of the American Academy of Child Psychiatry, 18,* 205–218.
9. Rosenberg, N.M., Meyers, S., & Shakleton, N. (1982). Prediction of child abuse in an ambulatory setting. *Pediatrics, 70,* 879–882.
10. Lealman, G.T., Haigh, D., Phillips, J.M., Stone, J., & Ord-Smith, C. (1983). Prediction and prevention of child abuse—An empty hope? *Lancet, 1,* 423–424.
11. Daniel, J.H., Newberger, E.H., Read, R.B., & Kotelchuck, M. (1978). Child abuse screening: Implications of the limited predictive power of abuse discriminants from a controlled family study of pediatric social illness. *Child Abuse and Neglect, 2,* 247–259.
12. Cook, J.V., & Bowles, R.T. (1980). *Child abuse: Commission and omission.* Toronto: Butterworths.
13. Schmitt, B.D., & Beezley, P. (1976). The long-term management of the child and family in child abuse and neglect. *Pediatric Annals, 5,* 165–176.
14. Bishop, F.I., & Moore, B.G. (1978). *Maltreating families,* Ministry of Health, Victoria, Australia.
15. Winkler, R.C., Ginn, D., & Miletic, R. (1979). Child abuse in the 24 hours after psychotherapy sessions. *Medical Journal of Australia, 1,* 239–240.
16. Rosen, B., & Stein, M.T. (1980). Women who abuse their children. *American Journal of Diseases of Children, 134,* 947–950.
17. Gray, J., & Kaplan, B. (1980). The lay health visitor programme: An eighteen-month experience. In C.H. Kempe & Helfer R.E. (Eds.), *The battered child* (3rd ed.). Chicago: The University of Chicago Press.
18. Lieber, L., & Baker, J.M. (1977). Parents Anonymous—Self-help treatment for child abusing parents: A review and an evaluation. *Child Abuse and Neglect, 1,* 133–148.
19. Besharov, D.J. (1983). Child protection: Past progress, present problems and future directions. *Family Law Quarterly, 17,* 151–164.
20. Bolton, F.G., Laner, R.H., & Gai, D.S. (1981). For better or worse? Foster parents and foster children in an officially reported child maltreatment population. *Children and Youth Services Review, 13,* 127–129.
21. Fischler, R.S. (1984). Child abuse treatment and follow-up: Can the pediatrician help improve the outcome? *Child Abuse and Neglect, 8,* 361–368.
22. Hensey, O.J., Williams, J.K., & Rosenbloom, L. (1983). Intervention in child abuse: Experience in Liverpool. *Developmental Medicine and Child Neurology, 25,* 606–611.

98 CHILD ABUSE AND NEGLECT

23. Kempe, R.S. (1981). Individual treatment planning for the child. *Child Abuse and Neglect, 5,* 317–323.
24. Carter, J. (1982). Family day centers and child abuse. In R.K. Oates (Ed.), *Child abuse—A community concern.* Sydney: Butterworths.
25. Lynch, M., Steinberg, D., & Ounsted, C. (1975). Family unit in a children's psychiatric hospital. *British Medical Journal, 2,* 127–129.
26. Coote, S. (1981). Beryl Booth Court—An innovative residential program in child maltreatment in Victoria. *Second Australasian conference on child abuse, Conference proceedings.* Queensland: Government Printer.
27. Brazier, J., Davis, A.A., & Shier, J. (1982). "Montrose" Child Life Protection Unit: A treatment and assessment model in child abuse intervention. *Child Abuse and Neglect, 6,* 389–394.
28. Petheram, R., & Thomson, J. (1981). Child abuse—The search for an effective service model. *Second Australasian conference on child abuse, Conference proceedings.* Queensland: Government Printer.
29. Morse, A.E., Hyde, J.N., Newberger, E.H., & Reed, R.B. (1977). Environmental correlates of pediatric social illness: Preventive implications of an advocacy approach. *American Journal of Health, 67,* 612–615.
30. Speight, A.N.P., Bridson, J.M., & Cooper, E.C. (1979). Follow-up survey of cases of child abuse seen at Newcastle General Hospital 1974–75. *Child Abuse and Neglect, 3,* 555–563.

7

The Development of Abused Children

Follow-up studies of abused children require careful interpretation as different researchers have studied different populations. For example, Elmer and Gregg's study (1) was of 50 children who had all multiple skeletal injuries. Martin and colleagues (2) included all inflicted injuries, including mild ones, while others have included some cases of neglect (3).

The sources of samples may also affect results. Cases identified in casualty departments are more likely to contain children who have had serious and perhaps life-threatening injuries. Loss to follow-up causes another problem. The results that finally appear in print are based on data from those members of the original sample who could be located and assessed. These families are notoriously difficult to locate after several years because of their high mobility. The widely quoted and valuable follow-up study by Martin and colleagues (2) contains only 37% of the original sample of 159 children admitted to Denver hospitals a minimum of one year previously. What we do not know is whether the characteristics of the families who were not evaluated are similar to those who were able to be located and who cooperated in the study.

Little attention was paid in the earlier literature to the long-term effects of abuse on the child. Early writers were content to describe the injuries and to speculate on the parental characteristics that led to the abuse. It was not until the paper by Elmer and Gegg (1) in 1967 that the high degree of neurological, developmental, and psychological disabilities in the child was realized. These researchers reviewed 20 children out of an original sample of 50 at a mean interval of five years after the abuse. They found that 40% were emotionally disturbed and that 50% had an IQ below 80. In 1970 Morse and co-workers (3) reviewed 25 abused children after three years and found that nine were mentally retarded, six were emotionally disturbed, and 15 were regarded as "problems" by their parents.

A review of 14 children in the program of the National Society for the Prevention of Cruelty to Children (N.S.P.C.C.) in London (4) was more optimistic, showing a mean intelligence quotient of 100 in the group and noting that this was a significant improvement on the findings when the children were first admitted to the program. However, this group was receiving intensive stimulation in either the N.S.P.C.C.'s therapeutic preschool or in another selected preschool, and the families were all receiving support from the N.S.P.C.C. team. This kind of treatment is unfortunately not available to the majority of abused children.

In 1972 Martin (5) reported on 42 children evaluated three years after their injuries. Thirty-three percent had an IQ below 80 and 38% had language delay. A later follow-up study by Martin and Beezley (6) of 50 children, some of whom had been only mildly injured, showed that 60% had an impaired capacity to enjoy life, 62% had behavioral problems, 62% had low self-esteem, and 30% had significant neurological impairment. The median IQ of this group was 98.

These six follow-up studies, none of which had a comparison group, are summarized in Table 1. Even though these studies are open to criticism because controls were not used, the impression given is that the outlook for maltreated children is not good.

Several groups of researchers have looked at the development of abused children in comparison with the development of a control group of children where abuse has not occurred. Elmer's (7) study of 17 matched pairs where abuse had occurred eight years previously failed to show a difference between the two groups in health, language development, intellectual status, self-concept, and behavior.

THE DEVELOPMENT OF ABUSED CHILDREN

Table 1
Follow-up Studies of Abused Children—Comparison Group Not Used

Author	Sample Size	Mean Follow-up (Years)	Outcome
Elmer & Gregg (1) (1967)	20	5	50% had IQ $<$ 80 40% emotionally disturbed
Morse et al. (3) (1970)	25	3	36% mentally retarded* 24% emotionally disturbed
Martin (5) (1972)	42	3	33% had IQ $<$ 80 38% language delay
Martin et al. (2) (1974)	58	4½	33 had IQ $<$ 85
N.S.P.C.C. (4) (1976)	14	2	Mean IQ 100—details not given
Martin & Beezley (6) (1977)	5	4½	66% impaired ability for enjoyment 62% behavioral disturbance 52% low self-esteem

* intelligence estimated by clinicians

The abused group had a somewhat greater level of impulsivity and of aggression. Both groups came from chaotic families with many emotional problems. It was suggested that social class membership may be a more handicapping feature than child abuse. This paper suggests that the subjects, and therefore the controls, were from an extremely deprived section of society which would not be representative of the general spectrum of child abuse. In a discussion of problems associated with control groups Lynch and Roberts (8) have pointed out that Elmer's study, which attempts to match for all factors, apart from afflicted injuries, may have simply obtained a control group of children who were abused but not actually identified as such.

A study by this author (9) and colleagues matched the abusive families and their children for education, employment, socioeconomic status, nationality, age, sex, and health of the child. Comparing the two groups on the Denver Developmental Screening Test, it was found that the abused group was significantly behind the comparison group in all areas, the difference being most marked in language development. The Denver Developmental Screening Test is only a crude measure of abilities; consequently, when the children were next reviewed (as described in Chapter 8), more sophisticated measures were used.

Kinard (10) concentrated on the emotional development of abused children and found that they had lower self-concept and more aggressive tendencies than controls. Lynch and Roberts used siblings as their controls in a follow-up study of 39 children seen by them at an average of four years previously (11). They showed delays in the siblings as well as in the abused children, although the delays in the siblings were not as marked. Those children who were under five at follow-up had a developmental assessment which showed 59% of the abused children and 39% of their siblings to be delayed. Thirty-six percent of the abused children under five years and 28% of their siblings were delayed in language ability. Forty-one percent of the abused children and 28% of their siblings had an IQ of less than 90. These four studies are summarized in Table 2.

Table 2
Follow-up Studies of Abused Children Using a Comparison Group

Author	Sample Size	Follow-up (Years)	Outcome Compared with Comparison Group
Elmer (7) (1977)	17	8	no difference in IQ, self-concept, language, or behavior
Oates et al. (9) (1980)	56	1–3	delayed in all areas on Denver, especially language
Kinard (10) (1980)	30	1–9	diminished self-concept, increased aggression
Lynch & Roberts (11) (1982)	39	4	under 5 yrs: 59% abused delayed 33% controls delayed over 3 yrs: 41% abused and 28% of controls had IQ < 90

THE DEVELOPMENT OF ABUSED CHILDREN

A study of the way in which maltreatment may affect a child's conception of transgressions of moral and social conventions (12) showed few differences between well-matched abused, neglected, and nonmaltreated childrens' judgments of familiar moral and social transgressions. Abused children were more likely than neglected children to consider psychological distress to be universally wrong for others, while neglected children were more likely than abused children to judge the unfair distribution of resources to be universally wrong for themselves.

A useful study, looking at the developmental consequences of different patterns of maltreatment, has come from Egeland and colleagues (13). These researchers followed 267 high-risk families for four years and looked at the characteristics of the children in relation to the pattern of maltreatment that had taken place. The four different patterns of maltreatment initially identified were: 1) physical abuse; 2) hostility and verbal abuse; 3) parents who were psychologically unavailable; and 4) parents who were neglectful. It was found that when these children were observed in a preschool situation, the physically abused children were distractible, lacked persistence, ego control, and enthusiasm, and experienced considerable negative emotions. Those children whose mothers were psychologically unavailable showed a marked increase in maladaptive patterns of functioning. The neglected children had considerable difficulty in dealing with the various tasks required in the preschool situation because of a lack of self-esteem. This study emphasizes the point that child abuse and neglect cover a wide range of behaviors with the outcomes depending on the initial problem and family characteristics. It also highlights the need for a careful assessment of the child, as well as the family, so that a specific treatment program to meet the child's needs can be formulated.

Despite differences in methodology, loss of some patients to follow-up, and abusive populations that cannot easily be compared, these studies suggest that many abused children do poorly both intellectually and emotionally. It is less likely to be the incident of physical abuse that leads to these problems than the continuation of the disturbed environment in which the child lives.

Trowell and Castle (14) have pointed out that in many cases, even

104 CHILD ABUSE AND NEGLECT

though the abuse stops, the emotional disturbances in the family remain—to the detriment of the child's development. Taitz (15) has confirmed this in a review of 47 at-risk children, in which he showed that the children who were making the least satisfactory progress were those whose family environment had not been able to be improved or changed. The crucial factor in determining a poor outcome for the child seems to be the continuation of the unsatisfactory environment. This is suggested by Lynch and Roberts' (11) follow-up study using sibling controls where it was shown that the siblings were also developing less than optimally.

In a review of the long-term effects of early experience, Rutter (16) concludes that it is possible for a major improvement in the environment in middle childhood to lead to substantial increases in IQ, speech, and language development, although some residual consequences of early adverse experiences may remain. This has implications for the management of child abuse. For many years much of the work has focused on the assessment and management of the parents. Often the needs of the child have been overlooked. Focus on the child is needed so that specific treatment programs to assist the child's intellectual and personality development can be provided. Also required is an awareness that in some cases the child may have to be reared in a more satisfactory environment if the long-term effects of abuse are to be prevented.

REFERENCES

1. Elmer, E., & Gregg, G. (1967). Developmental characteristics of abused children. *Pediatrics, 40,* 596–602.
2. Martin, H.P., Beezley, P., Conway, E.S., & Kempe, C.H. (1974). The development of abused children. *Advances in Pediatrics, 21,* 25–73. Chicago: Year Book Medical Publishers.
3. Morse, C.W., Sahler, O.J., & Friedman, S.B. (1970). A three-year follow-up of abused and neglected children. *American Journal of Diseases of Children, 120,* 439–446.
4. N.S.P.C.C. Battered Child Research Team (1976). *At risk.* London: Routledge & Kegan Paul.
5. Martin, H. (1972). The child and his development. In C.H. Kempe & R.E. Helfer, (Eds.), *Helping the battered child and his family.* Philadelphia: Lippincott.
6. Martin, H.P., & Beezley, P. (1977). Behavioral observations on abused children. *Developmental Medicine and Child Neurology, 19,* 373–378.

THE DEVELOPMENT OF ABUSED CHILDREN

7. Elmer, E. (1977). A follow-up study of traumatized children. *Pediatrics, 59*, 273–279.
8. Lynch, M.A., & Roberts, J. (1982). *Consequences of child abuse.* London: Academic Press, p. 5.
9. Oates, R.K., Davis, A.A., & Ryan, M.G. (1980). Predictive factors for child abuse. *Australian Paediatric Journal, 16*, 239–243.
10. Kinard, E.M. (1980). Emotional development in physically abused children, *American Journal of Orthopsychiatry, 50*, 686–696.
11. Lynch, M.A., & Roberts, J. (1982). *Consequences of child abuse.* London: Academic Press, pp. 79–97.
12. Smetana, J.G., Kelly, M., & Twentyman, C.T. (1984). Abused, neglected and maltreated children's concepts of moral and social-conventional transgressions. *Child Development, 55*, 277–287.
13. Egeland, B., Sroufe, L.A., & Erickson, M. (1983). The developmental consequence of different patterns of maltreatment. *Child Abuse and Neglect, 7*, 459–469.
14. Trowell, J., & Castle, R.C. (1981). Treating abused children. *Child Abuse and Neglect, 5*, 187–192.
15. Taitz, L.S. (1981). Follow-up of children at risk of child abuse: Effect of support on emotional and intellectual development. *Child Abuse and Neglect, 5*, 231–239.
16. Rutter, M. (1980). The long-term effects of early experience. *Developmental Medicine and Child Neurology, 22*, 800–815.

8

A Study of Children
Following Child Abuse and
Nonorganic Failure to Thrive

The remainder of this book is devoted to a study of two groups of children. One group had nonorganic failure to thrive in infancy; the other had suffered from maltreatment. There does seem to be a link between nonorganic failure to thrive and child abuse. Of the six cases of failure to thrive reported by Patton and Gardner (1) in 1962, one child was noted during the period of the study to have black and blue spots on more than one occasion. In 1969 Koel (2) reported three children admitted to hospital for nonorganic failure to thrive. All three children were subsequently readmitted suffering from physical abuse. Several other authors have since confirmed this link between the two conditions (3–6).

The aim of the study under discussion was to look at the intellectual and emotional development of children who had been abused or who had been diagnosed as having nonorganic failure to thrive. In addition to investigation of the development in these two groups and comparing them with children matched for important demographic characteristics who had not suffered from these conditions, a further aim was to look at the similarities and differences between these two groups of children and their families.

A FOLLOW-UP STUDY

The failure-to-thrive group was obtained from a cohort of 24 children admitted to the Royal Alexandra Hospital for Children, in Sydney, with a diagnosis of nonorganic failure to thrive between 1967 and 1969 and which was reviewed in 1970 (7). During 1975, 21 of these children were reviewed (8) at an average of seven years 10 months after presentation. Of those unable to be reviewed, one child had been taken overseas by his parents and two had died as a result of physical abuse. Two other children from the group had required hospital admission due to suspicious injury during this period. In that review it was found that 48% of the children were below average in their schoolwork, two-thirds had a delayed reading age, and 48% had behavior problems. A comparison group was not used in that review, although for some of the items sibling controls were used. The present study describes the characteristics of 14 of these children who were again reviewed, this time at an average of 12½ years after their initial admission to hospital with nonorganic failure to thrive.

The abuse group was derived from a group of 109 children admitted to the Children's Hospital over a 25-month period between 1974 and 1976. These children had suffered from physical abuse or from neglect severe enough to be referred to the hospital's Child Abuse Team. Fifty-six of these children were reviewed in 1978, the findings being considered in relation to those found in a nonabused comparison group (9). It was found that the children in the abuse group were significantly behind the comparison children in all developmental areas, the difference being most marked in language development. This study describes the characteristics of 39 of these children who were reviewed at an average of five-and-a-half years after the initial diagnosis of maltreatment. The overall design of the study, showing the section to be described in the remainder of this book, is shown in Figure 8.1.

BASELINE DATA

Some of the baseline data obtained at the initial presentation of these children may assist in obtaining an overview of these families. The 24 children who were diagnosed between 1967 and 1969 as hav-

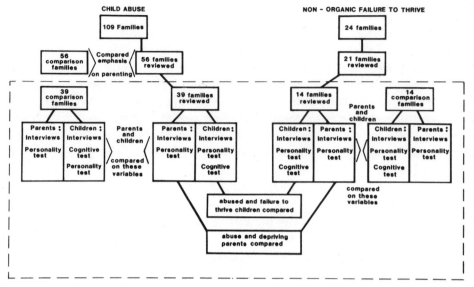

FIGURE 8.1 Research design.

ing nonorganic failure to thrive and the 109 abused children presenting over 25 months in 1974 through 1976 were seen in a clinical, rather than in a research, situation. This influenced the amount and type of data initially recorded in the clinical notes.

The Children from the Failure-to-Thrive Group

There were twice as many boys as girls in the group. Eleven of the 24 children were six months or less in age when they were admitted to hospital and an additional eight were between seven months and 24 months. Thirteen had been fully immunized. The average time spent in hospital was 4.9 weeks with a range from one to 22 weeks. The longer stays were for social rather than for medical reasons. These reasons included parents being reluctant to take the child home in several cases and the parents being unable to be contacted in another case. These findings are summarized in Table 1.

A FOLLOW-UP STUDY

Table 1
Characteristics of 24 Children Admitted to Hospital with Nonorganic Failure to Thrive, 1967–1969

Number of children	24	
Sex ratio (M:F)	16:8	
Age:		
2–6 months	11	(46%)
7–24 months	8	(33%)
Over 24 months	5	(21%)
Average time spent in hospital	4.9 weeks	
	(range 1 to 22 weeks)	
Health:		
Child fully immunized	13	(54%)
Attends baby health clinic	10	(42%)

The Parents from the Failure-to-Thrive Group

Sixty-seven percent of the mothers had married before 20 years of age. The pregnancy had been unplanned in 22 of the 24 cases and social stresses as well as obstetric complications had been common. Eleven of the children who had failed to thrive had been born within 18 months of a sibling. In 18 cases the child was the youngest in the family. Failure to thrive did not seem to be a problem in the siblings, the majority being over the 10th percentile for weight. The social class, based on the breadwinner's occupation, was predominantly class C or class D on the four-point scale of social class used for Australian families (10). The characteristics of the families, which were recorded at the initial presentation, are shown in Table 2.

The Children from the Maltreatment Group

The high proportion of males to females found in the failure-to-thrive children was also found in the abuse group, where there was a

Table 2
Family Data for 24 Children Admitted to Hospital with Nonorganic Failure to Thrive, 1967–1969

Family		
Mother married before 20 years	16	(67%)
Average number of children	3.8	
range	1–17	
Subject youngest child	18	(75%)
All siblings over 10th percentile for weight	20	(83%)
Family has family doctor	16	(67%)
Social class		
Class B	1	(4%)
Class C	13	(54%)
Class D	10	(42%)
Ethnic group of parents		
Australian	17	(71%)
U.K.	4	(17%)
European	3	(12%)
Pregnancy and birth		
Pregnancy unplanned	22	(92%)
Social stresses during pregnancy	11	(46%)
Absent or nonsupportive husband	8	(33%)
Obstetric complications	11	(46%)
Subject born within 18 months of a sibling	11	(46%)
Breast-feeding attempted	9	(38%)
Family uses contraception	8	(33%)

male-to-female ratio of almost 2:1. Forty-five percent of the children had presented in their first year of life, with over 60% being under three years. The child was the first born in almost half the cases.

Bruising was the commonest main presenting injury occurring in 38% of cases, while fractures other than skull fractures occurred in 17%. A further 17% had either skull fracture, subdural hematoma, or a combination of these injuries. Thirteen of the 109 children were considered at risk. These were either cases referred from the Outpatient Department to the Child Abuse Team because the parents had expressed fear that they might injure the child or cases where the

A FOLLOW-UP STUDY

Table 3
Features of 109 Abused and Neglected Children Admitted to Hospital During a 25-Month Period in 1974–1976

Number of children	109	
Sex ratio (M:F)	71:38	
Age at presentation		
6 months or less	31	(28%)
7–12 months	18	(17%)
1–2 years	17	(15.5%)
3–4 years	17	(15.5%)
5–8 years	15	(14%)
over 8 years	11	(10%)
Birth order		
First child	53	(48.5%)
Second child	28	(26%)
Third child	17	(15.5%)
Fourth or subsequent child	11	(10%)
Main presenting injury		
Bruising	42	(38%)
Fractures (other than skull)	19	(17%)
Skull fracture and/or subdural hematoma	18	(17%)
At risk	13	(12%)
Burns	4	(4%)
Other	13	(12%)

behavior of the parents or the state of the child was sufficient to alert the hospital staff to refer the child. Seventeen children had been previously admitted to hospital with what, on history, appeared to have been unrecognized episodes of abuse. The presenting features of these children are summarized in Table 3.

The Parents from the Maltreatment Group

At the time of presentation, 28% of the mothers were 20 years of age or less. Fifty percent of the mothers were married with both parents living together. In 24% of cases the mother was living in a common-law situation and in 26% she was either not married or separated. Forty-five percent of mothers gave a history of having been physically abused in their own childhood. Two of these revealed that they had been admitted to this same hospital in their infancy with a fractured skull. Seventeen of the parents had spent some part of their childhood in welfare institutions. The families came predominately from the lower two social classes, C and D. This reflects to some extent the social class of patients attending the Casualty and Outpatient Departments of the Children's Hospital. Forty-nine percent of the families were judged to be isolated from relatives, friends, and community supports. Table 4 gives the details of the family data.

Table 4
Family Data of 109 Abused and Neglected Children Admitted to Hospital During a 25-Month Period in 1974–1976

Age of mothers		
16–20 years	31	(28%)
21–25 years	49	(45%)
26–30 years	16	(15%)
over 30 years	13	(12%)
Marital status		
Married, both parents together	55	(50%)
De facto/common-law marriage	26	(24%)
Single parent, separated	14	(13%)
Mother never married	14	(13%)
Social class		
Class B	3	(3%)
Class C	25	(23%)
Class D	81	(74%)
Mother abused in own childhood	41	(45%)
Family judged to be socially isolated	53	(49%)

A FOLLOW-UP STUDY

METHODOLOGY ISSUES

Type of Study

The studies of these two groups of children could be regarded as longitudinal observation studies, the failure-to-thrive group being followed over 12½ years and the abuse group being followed over five-and-a-half years. However, they are not true observational cohort studies where two groups of children, one of whom has a risk factor thought to be associated with the occurrence of the problem, would be observed over time to determine the occurrence of the problem in question. Rather, they are prospective cohort studies with a contrived comparison group selected from other sources as described by Feinstein (11). Feinstein points out that the disadvantage of such a comparison group is that it does not act as a true nonexposed group since it may contain an unspecified number of both exposed and nonexposed cases. This is likely to create more difficulty when studying an exposure such as smoking or high fiber diet, both of which are common. However, even if the incidence of child abuse was 1%, this would mean that there was less than a 40% chance of just one abused child being inadvertently being included in the comparison group of 39. As nonorganic failure to thrive is a less common condition, the chances of a case being included in that comparison group are more remote.

Definition of Nonorganic Failure to Thrive

The criteria used for admission of children to the nonorganic failure-to-thrive study in 1970 were that the children should be over two months of age, be below the 10th percentile for weight, not have any discernible cause for their poor weight gain, and have factors in the family strongly suggestive of inadequate care. Although a weight below the 10th percentile was originally chosen for entry into the study, review of the charts and admission weights showed that the majority of the children meeting the study criteria were found to be either on or below the third percentile for weight.

Definition of Child Abuse

Children were admitted to the study if they had a diagnosis of physical abuse made by the Child Abuse Team at the Children's Hospital. Children who had bruising due to abuse but no other injuries were also included. Twelve percent of the original sample of 109 were children who were not physically abused but who were judged to be at marked risk of abuse. In the final sample of 39 children, 5% had originally been in this at-risk group.

Comparison Group

The term comparison group has been used throughout this study. When large groups are formed by means of random assignment of subjects, the groups are likely to be very nearly equal to one another on all conceivable variables. This gives true experimental and control groups. The groups being compared in this study have been matched for certain important variables, particularly social class, but they are nonequivalent groups so that the term comparison group is preferable to control group.

Statistical Analysis

A probability level of less than 0.05 has been chosen as the level of significance. It is important to be aware that this means that there is a 5% chance of the null-hypothesis (meaning there is no difference between the two groups) being true. In the study comparing the failure-to-thrive and abuse groups with their comparison groups and with each other, analysis of variance (ANOVA) was used. When ANOVA is used to test between only two samples, as in this case, the results are identical to the t-tests since ANOVA is based on the null-hypothesis that all means are equal. The chi-square test of significant differences was used for the majority of other calculations with Yates' correction for continuity for large numbers and the Fisher exact test being used for the smaller numbers, depending on the number in the sample and the expected frequencies.

A FOLLOW-UP STUDY   115

Instruments of Measurement

Information was obtained from the children and parents by structured interview. Personality tests and tests of cognitive abilities were done using standard psychological tests. In most cases tests were chosen that had been used for assessing these sorts of children and parents in the past so that the results could be compared with other studies.

LIMITATIONS

All studies have their limitations and this is no exception. Some of these limitations are listed below:

1) Length of follow-up. Because of the different lengths of follow-up of the children who failed to thrive (12½ years) and the abused children (five-and-a-half years), there must be some question about the validity of comparing the personality development and intellectual abilities of these two groups of children.

2) Definition. The definition of child abuse is broader than some other researchers have used as it contains some cases where the children were not actually abused, but were judged to be in significant danger of abuse. However, the factors that are more important for the child than the actual incident of physical abuse are the attitudes and childrearing practices of the family; in this regard the abusive and the severely at-risk families were similar.

3) Baseline data. Ideally, the information recorded about these families at the beginning of the studies should have been more closely related to the information sought when these families were reviewed. When the failure-to-thrive and the abuse families were initially seen, it was in a clinical situation, the concept of a long-term follow-up only coming later. Thus, the amount of baseline data available is

116   CHILD ABUSE AND NEGLECT

limited. This makes it difficult to be sure whether some of the variables that were found in the families later in the study were present at the start or whether the families changed over time.

4) Observer bias. Although strict interview protocols were used for the children and their families, the interviews were not done in a blind fashion and so there was the potential for observer bias in recording the answers. This problem was overcome when the psychological tests were performed, the psychologist not being informed as to which were the study and which the control families.

5) Hawthorne effect. When groups of people are being studied, there is always the possibility of a Hawthorne effect, i.e., the subjects giving atypical answers on some of the tests just because they are being studied. This effect is difficult to control, although a comparison group that may also experience a Hawthorne effect may compensate for any effect occurring in the study group.

6) Recall bias. Some of the questions asked of the mothers were about their recollection of their pregnancy with the child and of the child's infancy. It is known that recall of these events is not fully accurate (12–16). However, because these questions were designed to learn about parental attitudes, it is the parents' *perception* of these events rather than what actually happened that is being considered. The degree of inaccuracy in recall of events at the time of the child's birth was evaluated by comparing the parents' replies with information that had been recorded in the obstetric notes.

7) Loss to follow-up. A weakness of this study is that of the 109 abused children seen in 1974–1976, only 56 of the 100 still alive were seen in the 1978 review, a loss of 44%. Because these parents came from all over the state, an area in excess of 800,000 square kilometers, only those living within reasonable geographic access to the hospital were reviewed on that occasion. However, the possibility

A FOLLOW-UP STUDY

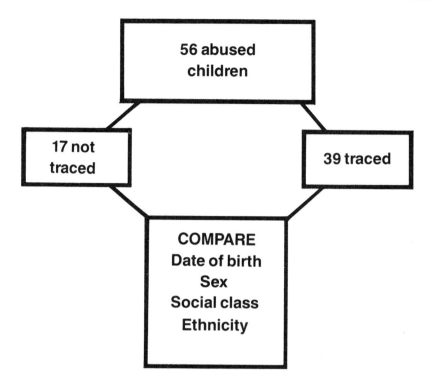

FIGURE 8.2 Comparison of reviewed abused children with those lost to follow-up.

remains that those cases that were not reviewed may have differed from the ones seen. This was less of a concern in the failure-to-thrive review in 1975 as 21 of the 22 children still living were reviewed. In the review to be described in the following chapters, 39 of the 56 abused children and 14 of the 21 failure-to-thrive children previously reviewed were able to be traced and reassessed. To see whether nonrespondent bias was a factor in this review, several known characteristics of the families who could not be traced were compared with these characteristics in the families who were reviewed. The characteristics available for both groups were the date of birth of the child, sex, social class, and ethnic group. The technique used is illustrated in Figures 8.2 and 8.3.

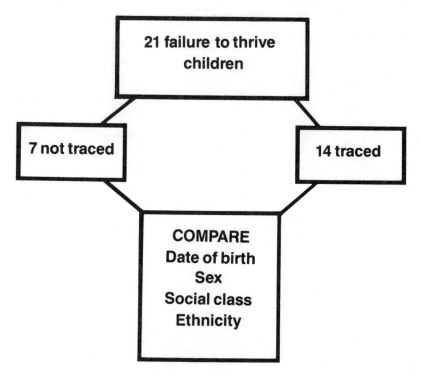

FIGURE 8.3 Comparison of reviewed failure-to-thrive children with those lost to follow-up.

TRACING THE FAMILIES

These families tend to be highly mobile (8, 17) and so considerable effort was required to trace them. The following procedures were used:

1) The last known addresses were checked against telephone directories. Families still at their last known address and who had the telephone connected were asked by telephone to participate in the study. This was followed by a letter confirming the arrangements and giving an appointment.
2) Letters were sent to the last known addresses of all other families, outlining some details of the study, asking for the parents' cooperation, and including a tear-off slip and reply-paid envelope.

A FOLLOW-UP STUDY

3) If no reply was received within two weeks, a follow-up letter was sent.

4) Inquiries were made to the local post offices about a forwarding address if the initial letter was returned "not known at this address."

5) Some families, known to be at their last address but not replying, were visited at home and asked to participate in the study.

6) The Child Life Protection Unit of the Department of Youth and Community Services, to which child abuse reports are made, was approached for information about those families that had not been able to be contacted otherwise. The Department approved of and cooperated with this approach on the grounds that the children being sought were ex-patients of the hospital.

7) For families that could not be traced by any of the above methods an approach was made to the Family Allowance Section of the Department of Social Security. This Department, while not able to divulge addresses to the investigators, was happy to forward letters asking the parents to participate in the study.

8) Approaches were made to community health centers, welfare agencies, schools, and other agencies known to have been involved with these families in the past to see if any contact was still being maintained.

As a result of these measures it was possible to trace 40 of the 56 families where child abuse had occurred and who had been reviewed in 1978. Of the 21 failure-to-thrive families reviewed in 1975, 15 were located. Two families, one from each group, refused to participate in the study, leaving 39 in the abuse group and 14 in the failure-to-thrive group. The other families not reviewed simply could not be found, despite the extensive efforts made to trace them. Of the total of 53 families reviewed, seven had moved to country areas up to 800 kilometers from the hospital and two other families had moved interstate. These families, together with their comparison families, were reviewed in the country towns and interstate capital cities in which they lived.

Considerable ingenuity was required to trace some of the families, particularly since many of them were not the type to respond readily to mail inquiries. One family was found to be living in a caravan park on the outskirts of a small country town several hundred kilometers from Sydney. There was no simple way of contacting them and they had not replied to the mail inquiry. It was learnt from the local post office that the mother came into the country town on a certain day each week to collect her mail. The number of the public telephone box which stood outside the post office was also obtained from the postmistress. She was prevailed upon, without knowing the reason for the request, to ask this mother to stand outside the call box at a fixed time on her next weekly visit to the post office and to step into the call box and answer the telephone should it ring. After having made this somewhat unusual arrangement, the research assistant working on this study then called the public telephone box on the appointed day and time. The subject's mother, who certainly must have wondered about the meaning of this strange request, was dutifully standing outside the call box as arranged, heard the telephone ring, took the call, and after a friendly discussion with the research assistant agreed to participate in the study.

SELECTION OF COMPARISON GROUPS

Permission was obtained from the New South Wales Director General of Education to ask schools to participate in the study. As each child in the study group was located, the principal from that child's school was contacted and asked for the names and addresses of two children from that school who matched the study child on age, sex, family ethnic background, and socioeconomic status based on the father's occupation. The principal was not given any other information about the study child's background or problems and was told, quite correctly, that the study was being conducted to assess the development of children who had been admitted to the Children's Hospital in the past and to compare these children with children from a similar background. The Principal was asked to contact the comparison family, saying that the Children's Hospital may contact them asking them to participate in this study, which Department of Education had approved.

A FOLLOW-UP STUDY

121

From the information supplied by the schools, one of the two comparison families was selected at random and asked to participate in the study. If the approach to the first family was not successful, the second family was contacted, although this was rarely necessary. In six cases it was not possible to obtain a suitably matched comparison group from the schools and over the period of the study suitably matched children were located from the surgical wards of the Children's Hospital. The assessments on these six children were carried out either on the day the child was to be discharged or after the child had been discharged and had convalesced.

METHOD OF ASSESSMENT

The same assessments were carried out on the nonorganic failure-to-thrive group, the abuse group, and the comparison groups. The assessment consisted of physical measurement of the child, a structured interview of the child and parent, and a battery of psychological tests.

Physical Measurement

Measurement of the height was made with the child barefoot, and weight was taken with the child in underclothing. Height was measured using a portable stadiometer which had been constructed for the study and which was suitable for use in those assessments that were done in Community Health Centers or in country hospitals. Heights and weights were plotted on standard percentile charts based on those prepared by Tanner, Whitehouse, and Takaishi (18) at the University of London in 1965. These same charts were in use when the study groups were previously assessed.

Interview

The interview schedules were constructed after consultation with the University of Sydney Sample Survey Center. In constructing the interview schedules, care was taken to use language familiar to the

122 CHILD ABUSE AND NEGLECT

respondents and to avoid value-laden terms and double-barreled questions. Before being used in the study, the interviews were pretested on six families of social classes C and D, since these comprised the social classes of the majority of families in the study. The interviews were modified as a result of this pretest.

Child Interview

The child interview consisted of 18 questions based on data from abuse and failure to thrive from the literature and from the researchers' own experience. Emphasis was placed on socialization skills, family relationships, the child's self-image, ambitions, and concepts of parenting.

Parent Interview

A parent interview schedule was prepared in the same way as the child interview. It contained 73 questions with emphasis on the following areas: family health; accommodation and family structure; employment patterns; family problems and relationships; the parents' relationships with others; the mothers' recollection of the pregnancy and birth for the subject child and the child's early years; attitudes toward the child's education; opinions of and expectations for the child; and the parents' own childhood experiences.

Psychological Tests

All tests were administered by the same psychologists who had wide experience in their use. The psychologist was not informed of which parents or children were in the study or comparison groups. The criteria for choosing the psychological tests were that they should be reputable, nonprojective, and not excessively time-consuming; where possible, there should have been used by others working in this area so that the results could be compared. For the parents Cattell's 16 Personality Factor Questionnaire (16PF) was used (19). This was administered to the mothers and in some instances to

A FOLLOW-UP STUDY

the fathers. It is a well-accepted measure of adult personality and has been used by other researchers studying child abuse (20–22) so that comparisons can be made. Where the child was in the care of foster parents, the test was not given.

The following tests were used to assess the children:

1) Cattell's High School Personality Questionnaire (HSPQ) for children between 12 and 18 years (23) and Cattell's Children's Personality Questionnaire (CPQ) for children between eight and 12 years (24) were chosen to provide an assessment of the child's personality.

2) The Piers-Harris Self Concept Scale (25), although not widely used, was chosen because it has been used in previous studies of abused children with conflicting results (26, 27).

3) The Wechsler Intelligence Scale for Children—Revised (WISC-R) (28) and the Wechsler Preschool and Primary Scale of Intelligence (WPPSI) for younger children (29) were used to obtain a level of general intelligence and to look for differences between verbal and performance scores that had been previously noted in the nonorganic failure-to-thrive children (8).

4) The Schonell Word Recognition Test (30) and the Verbal Language Development Scale (31) were used to see whether abused and failure-to-thrive children develop delays in their reading and language ability compared with other children.

5) The Vineland Social Maturity Scale (32) was used to obtain a quotient that gives an indication of social maturity in the subjects compared with other children.

6) Rutter's Children's Behavior Questionnaire (33) was designed to be completed by the child's teacher. When scored, it divided children into a normal and an abnormal group, with the abnormal group being further divided into predominately neurotic, antisocial, or undifferentiated groups. This questionnaire has been shown to have a re-test reliability of 0.89 and an interrater reliability of 0.72 and to agree with the findings of a blind psychiatric interview in 77% of cases (33). The questionnaire was also completed by the mothers. Evidence from the earlier, uncontrolled review of the children who had failed to thrive (8) had suggested

124   CHILD ABUSE AND NEGLECT

that the mothers saw more problems in their children than their teachers perceived.

Those children living within reasonable distance of the Children's Hospital were assessed at the Hospital, while those from outer suburbs and from country areas were seen by the assessment team at the local community health center or the local hospital. The data were analyzed by the University of Sydney Sample Survey Center, using the Statistical Package for the Social Sciences (34).

The study was approved by the Research Committee of the Children's Hospital and met with the guidelines laid down by the New South Wales Department of Education for conducting research in schools. Each family in the study gave permission for the child's teacher to be contacted for completion of the behavior questionnaire. Each family was given a written guarantee that any information obtained in the study would not be disclosed in any way that might identify the family without their permission. A code number, rather than a name, was used on all questionnaires and psychological tests. When the assessment revealed problems for which the family requested assistance or it was felt assistance was needed, this was discussed with the family at the conclusion of the assessment. Families who requested or agreed to assistance were then referred to an appropriate community agency, their family doctor, or to services at the Children's Hospital, depending on the need.

REFERENCES

1. Patton, R.G., & Gardner, L.I. (1962). Influence of family environment on growth: The syndrome of "maternal deprivation." *Pediatrics, 30,* 957-962.
2. Koel, B.S. (1969). Failure to thrive and fatal injury as a continuum. *American Journal of Diseases of Children, 118,* 565-567.
3. Oates, R.K., & Hufton, I.W. (1977). The spectrum of failure to thrive and child abuse. *Child Abuse and Neglect, 1,* 119-124.
4. Kreiger, I. (1974). Food restriction as a form of child abuse in ten cases of psychosocial dwarfism. *Clinical Pediatrics, 13,* 127-133
5. Galdston, E., Cadol, R.V., Fitch, M.J., & Umhauf, H.J. (1976). Non-accidental trauma and failure to thrive. *American Journal of Diseases of Children, 130,* 490-492.

A FOLLOW-UP STUDY

6. Kempe, R.S., Cutler, C., & Dean, J. (1980). The infant with failure to thrive. In C.H. Kempe & R.E. Helfer, (Eds.), *The battered child* (3rd ed). Chicago: The University of Chicago Press.
7. Oates, R.K., & Yu, J.S. (1971). Children with non-organic failure to thrive—A community problem. *Medical Journal of Australia, 2*, 199-203.
8. Hufton, I.W., & Oates, R.K. (1977). Nonorganic failure to thrive: A long-term follow up. *Pediatrics, 59*, 73-77.
9. Oates, R.K., Davis, A.A., & Ryan, M.G. (1980). Predictive factors for child abuse. *Australian Paediatric Journal, 16*, 239-243.
10. Congalton, A.A. (1963). Social standing of occupations in Australia. *Studies in Sociology*, No. 3. School of Sociology, The University of New South Wales.
11. Feinstein, A.R. (1979). Clinical Biostatistics: XLVIII. Efficacy of different research structures in preventing bias in the analysis of causation. *Clinical Pharmacology and Therapeutics, 26*, 129-141.
12. Pyles, M.K., Stolz, H.R., & McFarlane, J.W. (1935). The accuracy of mother's reports on birth and developmental data, *Child Development, 6*, 165-176.
13. Goddard, K.E., Broder, G., & Wenor, C. (1961). Reliability of pediatric histories. *Pediatrics, 28*, 1011-1018.
14. Mednick, S.A., & Shaffer, J.B.P. (1963). Mothers' retrospective reports in child-rearing research. *American Journal of Orthopsychiatry, 33*, 457-461.
15. Hoekelman, R.A., Kelly, J., & Zimmer, A.W. (1976). The reliability of maternal recall. *Clinical Pediatrics, 15*, 261-265.
16. Hart, H., Bax, M., & Jenkins, S. (1978). The value of a developmental history. *Developmental Medicine and Child Neurology, 20*, 442-452.
17. Lauer, B., Broeck, E.T., & Grossman, M. (1974). Battered children: Review of 130 patients with controls. *Pediatrics, 54*, 67-70.
18. Tanner, J.M., Whitehouse, R.H., & Takaishi, M. (1966). Standards from birth to maturity for height, weight, height velocity and weight velocity; British children 1965. *Archives of Disease in Childhood, 41*, 454-463.
19. Cattell, R.B., Eber, H.W., & Tatsuoka, M.M. (1970). *Handbook for the 16PF.* Champaign, IL: Institute for Personality and Ability Testing.
20. Hyman, C.A. (1977). A report on the psychological test results of battering parents. *British Journal of Social and Clinical Psychology, 16*, 221-224.
21. Hyman, C.A., & Mitchell, R. (1975). A psychological study of child battering. *Health Visitor, 48*, 294-296.
22. N.S.P.C.C. Battered Child Research Team (1976). *At risk.* London: Routledge & Kegan Paul.
23. Cattell, R.B., & Cattell, M.D.L. (1975). *Handbook for the High School Personality Questionnaire "HSPQ."* Champaign, IL: Institute for Personality and Ability Testing.
24. Porter, R.B., & Cattell, R.B. (1979). *Handbook for the Children's Personality Questionnaire.* Champaign, IL: Institute for Personality and Ability Testing.
25. Piers, E.V. (1976). *The Piers-Harris Children's Self-Concept Scale.* Nashville, TN: Counselor Recordings and Tests.
26. Elmer, E. (1977). A follow-up study of traumatized children, *Pediatrics, 59*, 273-279.
27. Kinard, E.M. (1980). Emotional development in physically abused children. *American Journal of Orthopsychiatry, 50*, 686-696.

28. Wechsler, D. (1966). Wechsler Intelligence Scale for Children—Revised. New York: The Psychological Corporation.
29. Wechsler, D. (1966). Wechsler Preschool and Primary Scale of Intelligence. New York: The Psychological Corporation.
30. Schonell, A.J., & Schonell, F.E. (1952). *Diagnostic and attainment testing* (2nd Ed.). Edinburgh: Oliver and Boyd.
31. Mecham, M.J. (1971). *Verbal Language Development Scale.* Circle Pines, MN: American Guidance Service Inc.
32. Doll, E.A. (1953). *Measurement of Social Competence.* Circle Pines, MN: American Guidance Service, Inc.
33. Rutter, M. (1967). A child's behavior questionnaire for completion by teachers. *Journal of Clinical Psychology and Psychiatry, 8,* 1-11.
34. Nie, N.H. (1975). *Statistical package for the social sciences.* New York: McGraw-Hill.

9

Interviews with Parents and Children

PRELIMINARY INFORMATION

Thirty-nine children who had suffered from child abuse at an average of five-and-a-half years previously and 14 children who had been diagnosed as having nonorganic failure to thrive at an average of 12½ years previously were reviewed.

The mean age of the abused children at the time of reassessment was 8.9 years with a range of 4.6 to 14.4 years. The mean age of the comparison group was nine years, the range being from 4.8 to 14 years. In the study group eight families were from social class C and 31 were from class D. The comparison group was made up of class B two cases, class C nine cases, and class D 28 cases. This was not a significant difference. There were 24 boys and 15 girls in the group. The original major injury for each child at the time of diagnosis is shown in Figure 9.1. This shows diagnostic categories of the 56 children previously reviewed along with the diagnosis of 39 of these children able to be traced for the present review. It can be seen that the distribution of injuries is similar, with bruising being the most common injury.

The mean age of the children who had failed to thrive was 13.8 years with a range of 12 to 16.6 years, the mean age of the comparison group being 13.4 years with a range of 11.6 to 16.4 years. There

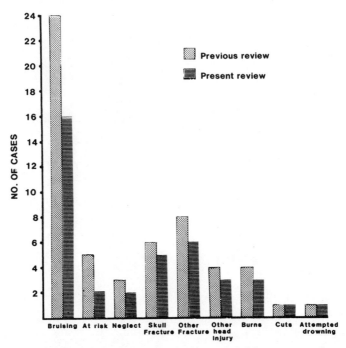

FIGURE 9.1 Major diagnostic findings in 56 abused children previously reviewed and in 39 of those children seen in the present review.

was no significant difference in social class; eight of the study group were in class C and six in class D compared with seven in each of class C and D for the comparison group. Each group was made up of eight boys and six girls.

In order to see if there was any bias due to loss to follow-up between the last and the present review, the year of birth and sex of child and social class and ethnic group of the parents of the 39 abuse-group families able to be traced were compared with these characteristics in the 17 families who could not be found. No significant differences were detected between the lost and found groups on any of these variables (Tables 1-4).

A similar comparison was made, using the same four variables on the 14 failure-to-thrive families able to be found and the seven families lost to follow-up. There was a significant difference in the sex of the children in the two groups, a higher proportion of males being

INTERVIEWS WITH PARENTS AND CHILDREN

Table 1
Comparison of Year of Birth of Child in Found and Lost-to-follow-up Abuse Families

Year of birth	Found	Lost
1967-1972	21	4
1973-1974	11	8
1975-1976	7	5
TOTAL	39	17

$X^2 = 4.4$, not significant

Table 2
Comparison of Sex of Child in Found and Lost-to-follow-up Abuse Families

Sex	Found	Lost
Male	24	13
Female	15	4
TOTAL	39	17

$X^2 = 0.605$, not significant

Table 3
Comparison of Social Class in Found and Lost-to-follow-up Abuse Families

Social class	Found	Lost
Class C	8	4
Class D	31	13
TOTAL	39	17

$X^2 = 0.01$, not significant

Table 4
Comparison of Ethnic Group in Found and Lost-to-follow-up Abuse Families

Ethnic group	Found	Lost
Australian born	28	14
U.K. born	2	1
European and other	9	2
TOTAL	39	17

$X^2 = 0.95$, not significant

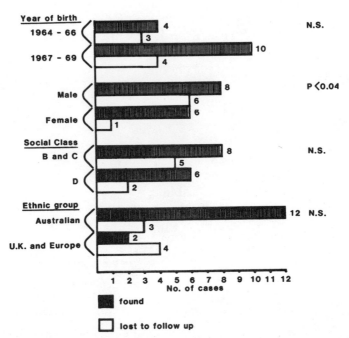

FIGURE 9.2 Comparison of failure-to-thrive families found and lost to follow-up.

lost to follow-up. There were no differences at the 5% level between the two groups on year of birth of child, social class, or ethnic group. These findings are summarized in Figure 9.2.

In some of the information presented in the tables in this chapter it will be seen that the total number of respondents differs. This is because not all of the interview questions were answered precisely enough for analysis so that the total number of respondents to different questions varies slightly. Three of the abused children were in foster care and so the parent interview was not carried out in these cases.

PARENT INTERVIEW

Age of Mothers

Although the mean age of the abused children (8.9 years) and the mean age of the comparison children (9.0 years) were similar, the

INTERVIEWS WITH PARENTS AND CHILDREN

Table 5
Ages of Abuse and Comparison Mothers

Age	Study Group	Comparison Group
25 years or less	6	1
26–30 years	19	14
31 years or more	11	24
TOTAL	36	39

$X^2 = 9.05$, d.f. $= 2$, P < 0.02

mothers of the abused children were significantly younger than those in the comparison group, as shown in Table 5. There were no significant differences between the ages of the failure to thrive mothers and their comparison group.

Health of the Family

The parents were asked about the number of illnesses the child had suffered in the past six months, the number of visits made to the doctor, whether the child had any episodes of accidental poisoning, and whether they thought the child was clumsier than other children. The mothers were also asked whether they thought their children were more or less healthy or the same as other children. There were no significant differences, with only one mother in each group feeling that her child was less healthy than other children.

The mothers were asked about the frequency of headaches, backaches, nausea, and general feelings of malaise in themselves and in their partners. They were also questioned about the frequency of visits to the doctor in the past six months and whether they or their partner had received professional help for an emotional problem.

A significant difference was found between the abuse-group mothers and the comparison group in the amount of help needed for emotional problems during the previous three years. Forty-nine percent of abuse-group mothers had received professional help for an emotional problem compared with 13% of comparison mothers (Table 6). The majority of these consultations had been with a psy-

Table 6
Mothers from Abuse Group Who Have Received Help for Emotional Problems

Professional Help for Emotional Disorder		Study Group	Comparison Group
Yes		19	5
No		17	34
	TOTAL	36	39

$X^2 = 11.96$, d.f. $= 1$, $P < 0.001$

chiatrist, 42% of abusive mothers having had at least one psychiatric consultation compared with 4% of comparison mothers (Table 7). There were no other significant differences in health.

In the failure-to-thrive group the only significant difference in health was found in the fathers of the study group who were reported to have suffered more headaches than the comparison fathers ($p < 0.05$). No difference in emotional disorders was found in this group.

Accommodation and Family Structure

The parents were asked about the number of bedrooms in the house and whether they thought this was adequate, the number of children in the family, the number of adults living in the family, and

Table 7
Mothers from Abuse Group Who Have Had at Least One Psychiatric Consultation

Psychiatric Consultation		Study Group	Comparison Group
Yes		15	4
No		21	35
	TOTAL	36	39

$X^2 = 9.75$, d.f. $= 1$, $P < 0.005$

INTERVIEWS WITH PARENTS AND CHILDREN

Table 8
Number of Times Abuse Families Have Moved House in the Past Five Years

No. of Moves		Study Group	Comparison Group
None		6	16
One		18	19
Two or more		10	4
	TOTAL	34	39

$X^2 = 6.83$, d.f. $= 2$, $P < 0.04$

the number of times the family had changed address in the last five years. As a possible indicator of social isolation, a question was included about whether the telephone was connected. Because of a clinical impression that some abusive families do not list their telephone numbers, a question was also included about whether the number was listed or unlisted.

The abuse families moved house more frequently than their comparison group. Twenty-nine percent of parents had changed their address two or more times in the past five years compared with 10% of the comparison group. Fifteen percent of the abuse group had moved on more than three occasions (Table 8).

Significant differences were also found when inquiry was made about the number of adults living with the family. Fifty-six percent of the abuse-group mothers were living alone compared with 13% of comparison mothers ($p < 0.001$). The abuse group was also less likely to have the telephone connected (Table 9). Very significant

Table 9
Number of Abuse Families with Telephone Connected

Telephone Connected		Study Group	Comparison Group
Yes		25	36
No		11	3
	TOTAL	36	39

$X^2 = 5.03$, d.f. $= 1$, $P < 0.025$

Table 10
Number of Abuse Families with Unlisted Telephone Number

Telephone Number Unlisted		Study Group	Comparison Group
Yes		12	1
No		13	35
	TOTAL	25	36

$X^2 = 15.4$, d.f. $= 1$, $P < 0.0001$

differences emerged when listed and unlisted telephone numbers were compared. Of the 25 abuse families with a telephone, 12 had an unlisted number compared with one of the 36 comparison families (Table 10). There were no significant differences in the number of bedrooms in the house or in the mothers' opinion about whether this was adequate.

In contrast with these findings, for the failure-to-thrive group a significant difference was only found for the number of adults living in the family. Forty-five percent of the failure-to-thrive mothers were living alone compared with 7% of the comparison mothers ($p < 0.04$).

Employment

There was a higher incidence of job instability in the abuse families. In those families that had a wage earner, 35% had held the same job for the last three years compared with 62% in the comparison group. Thirty-eight of the abuse families were on some form of social security benefits at the time of the interview compared with 10% of the comparison familes ($p < 0.02$). Two parents from the abuse group were prison warders and one served in the armed forces. Four of the fathers in this group were known to have served prison sentences unrelated to child abuse and one father was currently in prison.

Although the failure-to-thrive parents did not have a greater level of job instability than the comparison familes, 36% were on social security benefits, while all of the comparison families had some form of employment ($p < 0.001$).

Family Problems

Questions were asked about whether finances, domestic and marital relationships, housing, employment, and health in the family members were causing problems for the family. While there was a high incidence of concerns about several of these problems in all groups, no significant differences were found between the study and comparison families in either the abuse or the failure-to-thrive groups. These data are summarized in Figure 9.3.

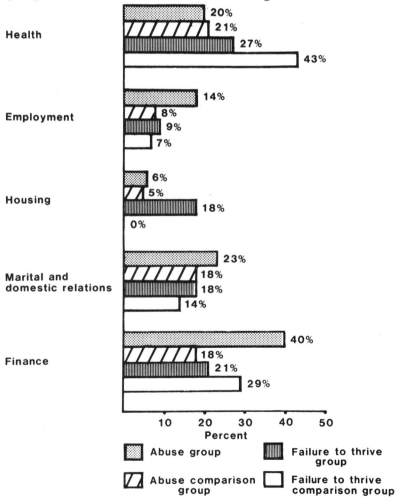

FIGURE 9.3 Problems in abuse and failure-to-thrive families

136   CHILD ABUSE AND NEGLECT

Although not significantly different, the abuse group had a greater percentage of problems than the comparison group in all areas and the failure-to-thrive group had a greater percentage of problems than their comparison group in domestic relationships and in housing. Although the abuse group had a higher incidence of being separated from their partners and while the abuse and failure-to-thrive groups both had a high incidence of dependence on social security benefits, these were not seen as being problems by these parents.

Family Relationships

The mothers were asked how they got on with their partners, the number of partners they had lived with during the last five years, and how much agreement there was in the family on childrearing techniques. To gain some idea of the mother's own self-esteem and regard for her own partner, she was asked whether she would like the index child to grow up to be like herself or like her partner.

There were no differences between either group and their comparison groups about the number of partners they had lived with during the last five years and no significant differences about how the mothers said they got on with their partners. Although 43% of abuse-group families disagreed about childrearing practices compared with 22% disagreement in the comparison group, this did not reach statistical significance.

The abuse-group mothers were significantly less likely to want the child to be like them or their partners. It can be seen in Table 11 that

Table 11

Abuse-Group Mothers' Opinions About Whether They Would Like Their Child to Grow Up Like Themselves or Their Partner

Mother's Wish for Child		Study Group	Comparison Group
To be like mother, partner, or either		12	26
To be like neither		17	4
	TOTAL	29	30

$X^2 = 11.3$, d.f. $= 1$, $P < 0.001$

INTERVIEWS WITH PARENTS AND CHILDREN

over half of the mothers in the abuse group wanted the child to be like neither themselves nor their partners compared with less than one sixth of the comparison mothers saying this. This ambivalent or even rejecting attitude from some of the mothers in the abuse group is illustrated by comments made by one mother in the study group and by her comparison mother. The study group mother's comment about her daughter was: "I can see so much of myself in J—and I don't like any of it." In contrast, the comparison mother volunteered: "I can see so much of myself in her at this stage and I really love it." Nine of the mothers from the study group and one of the comparison mothers openly admitted, without prompting, that they really could not stand their children.

In the failure-to-thrive families there was no significant difference between the study and comparison groups on the degree of agreement between the partners on childrearing practices. Although 50% of the failure-to-thrive mothers claimed that they did not want the child to grow up to be like them or their partners compared with 29% of the comparison mothers having this feeling, this difference was not significant.

Parents' Relationships with Others

The mothers were asked to rate themselves on a four-point scale ranging from outgoing and easy to get to know to shy and retiring. They were also asked about whether they thought other people were easy to get along with. Questions were asked about the frequency of opportunities to go out and relax and the number of occasions to have a break from caring for their children. They were also asked about any sources that they had turned to for financial or emotional help in the past five years.

Forty-two percent of the abuse-group mothers rated themselves as easy to get to know compared with 64% of the comparison group. This was not a significant difference. The majority of mothers in both the study group and the comparison group felt that most people were easy to get along with. Although the mothers from the abuse group claimed to relate readily to other people, it became clear that some

138 CHILD ABUSE AND NEGLECT

were very dependent. After a single interview with the psychologist, four of the mothers tried to form some sort of dependent relationship, calling him regularly at work for advice and help with relatively simple everyday problems. All this occurred despite the psychologist's best professional intentions and is an example of the deep need of some of these parents. There were no such instances from the comparison group. No differences were found in opportunities for mothers to relax (approximately 90% of the study group and 90% of the comparison group) or to have a break from caring for their children, which was available to 50% of the study and comparison mothers.

Sixty-nine percent of the abuse and 74% of the comparison mothers had sought financial or emotional help in the past five years. However, of those who sought help, 64% of the abuse families had contacted social work agencies compared with 45% of the comparison families. In response to the question, who would you be more likely to see to discuss personal problems, the abuse mothers were more likely to avoid discussing them with anyone, while the comparison mothers were more likely to approach a friend or relative (Table 12).

Thirty-eight percent of the failure-to-thrive mothers felt that other people were not easy to get along with compared with none of the mothers in the comparison group ($p < 0.05$). There was no significant difference between the failure-to-thrive mothers and the comparison group in their perception of how they related to others. Similarly there were no differences in the frequency of opportunities to

Table 12
People with Whom Abuse-Group Mothers Would Be Most Likely to Discuss Personal Problems

Most Likely Person		Study Group	Comparison Group
No one		13	3
Spouse		12	24
Parent or family friend		10	8
	TOTAL	35	35

$X^2 = 10.47$, d.f. $= 2$, $P < 0.006$

INTERVIEWS WITH PARENTS AND CHILDREN

go out and relax or to have a break from caring for their child, with approximately 50% having this opportunity at least once each week. There was no significant difference in the 75% of failure-to-thrive families and the 57% of comparison families who sought financial or emotional help in the past five years; assistance was sought equally from family, friends, and agencies.

Mothers' Recollection of Pregnancy and Child's Early Years

The mothers were asked whether the pregnancy and the birth of the child were a pleasant, average, or difficult experience. They were also questioned about their recollection of what it was like to look after the subject child in the first year after birth, during the subsequent four years, and at present.

Twenty-five percent of mothers from the abuse group recalled that the pregnancy was difficult and 37% found the birth unpleasant. The comparison mothers were not significantly different, with 33% saying the pregnancy was difficult and 28% remembering the birth as unpleasant.

The experience of the child's birth given by 30 of the study-group mothers at this interview was compared with the response that the same 30 mothers had given when asked this question when they had been reviewed three years previously (Table 13). There is a trend for the memory of the birth to have mellowed during the intervening

Table 13
Attitudes of 30 Abuse Mothers to Child's Birth Given Three Years Previously Compared with Answers Given in Present Study

Attitudes to Birth	Previous Response	Present Response
Birth easy or "average"	13	19
Birth difficult or unpleasant	17	11
TOTAL	30	30

$X^2 = 2.4$, not significant

140   CHILD ABUSE AND NEGLECT

three years. However, with 37% of the mothers seeing the birth as unpleasant on this review, compared with 57% having this opinion three years earlier, the difference was not significant.

The first 12 months of their child's life was reported as being difficult by 35% of mothers from the abuse group and by 16% of comparison mothers, an insignificant difference. A significant difference did emerge in the reported ease of caring for the child over the next four years. While only 5% of the comparison mothers recalled any problems, 38% of the study-group mothers experienced difficulties (Table 14). One of the comparison mothers recalled experiencing many problems during these early years. She had not planned to have a baby and had intended to give him up at birth, but at the last moment decided not to do so. This high level of ambivalence remained so that even when the child was eight-and-a-half years of age, at the time of this study, the mother was still expressing some confusion about whether she should keep the child or place him in foster care.

The answers from the 34 abuse-group mothers who responded to the question about ease of caring for the child after the first year of life are compared in Table 15 with the answers to the same question given by the same 34 mothers three years earlier. Although two of the mothers who previously described the child's early years as difficult have since changed their minds, there is no significant difference between the two sets of responses.

In the group of mothers whose children had failed to thrive, 41% recalled the pregnancy as being difficult and 17% found the actual

Table 14

Abuse Mothers' Reports of Ease of Caring for Child Between
First and Fifth Year of Life

Ease of Care		Study Group	Comparison Group
Easy to average		21	36
Difficult		13	2
	TOTAL	34	38

$X^2 = 9.91$, d.f. $= 1$, $P < 0.002$

INTERVIEWS WITH PARENTS AND CHILDREN

Table 15
Reports Given Three Years Previously by Abuse Mothers on Ease of Caring for Child Between One and Five Years Compared with Report Given by Them in Present Study

Ease of Caring for Child		Previous Study	Present Study
Easy or acceptable		19	21
Difficult		15	13
	TOTAL	34	34

$X^2 = 0.245$, not significant

birth unpleasant. This was not significantly different from the answers of the comparison group for whom the pregnancy was remembered as difficult and the birth as unpleasant in 25% of cases. However, in the first year of life, the year when the majority of children with failure to thrive presented, 42% of the study-group mothers reported this as being a difficult year in which to look after the child compared with this response in only 7% of the comparison group. There was no significant difference between the study and comparison groups in their memory of ease of looking after the child between one and five years of age.

The responses of the abuse and failure-to-thrive groups to the way they remembered the pregnancy, birth, and first five years of life of the children in the study are compared in Figure 9.4.

Attitude Toward Child's Education

The mothers were asked whether the child had attended organized play groups and preschool, who had organized the child's attendance, and whether they thought attendance had been helpful to the child and to themselves. They were also asked about what school class their child currently attended, the name of the class teacher, and whether they had voluntarily spoken to the child's teacher in the last 12 months.

Approximately one-third of the abused children and one-third of their comparison group had attended preschool or play group. How-

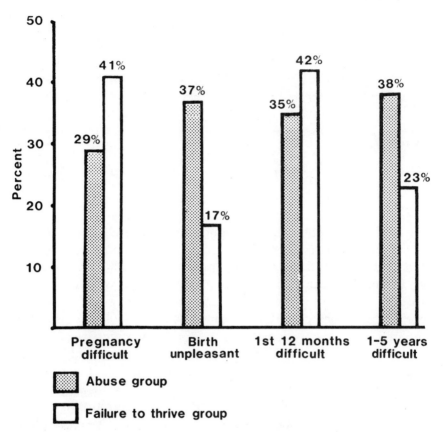

FIGURE 9.4 Comparison of abuse and failure-to-thrive groups on mothers' experiences during pregnancy, birth, and the child's first five years.

ever, the stimulus for enrolling was different. Of the abused children who attended preschool, in 30% the arrangements for their enrollment had been made by social welfare agencies compared with this happening for 11% of the comparison children. For play-group attendance this had been organized by welfare agencies in 50% of cases, compared with 8% for the comparison children. The majority of parents from the abuse and comparison groups whose children had attended felt that play group and preschool had been beneficial for them and their child.

It was found that 85% of abuse-group mothers knew their child's

INTERVIEWS WITH PARENTS AND CHILDREN

143

class and teacher's name compared with 97% of comparison mothers knowing the child's class and 87% knowing the teacher's name, an insignificant difference. In contrast, only 67% of abuse-group mothers had voluntarily approached the child's teacher in the past 12 months to discuss school progress compared with 97% of the comparison mothers ($p < 0.015$).

Four of the 14 children who had failed to thrive and eight of their comparison group had attended preschool. There was no significant difference between the two groups in the stimulus for enrollment. Ten of the failure-to-thrive mothers knew in what class their child was currently enrolled compared with all of the comparison mothers knowing this, although this difference did not reach significance.

Only four (29%) of the failure-to-thrive mothers knew the name of the child's present class teacher compared with 11 (79%) of the comparison mothers ($p < 0.01$) and only four had spoken to the class teacher compared with 100% of the comparison group ($p < 0.01$). The attitudes of the abuse and failure-to-thrive groups toward their child's education are shown in Table 16.

Parental Opinions on and Expectations for the Child

The parents were asked whether they thought their child was doing as well at school as could be expected and what sort of job they

Table 16
Comparison of Attitudes Toward Child's Education in Abuse and Failure-to-thrive Families

Education Involvement	Abuse Group (N = 39)	Failure-to-thrive Group (N = 14)
Attended playgroup	28%	0%
Attended preschool	67%	29%
Attendance organized by agency other than parents	30%	0%
Mother knows child's school class	85%	71%
Mother knows teacher's name	85%	29%
Mother spoken to teacher in past 12 months	67%	29%

144 CHILD ABUSE AND NEGLECT

thought the child would be likely to obtain. They were asked how they thought their child got on with other children and whether they thought their child was outgoing compared with others. In order to gain information about their attitudes to supervision, the mothers were asked at what age they would let their children travel up to one kilometer by themselves to play at a friend's house.

Sixty-six percent of the abuse-group mothers felt that their child was not performing up to their expectations at school compared with 24% of comparison mothers expressing this (Table 17).

There were no significant differences between the abuse and comparison mothers' views on the types of jobs they thought their children would be able to get or the types of jobs they would like their children to obtain. Figure 9.5 shows that the majority of parents did not have any firm ideas about what their child was likely to do and most did not have any definite ambitions for their child, although there was a trend for the comparison parents to have higher expectations and ambitions.

There were no significant differences in the way parents from the abuse and comparison groups thought their children related to other children or about whether they thought their child was outgoing compared with others (Table 18). Table 19 shows that the majority of parents regarded their children as being outgoing compared with other children.

Significantly more mothers from the abuse group would let their children travel one kilometer without supervision. Twenty-two per-

Table 17
Abuse-Group Mothers' Expectations for Child's Performance at School

Child Performing up to Expectation at School		Study Group	Comparison Group
Yes		11	25
No		21	8
	TOTAL	32	33

$X^2 = 9.65$, d.f. $= 1$, $P < 0.002$

INTERVIEWS WITH PARENTS AND CHILDREN 145

cent of these mothers said they would let a child under six years of age travel this distance unsupervised. None of the comparison mothers would allow this. At the other end of the scale 42% of comparison mothers felt the child should be over nine years of age before allowing this amount of unsupervised travel compared with 28% of parents from the abuse group having this view (Table 20). This difference between the abuse and comparison group mothers is an

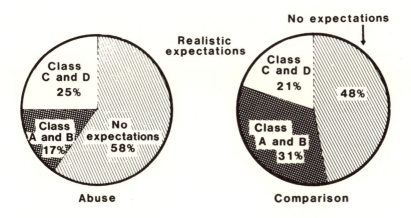

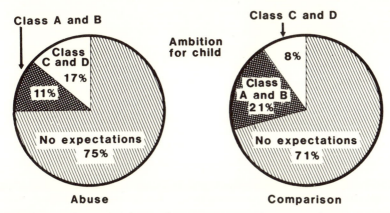

FIGURE 9.5 Parents' realistic job expectations and parent ambitions for their children as shown by social class of occupation chosen.

Table 18
Abuse-Group Mothers' Perception of Ability of Child to Get on with Other Children

Ability to Get on with Other Children		Study Group	Comparison Group
Better		6	8
Average		22	28
Worse		8	3
	TOTAL	36	39

$X^2 = 3.16$, not significant

Table 19
Abuse-Group Mothers' Perception of Child's Personality

Child's Personality		Study Group	Comparison Group
Outgoing		18	24
Average		5	8
Shy		13	7
	TOTAL	36	39

$X^2 = 3.23$, not significant

Table 20
Age When Abuse-Group Mothers Would Let Their Child Travel Up to 1 km Without Supervision

Age when Unsupervised Travel Allowed		Study Group	Comparison Group
Under 6 years		7	0
7–9 years		16	22
over 9 years		9	16
	TOTAL	32	38

$X^2 = 9.46$, d.f. $= 2$, $P < 0.01$

example of the high expectations that abusive parents often have for their children in being able to perform tasks. This is often coupled with a lack of supervision that may lead to a situation where the high parental expectations are less likely to be met.

INTERVIEWS WITH PARENTS AND CHILDREN

Differences between the failure-to-thrive group of parents and their comparison parents were much less marked than the differences seen between the abuse and comparison groups. Here, there was no significant difference between the study and comparison groups in the parents' expectations for their child's performance at school, with the majority of parents feeling that their child's performance was satisfactory. The expectations and ambitions for the sort of occupation the mothers thought their child would obtain did not differ significantly from the comparison group nor were their any differences in their opinions of the child's relationships with others, the child personality, or the degree of supervision they would allow.

Parents' Own Childhood

The mothers were asked with whom they had mainly lived during the first five years of their own childhood, how they felt about their mothers and fathers when they were children, and how they felt about them now.

There was a signficant difference between the abuse group and their comparison group, with seven of the abuse-group mothers not having lived with their natural parents compared with only one of the comparison mothers (Table 21). Although 27% of the abuse-group mothers felt negatively toward their own mothers when they were children and 27% still had negative feelings compared with 14% of comparison mothers having these feelings in the past and 8% having them at present, this difference was not significant.

Table 21
People with Whom Abuse-Group Mothers Mainly Lived During Their First Five Years of Life

Where Mothers Mainly Lived	Study Group	Comparison Group
With one or both natural parents	26	34
With relatives or in institution	7	1
TOTAL	33	35

$X^2 = 3.89$, d.f. $= 1$, $P < 0.05$

Table 22
Abuse-Group Mothers' Childhood Feelings Toward Their Fathers

Feeling Toward Father		Study Group	Comparison Group
Warmly		11	24
No particular feeling		9	9
Negatively		14	4
	TOTAL	34	37

$X^2 = 10.28$, d.f. $= 2$, P < 0.006

In contrast, the negative feelings the abuse-group mothers had toward their fathers, both in the past and at present, were significantly different between the two groups. Forty-one percent of abuse-group mothers had negative feelings toward their fathers during childhood compared with 11% of comparison mothers (Table 22). At the time of the review, 29% still felt negatively toward their fathers (Table 23).

In contrast with these findings, in the group whose children had failed to thrive, no significant differences between the study group and comparison mothers were found on any of these measures.

The areas where significant differences were found between the study and comparison groups for both the abuse and failure-to-thrive group parents are summarized in Table 24. This table also allows the abuse group and failure-to-thrive group to be compared. The only areas where the abuse and failure-to-thrive groups both differ from their comparison groups are in the higher incidence of

Table 23
Abuse-Group Mothers' Present Feelings Toward Their Fathers

Feeling Toward Father		Study Group	Comparison Group
Warmly		13	26
No particular feeling		11	5
Negatively		10	6
	TOTAL	34	37

$X^2 = 7.47$, d.f. $= 2$, P < 0.025

Table 24
Significant Differences Found Between Abuse and Comparison Families and Between Failure-to-thrive and Comparison Families

Characteristics of Study Group Families	Abuse Group Difference from Comparison Group	F.T.T. Group Difference from Comparison Group
Mothers were younger	*	N.S.
Psychiatric treatment for mothers	***	N.S.
Family more mobile	*	N.S.
Only one adult in family	***	*
Less likely to have a telephone	*	N.S.
Telephone number unlisted	****	N.S.
Higher incidence of Social Security payments	*	**
Problems in childrearing between 1 and 5 years	**	N.S.
Playgroup arranged by agencies	*	N.S.
Preschool arranged by agencies	*	N.S.
Mother less likely to know teacher's name	N.S.	**
Less likely to have spoken to teacher	N.S.	**
Teacher interview less likely to have been at mother's instigation	*	N.S.
Child's school work not up to mother's expectations	**	N.S.
Less likely to supervise distance child travels to play	**	N.S.
Mothers brought up by people other than natural parents	*	N.S.
Mothers felt negative toward their fathers in childhood	**	N.S.
Mothers feel negative toward their fathers now	*	N.S.
Mothers wary of other people	N.S.	*
Mothers more likely to keep problems to themselves	**	N.S.
Group rather than individual family decisions more likely	N.S.	*
Mothers do not want child to be like them or their partner	***	N.S.

$*P < 0.05$; $**P < 0.01$; $***P < 0.001$; $****P < 0.0001$
N.S. = not significant

150 CHILD ABUSE AND NEGLECT

single-parent families and the higher dependence on social security benefits.

The abuse group differed significantly from the comparison group in 18 of the 22 items listed in Table 24, while the failure-to-thrive group differed in only six of these areas. The failure-to-thrive group are less likely than comparison group families to know details about the child's school, to be more wary of other people, and to make group rather than individual family decisions. The abuse families are more likely to be mobile, to have had psychiatric help, to not have a telephone, and when they do have a telephone to have an unlisted number. They have high standards for their child's work at school but are likely to supervise their children less frequently. They tend to keep problems to themselves and are more likely to have been raised by people other than their natural parents. They retain early negative childhood feelings toward their fathers and are less likely than comparison mothers to want their child to grow up to be like themselves or like their partners.

CHILD INTERVIEW

Physical Characteristics

There was no significant difference in either the height or weight of the abuse children and their comparison children or between the children who had failed to thrive and their comparison group (Table 25). However, a difference did emerge when the relationship between the height ages and weight ages of the children who had failed to thrive were compared with their chronological ages.

The height age is calculated by plotting the child's height on the percentile chart and looking across the horizontal line on which the height lies to see at what point that line crosses the 50th percentile curve. The age represented where the 50th percentile curve is crossed represents that child's height age. Thus a child taller than the 50th percentile will have a height age greater than his chronological age and a child shorter than the 50th percentile for his age will have a height age less than his chronological age. The weight age is calcu-

INTERVIEWS WITH PARENTS AND CHILDREN

Table 25

Physical Characteristics of Children Who Had Been Physically
Abused 5½ Years Previously and of Children Who Had Failed to
Thrive 12½ Years Ago

	Abused		Failure-to-thrive	
Physical Characteristics	*Study group*	*Comparison group*	*Study group*	*Comparison group*
Height below 3rd percentile	2	1	1	0
Height 3rd–10th percentile	4	1	2	0
Height above 10th percentile	33	37	11	14
TOTAL	39	39	14	14
Weight below 10th percentile	2	3	0	0
Weight 3rd–10th percentile	5	3	3	0
Weight above 10th percentile	32	33	11	14
TOTAL	39	39	14	14

lated in a similar way. When this calculation was made, it was found that six of the children who had failed to thrive, compared with one comparison child, were one or more years below their chronological age for height and also for weight ($p < 0.04$) (Figure 9.6).

Relationships with Others

The children were asked to which person in the family they felt closest and were given an opportunity to say if they did not feel particularly close to anyone. They were asked how they described themselves in relation to other children of their age, about their membership of clubs or organizations, about the number of friends they had, how often they played with or went out with their friends, and whether they enjoyed school.

In the abuse group there were no significant differences in whom the children felt closest to in their families, with 36% of the abuse group and 51% of the comparison group choosing their mother. Thirteen percent of the abuse group and 5% of the comparison group claimed that there was no one in the family to whom they felt particularly close. A majority of the abused children (67%) and their com-

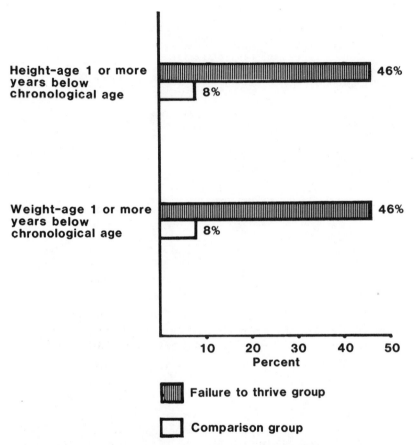

FIGURE 9.6 Height age and weight age of children who failed to thrive.

parison group (57%) described themselves as being more friendly and outgoing than other children. The answers to this question, which showed no significant difference, are shown in Table 26.

There were no differences in the number of clubs or organizations to which the abused and comparison children belonged and no differences in the size of the sample (almost three-quarters) who said they enjoyed school. There was a significant difference in the number of friends the abused children saw themselves as having compared with the number that the comparison children perceived they had.

INTERVIEWS WITH PARENTS AND CHILDREN

Table 26
How Children Abused 5 Years Previously Describe Themselves in Comparison with Other Children

Child's Description of Self	Abuse Group	Comparison Group
Same as others	5	10
Friendlier than others	24	21
Shyer than others	7	6
TOTAL	36	37

$X^2 = 2.97$, not significant

Sixteen (43%) of 37 abused children said that they did not have many friends compared with four (11%) of the comparison children believing this (Table 27).

This result was confirmed when the children answered a question about how often they played with or went out with friends. Fourteen out of 37 of the abused children played with friends less than once each week compared with six out of 37 comparison children. While 20 (54%) of the comparison children played with friends daily, this was so for only seven (19%) of the abused children (Table 28).

The only significant difference between the failure-to-thrive children and their comparison group was related to enjoyment of school. On this occasion the difference lay with the comparison group. While only one failure-to-thrive child said he did not enjoy school, this claim was made by six of the comparison children ($p < 0.05$). No significant differences between the failure-to-thrive children and

Table 27
Number of Friends Claimed by Abused Children

Number of Friends	Abuse Group	Comparison Group
A lot	17	26
Average number	4	7
Not many	16	4
TOTAL	37	37

$X^2 = 9.9$, d.f. $= 2$, $P < 0.01$

154 CHILD ABUSE AND NEGLECT

their comparison group was noted in their family or outside relationships.

Ambitions

The children were asked whether they would like to work in the
same sort of job as one of their parents. They were also asked what
sort of job they would really like to get and what sort of job they
realistically thought they would be able to obtain when they grew up.

Just over 50% of the abused and their comparison children thought
that they would probably have a different job from their father.
When asked about the sort of job they would like to have, the
abused children had lower job ambitions with regard to the social
standing of the job they selected than the comparison group. While
17 out of 37 comparison children nominated jobs that were in social
classes A or B on the Congalton four-point scale, only seven of 37
children from the abuse group nominated occupations in these
higher social classes (Table 29). The abuse group also had lower
ambitions for the job they realistically thought they would be able
to obtain, with only five (14%) nominating an occupation in social
class A or B compared with 16 (43%) of the comparison children
(Table 30).

In contrast to these findings, there was no significant difference
between the children who had failed to thrive and their comparison
group in the sort of job they would like to have. Like the abuse

Table 28
Frequency with Which Abused Children Play
or Go Out with Friends

Frequency of Play with Friends	Abuse Group	Comparison Group
Daily	7	20
Every 3 days	6	6
Weekly	10	5
Less than weekly	14	6
TOTAL	37	37

$X^2 = 11.13$, d.f. $= 3$, $P < 0.02$

INTERVIEWS WITH PARENTS AND CHILDREN

Table 29
Abused Children's Ideas of the Sort of Occupation They Would Like to Have as an Adult

Social Class of Job Chosen	Abuse Group	Comparison Group
A or B	7	17
C or D	19	14
Don't know	11	6
TOTAL	37	37

$X^2 = 6.39$, d.f. $= 2$, $P < 0.05$

group, the failure-to-thrive children had lower ambitions for the sort of job they realistically thought would be possible. While 29% of the comparison children nominated occupations in social classes A or B, none of the failure-to-thrive children nominated occupations in these classes ($p < 0.05$).

Childrearing Attitudes

The children were asked if they thought they would marry and, if they had children, whether they would be as strict or as easygoing in childrearing as their parents had been with them. They were also asked whether they thought they would bring their children up differently or in the same way as their own parents were rearing them.

In the abuse group no significant differences were found in the

Table 30
Abused Children's Ideas of the Sort of Occupation They Think They Will Be Able to Have as an Adult

Social Class of Job Chosen	Abuse Group	Comparison Group
A or B	5	16
C or D	19	15
Don't know	13	6
TOTAL	27	37

$X^2 = 8.81$, d.f. $= 2$, $P < 0.02$

156   CHILD ABUSE AND NEGLECT

numbers who thought they would marry, the number of those marrying who thought they would have children, or in the degree of strictness they would use compared with that used by their own parents. Most thought that they would bring up their children the way that they were brought up. Similarly, between the failure-to-thrive children and their comparison group there were no significant differences except for the number of children who thought that they would have children of their own. Only eight of 13 failure-to-thrive children thought they would have children compared with all 13 in the comparison group.

The areas where significant differences occur between the study and comparison groups for the abuse and failure-to-thrive children are shown in Table 31. It can be seen that the children who were abused at an average of five-and-a-half years previously have fewer friends than the children in their comparison group and have lower ambitions for their future occupations. The children who failed to thrive almost 13 years ago, while within the normal range for height and weight, are more likely to have a height age and weight age

Table 31

Significant Differences Found Between Abused Children and Their Comparison Group and Between Children Who Failed to Thrive and Their Comparison Group

Characteristics of Child in Study Group	Abuse Group, Differences from Comparison Group	Failure-to-thrive Group, Differences from Comparison Group
Height age more likely to be below chronological age	N.S.	*
Weight age more likely to be below chronological age	N.S.	*
More likely to enjoy school	N.S.	*
Does not have many friends	**	N.S.
Less likely to play with friends	*	N.S.
Adult job child would like more likely to be in a lower social class	*	N.S.
Adult job child thinks he will get more likely to be in a lower social class	*	*
Less likely to think he will have children of his own	N.S.	*

*P $<$ 0.05; **P $<$ 0.01**; N.S. = not significant

INTERVIEWS WITH PARENTS AND CHILDREN

below their chronological age than the comparison children. They enjoy school more than their comparison group, are less likely to want children of their own, and, like the abused children, have lower ambitions for their future occupations.

It is clear that some disturbing features persist in abusive parents and in their children as long as five-and-a-half years after the event. Comparison of these children and their families with the nonorganic failure-to-thrive group show that the disturbances seem to be less in the group where there was failure to thrive and that some of the differences are in different areas (Tables 24 and 31). These data suggest that while nonorganic failure to thrive and child abuse do have some features in common, there are also similarities and differences between these parents and their children. These features can be further evaluated by psychological testing as demonstrated in the following chapter.

10

Psychological Testing of Parents and Children Following Child Abuse and Nonorganic Failure to Thrive

In the previous chapter information was given about the interviews with parents and 39 children who had been abused at an average of five-and-a-half years previously and about the interviews with parents and 14 children who had been admitted to hospital with nonorganic failure to thrive 12½ years previously. This chapter describes the psychological testing on the parents and children in these two groups.

THE PARENTS

In the abuse group the Cattell 16 Personality Factor Test (16PF) was given to 32 study and 32 comparison mothers. Six fathers and six comparison fathers from this group also had the test administered. In the nonorganic failure to thrive group, 11 of the study group and 12 of their comparison mothers, as well as two fathers from the study group and three comparison fathers, completed the test.

PSYCHOLOGICAL TESTING OF PARENTS AND CHILDREN

159

The original aim had been to perform the 16PF only on the mothers. Fathers were only tested when they happened to be available on the testing day. The commonest reason for not being able to test the seven mothers from the abuse group and the three mothers from the failure-to-thrive group were difficulty in understanding English, inability to comprehend the requirements to complete the test, or the mother being unavailable if the child was in foster care, as occurred in three cases.

The 16PF is an objective, scorable test designed to give a complete coverage of personality in a brief time (1). It measures 16 different personality dimensions, each of which is referred to by a letter. In addition to these 16 primary factors, the test can be used to measure second-order factors which give broader personality categories.

In the abuse group significant differences were found between the study and comparison mothers on factors E and L (Table 1). People with a low score on factor E are described as being more submissive, docile, and accommodating, while those with a high score are described as assertive and aggressive (1). The mean score for the abuse-group mothers on factor E was 5.7 and the mean score for the comparison group was 4.4. While both of these scores are within the normal range, analysis of scores between the study and comparison mothers showed the abuse-group mothers to be significantly more assertive ($p < 0.02$).

Those who score low on factor L are described as being easygoing, relaxed, and perhaps lacking in ambition, while those high on this factor are said to be more demanding, jealous, and suspicious (1). The mean score on factor L for the comparison mothers was 6.1,

Table 1
Factors Showing Differences Between Abuse- and Comparison-Group Mothers on Mean Sten Scores of 16PF Test

	Abuse Group (N=32)		Comparison Group (N=32)		
FACTOR	Mean	S.D.	Mean	S.D.	Significance
E	5.7	2.1	4.4	1.8	F = 7, P < 0.02
L	7.0	1.4	6.1	2.0	F = 4.2, P < 0.05

while the abuse mothers were significantly higher with a mean score of 7.0 ($p < 0.05$).

The broader, second-order factors were also calculated for the 16PF. When this was done, there was a significant difference between the abuse and comparison mothers on factor Qiii. People with a low score on this factor are said to be sensitive and thoughtful, while those with high scores are more enterprising, decisive, and liable to act with insufficient consideration and thought (2). The abuse mothers' score of 6.5 (standard deviation 1.7) on this factor was significantly higher than the comparison mothers' score of 5.4 with a standard deviation of 1.6 ($p < 0.03$).

In summary, the 16PF showed that the abuse-group mothers were more assertive than the comparison mothers and were more likely to have characteristics associated with demanding, suspicious, and assertive personalities.

Although the sample of six fathers from the abuse group was small, some differences did emerge between these fathers and their comparison fathers. As with the mothers, a significant difference occurred with factor E, although the trend was opposite to that observed with the mothers. Here it was the comparison fathers who scored higher, toward the more assertive end of the scale, with mean score of 7.2, while the fathers from the abuse group were significantly lower with a mean score of 4.8 ($p < 0.04$). The fathers from the abuse families were also significantly lower than their comparison fathers on factor G and factor M. People low on factor G are said to have weaker superego strength, to have a tendency to evade rules, and to feel few obligations. Those low on factor M are said to be more practical and to be concerned with immediate interests compared with those with higher scores who are less practical and tend to be absorbed in inner ideas (1). The details of the scores and standard deviations on these three factors showing the differences between the fathers from the abuse and comparison families are shown in Figure 10.1.

In the failure-to-thrive group a significant difference was found between the failure-to-thrive and comparison mothers only on factor B, where the failure-to-thrive mothers had lower scores. People scoring low on this factor tend to be less intelligent and to have difficulty

PSYCHOLOGICAL TESTING OF PARENTS AND CHILDREN

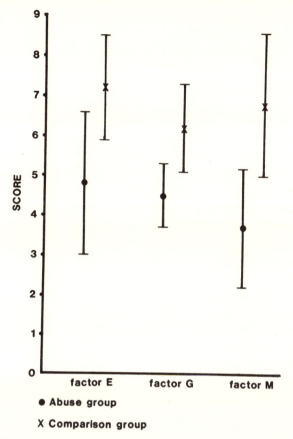

FIGURE 10.1 Mean sten scores and standard deviations for six abuse-group and six comparison fathers on 16PF test.

in handling abstract problems, while those with high scores are of higher mental capacity (2). The mean score for the failure-to-thrive mothers on factor B was 4.2 with a standard deviation of 1.1, while the comparison mothers had a mean score of 5.4 and standard deviation of 1.6 ($p < 0.05$).

The second-order factor Qii was significantly higher in the mothers from the failure-to-thrive group. People with high scores on this factor tend to have high levels of anxiety (1). The failure-to-thrive group of mothers had a mean score of 7.0 (standard deviation, 1.2) on this factor compared with 4.5 (standard deviation, 1.6) for the comparison mothers (p < 0.002).

In summary, the 16PF results suggest that this group of mothers, whose children failed to thrive for no organic cause 12½ years previously, have a tendency to lower intelligence, to concrete thinking, and to higher anxiety levels than the comparison mothers. The number of fathers tested in the failure-to-thrive group was too small for any valid comparison to be made.

A comparison was made between the 16PF scores of the abuse group and the failure-to-thrive group of mothers to see if there were any significant differences. A difference was found on factor G, the mean score for the abuse group being 5.5, while the failure-to-thrive mothers had a higher mean score of 6.5 (p < 0.02). Factor G is related to superego strength, with higher scores suggesting higher strengths in this area. While both groups scored within the normal range on this factor, the abusive mothers were significantly lower than the failure-to-thrive mothers.

A comparison of second-order factors between the abuse and failure-to-thrive groups of mothers showed that the failure-to-thrive mothers had a higher score on factor Qi. People with higher scores on this factor are said to be outgoing and good at making interpersonal contacts compared with those with low scores who are said to be shyer and more inhibited (1). The failure-to-thrive mothers' mean score of 5.7 is in the middle of the normal range, while the abuse-group mothers had significantly lower scores, tending toward introversion, with a mean score of 4.7 (p < 0.05).

A summary of the significant differences between the abuse parents and their comparison group and between the failure-to-thrive parents and their comparison group is shown in Table 2. The abuse group mothers were found to be more assertive (factor E), more demanding, jealous, and suspicious (factor L), and more likely to act without thinking (factor Qiii) than their comparison mothers. The fathers from the abuse group were more likely to be submissive, in contrast to their assertive wives, to evade rules and obligations (factor G), and to be more practical than the comparison fathers.

The mothers whose children failed to thrive had a tendency to be less intelligent, to be less able to handle abstract problems, and to

PSYCHOLOGICAL TESTING OF PARENTS AND CHILDREN

Table 2

Summary of Significant Differences Found Between Abuse-Group Parents and Their Comparison Group and Between Failure-to-thrive Parents and Their Comparison Group on the 16PF Test

Characteristics of parents in study groups	Child-abuse Group	Failure-to-thrive Group
Mothers higher on factor E (submissive—dominance)	*	N.S.
Fathers lower on factor E	*	—
Mothers higher on factor L (trusting—suspicion)	*	N.S.
Mothers lower on factor B (intelligence)	N.S.	*
Fathers lower on factor G (superego strength)	*	—
Fathers lower on factor M (practical—imaginative)	**	—
Mothers higher on 2nd order factor Qii (anxiety)	N.S.	**
Mothers higher on 2nd order factor Qiii (tender-minded—tough poise)	*	N.S.

*$P < 0.05$; **$P < 0.01$; N.S. = not significant

have higher anxiety levels than their comparison mothers. The abuse-group mothers were much more introverted than the failure-to-thrive mothers.

THE CHILDREN

The following tests were used for assessment of the children:

1) Cattell's Children's Personality Questionnaire (CPQ)
2) Cattell's High School Personality Questionnaire (HSPQ)
3) The Piers-Harris Children's Self-Concept Scale
4) The Wechsler Intelligence Test for Children—Revised (WISC-R) and the Wechsler Preschool and Primary Scale of Intelligence (WPPSI)
5) The Schonell Reading Age
6) The Vineland Social Maturity Scale

164 CHILD ABUSE AND NEGLECT

7) The Verbal Language Development Scale
8) Rutter's Children's Behavior Questionnaire

Cattell's Children's Personality Questionnaire (CPQ)

This is designed for children between eight and 12 years of age. Fourteen abused children were of appropriate age for this test. Their results were compared with those of 17 comparison children. An insufficient number of children who had failed to thrive were of appropriate age for this test.

In the abused children the only significant difference between the study and comparison children was on factor F. Children who score low on this factor are described as being serious, cautious, and subdued, compared with those scoring at the higher end of the scale who are said to be lighthearted. The abused children had a mean score of 3.5 (standard deviation, 1.9) on this factor. This was significantly lower than the comparison children whose mean score of 5.2 on factor F (standard deviation, 2.1) was in the middle of the normal range ($p < 0.03$).

When the broader, second-order factors were calculated from the Children's Personality Questionnaire, a significant difference emerged on the extraversion factor. Lower scores on this factor are associated with the child being shy and inhibited in interpersonal contacts, whereas children with high scores are socially outgoing (3). The abused childrens' mean score of 4.5 (standard deviation, 0.95) was significantly lower than the comparison children whose mean score was 5.6 (standard deviation, 0.79) ($p < 0.004$).

Cattell's High School Personality Questionnaire (HSPQ)

The HSPQ is designed for children aged between 12 and 18 years. It was given to 10 of the children who had failed to thrive and 11 children in their comparison group. An insufficient number of the abused children were of the appropriate age for this test.

The children who had failed to thrive showed a significant difference from their controls on factor C. Children scoring highly on this

PSYCHOLOGICAL TESTING OF PARENTS AND CHILDREN

factor are said to have higher ego-strength and emotional stability (4). While the mean score for the comparison children was 7.2 (standard deviation, 1.4), the mean score for the study-group children was significantly lower at 5.5 (standard deviation, 1.8), although this score is still within the normal range ($p < 0.03$).

There were no significant differences on the second-order factors between the failure-to-thrive and comparison children, although there was a trend for the study group to be lower on factor Qiv, a factor relating to independence. The study group's mean was 3.4 (standard deviation, 0.8) in contrast with the comparison group's mean of 5.9 (standard deviation, 1.4) ($p < 0.076$).

In summary, the CPQ and HSPQ results suggested that the abused children were more likely than their comparison group to be serious, subdued, and more inhibited in interpersonal relationships, while the children who failed to thrive were more likely to have lower ego-strength and emotional stability than their comparison group.

The Piers-Harris Children's Self-Concept Scale

This scale, subtitled "The way I feel about myself," is a pencil and paper test which is completed by the child and takes about 20 minutes. Average scores are usually considered to be those between the 31st and 70th percentiles or raw scores between 46 and 60 (5). High scores suggest high self-concept, with low scores suggesting the reverse.

The test was administered to 37 of the abused children and to 37 of their comparison children. The comparison group had significantly higher scores. The study group's raw score of 51.4 fell toward the lower end of the normal range, while the comparison group's mean of 60.9 was just above the normal range. Table 3 shows the raw scores, sten scores, percentiles, and standard deviations for the abused and comparison children.

In the failure-to-thrive group all 14 of the study children and their comparison children completed the test. In contrast to the results for the abused children, no significant difference was found between the failure-to-thrive children and their comparison group, with both

Table 3
Piers-Harris Children's Self-Concept Scale Scores for Abused and Comparison Children

Type of Score	Study Group (N = 37)	Comparison Group (N = 37)	Significance
Raw score	51.4 (S.D. 13.2)	60.9 (S.D. 9.2)	F = 12.9, P < 0.001
Sten score	5.0 (S.D. 2.2)	6.2 (S.D. 1.5)	F = 7.9, P < 0.007
Percentile	47.2 (S.D. 28.9)	69.7 (S.D. 23.2)	F = 13.6, P < 0.001

groups falling within the normal range for the test. However, like the comparison children from the abuse group, the failure-to-thrive comparison children tended to have scores toward the upper end of the normal range. The results for the failure-to-thrive children, which contrast with the abuse group, are shown in Table 4.

The Wechsler Intelligence Scale for Children—Revised (WISC-R).

The WISC-R was performed on 34 abused and 34 comparison children. Four abused children and four comparison children who were under the age range for the test were given the Wechsler Pre-school and Primary Scale for Intelligence (WPPSI). Another child, who was severely retarded, was excluded. The results for the WISC-R and WPPSI have been considered together.

The WISC-R is divided into verbal and performance sections to identify the two principal modes by which human abilities are ex-

Table 4
Piers-Harris Children's Self-Concept Scale Scores for Failure-to-Thrive Children

Type of Score	Study Group (N = 14)	Comparison Group (N = 14)	Significance
Raw scores	52.9 (S.D. 10.5)	57.4 (S.D. 10.5)	N.S.
Sten scores	4.9 (S.D. 1.6)	5.8 (S.D. 1.6)	N.S.
Percentile	50.4 (S.D. 25.8)	61.2 (S.D. 26.6)	N.S.

N.S. = not significant

PSYCHOLOGICAL TESTING OF PARENTS AND CHILDREN

pressed. Thus a verbal score, a performance score, and a full-scale intelligence score can be obtained from the test.

The mean score on the verbal scale for the abused children was 95. This was significantly lower than the mean score of 106 for the comparison children. Another way of looking at these differences is to consider the standard error of measurement of these scores. This is a function of the reliability coefficient and variability of the test scores and provides an indication of the confidence one can have in making judgments about a child's true ability on a particular test (6). The standard error of measurement for children eight-and-a-half years to nine-and-a-half years (the mean age of the abused and comparison children) is between 3.9 and 3.7. As the difference between the mean verbal scores in the study and comparison group was 11, this could not be accounted for purely by differences in the standard error of measurement.

The abused children had a mean performance score of 95. This was significantly lower than the comparison group's mean of 106. The standard error of the performance score for children of this age is 4.5 to 4.7 which would not be enough to account for the difference observed.

The full scale also showed a significant difference, with the abused children having a mean full scale score of 95 and the comparison children having a mean of 107. The standard error of measurement on the full scale for this age range is 3.1 to 3.2. The range of full-scale scores for the study group was 65 to 127 and for the comparison group, 61 to 130. The findings on the intelligence scales for the abused children are summarized in Table 5. Although the children who had been abused showed significantly lower scores than the comparison children on the verbal, performance, and full scales, they

Table 5
Summary of Wechsler Intelligence Scores of Abused Children

I.Q. score	Study Group (N = 38)		Comparison Group (N = 38)		Significance
	Mean	S.D.	Mean	S.D.	
Verbal IQ	95	15.5	106	14.8	$F = 10.31, P < 0.003$
Performance IQ	95	17.1	106	16.2	$F = 7.99, P < 0.007$
Full Scale IQ	95	16.8	107	15.3	$F = 11.35, P < 0.002$

168   CHILD ABUSE AND NEGLECT

had no significant discrepancy between their own verbal and performance scores.

To see whether head injury may have accounted for the difference in intelligence between the abused and comparison children, the intelligence quotients of the group with head injuries were considered. Eight of the 39 abused children had suffered head injuries comprising five children with a fractured skull, two with a subdural hematoma, and one with marked bruising to the head. The full-scale intelligence scores for these children are shown in Table 6. The mean IQ of this group is 90. Although this is lower than the mean score for the total group, it is not enough to account for the difference in IQ between the abused and comparison children. Of the 12 children from the abused group who had an IQ below 85, only four are known to have suffered head injury at the time of diagnosis.

In the failure-to-thrive group, all of the children and their comparison children were given the WISC-R. The mean score on the verbal scale for the children who failed to thrive was 90. This was significantly lower than the mean score of 102 for the comparison children. The standard error of measurement on the verbal scale for children aged 13½ years (the mean age of children in this group) of 3.4 is not enough to account for this difference. The mean performance score for the failure-to-thrive group was 98 compared with 104 for the comparison children, and the mean full score was 93 compared with 103 for the comparison group. The standard error of

Table 6

Full-Scale Intelligence Scores of 8 Children Whose Diagnosis of
Child Abuse Was Made on the Basis of Head Injury

Type of head injury	IQ
Fractured skull	68
Fractured skull	82
Fractured skull	84
Severe bruising to head	84
Fractured skull	92
Fractured skull	92
Retinal hemorrhages/subdural hematoma	95
Subdural hematoma	121
MEAN IQ	89.8

PSYCHOLOGICAL TESTING OF PARENTS AND CHILDREN

measurement on the full scale for children of this age is 3.2. Although the performance and full-scale scores of the children who failed to thrive are lower than those of the comparison group, these differences did not reach statistical significance (Table 7).

The study-group children had an average discrepancy of eight points between their verbal IQ of 90 and performance IQ of 98. Wechsler regards a difference of 8.7 points at this age as being significant at the 15% level and 11.8 points being significant at the 5% level of confidence (6), so that the discrepency noted between the verbal and performance scores when these children were reviewed six years earlier (7) has become less marked with time.

The Schonell Reading Age

The Schonell Reading Age test consists of a list of words of increasing difficulty. The child is asked to read the words from the list until 10 consecutive failures are made. The reading age is calculated from the number of words correctly read in relation to the child's chronological age. The maximum attainable reading age is 12.5 years (8).

Thirty-five abused and 35 comparison children under 12.5 years of age were tested. The reading age of the abused children was an average of 14.3 months behind their chronological age. In the comparison group there was an average delay of 4.8 months. This difference was significant at the 5% level. The discrepancies in reading age between the two groups broken down into the number of children

Table 7

Summary of Wechsler Intelligence Scale Scores of Children Who Failed to Thrive

IQ Scale	Study Group (N = 14)		Comparison Group (N = 14)		Significance
	Mean	S.D.	Mean	S.D.	
Verbal IQ	90	13.8	102	10.2	F = 6.25, P < 0.02
Performance IQ	98	14.9	104	15.2	F = 1.27, P = 0.27
Full scale IQ	93	14.7	103	11.9	F = 3.79, P = 0.06

Table 8
Reading Age of Abused and Comparison Children in Relation to Their Chronological Age

Reading Age in Relation to Chronological Age	Study Group	Comparison Group
13 months or more ahead	0	4
12 months either side of chronological age	18	21
13–24 months behind	9	4
25–36 months behind	2	3
More than 36 months behind	6	3
TOTALS	35	35

who are two, three, or more than three years behind their chronological age are shown in Table 8. Seventeen children from the abuse group and 10 from the comparison group had a reading age more than one year below their chronological age.

Although the failure-to-thrive children comprised an older age group, all children were tested. Those who were aged 12.5 years or more and who were reading at the test's ceiling were then excluded. In children who were older than 12.5 years but who had a reading age below this level, the discrepancy was taken as the number of months their reading age was below 12.5 years rather than the number of months it was below the child's chronological age. With these criteria, the comparison group was an average of 23.5 months behind their chronological age. The study group was further behind with an

Table 9
Reading Age in Relation to Chronological Age for Failure-to-Thrive and Comparison Children

Reading Age in Relation to Chronological Age	Study Group	Comparison Group
12 months either side of chronological age	3	7
13–24 months behind	1	4
25–36 months behind	2	2
More than 36 months behind	8	1
TOTALS	14	14

PSYCHOLOGICAL TESTING OF PARENTS AND CHILDREN 171

average delay of 34.7 months. This difference did not reach statistical significance.

Eleven of the failure-to-thrive children compared with seven of the comparison children had a reading age of more than one year below their chronological age. This difference was significant at the 5% level. In eight of these children from the study group, their reading age was three years or more behind their chronological age. The reading ages of the children who had failed to thrive are summarized in Table 9.

The Vineland Social Maturity Scale

This scale measures performances in which children show a progressive capacity for looking after themselves and for participating in those activities that lead toward ultimate independence as adults. The degree of social independence measured by the scale may be taken as an indication of progressive development of social competence (9). Thirty-eight abused and 38 comparison children and 14 failure-to-thrive and 14 comparison children were tested.

No significant differences were found in the abused children between their scores and those of their comparison group. The abused children had a mean social maturity quotient of 103, the mean of the comparison children being 105. Why is it that the abused children, who performed less well than their comparison children on all other parameters including intelligence, have a social maturity quotient no different from the comparison children? The answer became apparent during the interviews with the mothers when it became clear that many of the abused children had to, of necessity, develop certain social skills. Because they were often left to fend for themselves, they became adept at some of the skills that the Social Maturity Scale measured. For example, in administering the scale one mother was asked whether her eight-year-old daughter could do certain household tasks. Her reply was: "She . . . has to! I'm not . . . doing it!" Many of the children were left unsupervised, allowed to wander the streets, or sent shopping, thus acquiring a variety of skills that could be regarded as showing some degree of social competence. One

Table 10
Vineland Social Maturity Scale of Abused Children and Children Who Failed to Thrive

Test	Abused (N=38)	Comparison (N=38)	Failure to Thrive (N=14)	Comparison (N=14)
Social maturity quotient	103	105	98	107
S.D.	17.8	11.4	10.6	10.0
Significance	F = 1.41, P = 0.24 N.S.		F = 5.15, P < 0.04	

seven-year-old would truant from school and enter other people's houses, stealing minor items and food. The older children were often given the responsibility of looking after their younger siblings so that they acquired a number of the skills tested by the Social Maturity Scale.

The failure-to-thrive children did not seem to have been put into a situation where social skills were prematurely developed. These children had a social maturity quotient of 98 compared with 107 for the comparison group. The results for the abused and failure-to-thrive children are summarized in Table 10.

The Verbal Language Development Scale

This is an extension of the communication portion of the Vineland Social Maturity Scale. It does not have the precision of direct testing methods and is carried out in an interview situation with the child, the examiner scoring the child on items on the test sheet appropriate to the child's age. The scale was administered to 38 abused and comparison children and to 14 failure-to-thrive and comparison children.

The abused childrens' mean score of 92 was significantly lower than the comparison children's mean of 100. A difference was also found between the failure-to-thrive children and their comparison group. Here the study group's mean score was 80, significantly lower than the comparison group's mean of 91. Details of the Verbal Lan-

PSYCHOLOGICAL TESTING OF PARENTS AND CHILDREN

Table 11
Verbal Language Development Scale (VLDS) of Abused Children and Children Who Failed to Thrive

Test	Abused (N=38)	Comparison (N=38)	Failure to Thrive (N=14)	Comparison (N=14)
VLDS	92	100	80	90
S.D.	18.1	15.9	12.6	14.3
Significance	F = 5.45, P < 0.03		F = 4.91, P < 0.04	

guage Development Scale results for the abused and failure-to-thrive children are shown in Table 11.

Rutter's Children's Behavior Questionnaire

This questionnaire was designed to be completed by the child's teacher. When scored it divides children into a normal and an abnormal group, with the abnormal group being further divided into predominantly neurotic, antisocial, or undifferentiated groups. In a general population in England, Rutter found that 11% of boys and 3.5% of girls obtained abnormal scores.

In 38 of the abused children and 38 of their comparison children the questionnaire was completed by the children's class teachers. Twenty-one (55%) of the abused children received abnormal scores compared with seven (18%) of the comparison children (p < 0.001). The results for the abused and comparison children with further breakdown of the abnormal scores into predominantly antisocial, neurotic, or undifferentiated categories are shown in Figure 10.2. Thirty-four percent of the study-group children fell into the antisocial group, 16% into the neurotic group, while 5% were abnormal, but undifferentiated.

The mothers were then asked to complete the questionnaire on their own child to see if their perceptions were similar to those of the teachers. Both the study and comparison mothers perceived their children as having more deviant behavior than did the teachers, with 30 out of 37 abuse-group mothers (81%) and 13 out of 38 comparison

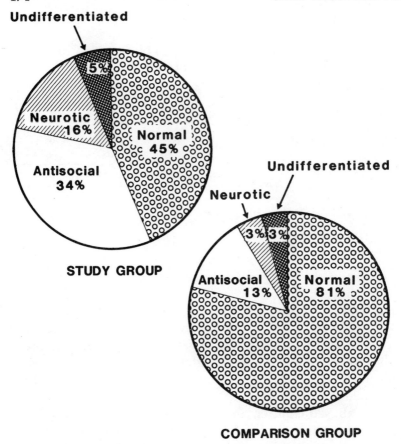

FIGURE 10.2 Results of Rutter Children's Behavior Questionnaire completed by teachers of abused and comparison children.

mothers (34%) completing the questionnaire in a way that gave the child an abnormal score ($p < 0.005$). Figure 10.3 shows these results with the further breakdown of the abnormal group into predominantly neurotic, antisocial, and undifferentiated categories.

The failure-to-thrive children, like the abused children, were more likely than the comparison children to receive abnormal scores from their teachers. Seven (50%) of the study group received an abnormal score compared with two (14%) of the comparison children ($p < 0.05$).

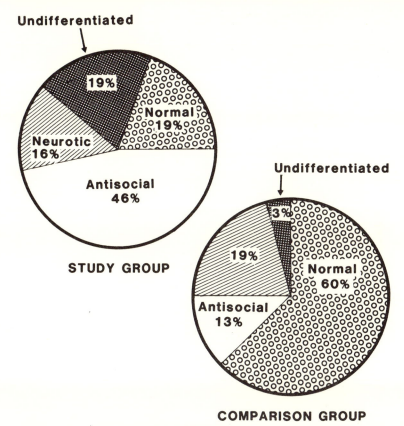

FIGURE 10.3 Results of Rutter Children's Behavior Questionnaire completed by mothers of abused and comparison children.

When the failure-to-thrive mothers completed the same questionnaire, the results were similar to those found in the abuse group of mothers. More abnormal behavior was perceived by the mothers than by the teachers with nine (64%) of the study-group mothers and four (29%) of the comparison mothers giving their children an abnormal score, although this difference did not reach statistical significance. The results of the behavior questionnaire for the children who had failed to thrive are shown in Figure 10.4.

The areas where significant differences occurred between the abused children, those who failed to thrive, and their respective com-

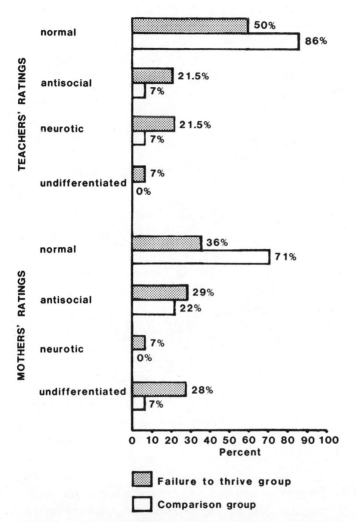

FIGURE 10.4 Results of Rutter Children's Behavior Questionnaire completed by teachers and mothers of children who failed to thrive.

parison groups are shown in Table 12. The children who had been abused differed significantly from their comparison group on 10 of the 11 variables tested. The failure-to-thrive children differed from their comparison group on six of the 10 variables tested.

The abused children were found to be more cautious, subdued,

PSYCHOLOGICAL TESTING OF PARENTS AND CHILDREN

Table 12
Summary of Significant Differences Found on Psychological Testing Between Abused Children and Their Comparison Group and Between Children Who Failed to Thrive and Their Comparison Group

Characteristics of Children in Study Group	Abuse Group	Failure-to-thrive Group
Children lower on factor F of CPQ (serious-enthusiastic)	*	—
Children lower on CPQ second-order factor for extraversion	**	—
Children lower on factor C of HSPQ (superego strength)	—	*
Lower self-concept (Piers-Harris Scale)	***	N.S.
Lower on WISC-R verbal scale	**	*
Lower on WISC-R performance scale	**	N.S.
Lower on WISC-R full score	**	N.S.
Lower reading age	*	*
Lower social maturity quotient (Vineland)	N.S.	*
Lower Verbal Language Development scale	*	*
More personality abnormalities when teachers completed Rutter's Behavior Questionnaire	**	*
More personality abnormalities when mothers completed Rutter's Behavior Questionnaire	**	N.S.

$*P < 0.05$; $**P < 0.01$; $***P < 0.001$; N.S. = not significant

and inhibited in interpersonal contact than their comparison children. They had a low self-concept, were lower on all of the measures of intelligence, reading, and verbal ability, and were perceived by their teachers and mothers in such a way that they were more likely than the comparison group to receive an abnormal personality profile. They were no different from their comparison group on social maturity, although it seems likely that some of the less desirable features of their homes had forced them into situations where social maturity skills had to be developed.

The children who had failed to thrive were lower than their comparison children on superego strength and emotional stability. They were lower in verbal abilities, reading and social maturity, and were more likely than the comparison children to receive an abnormal personality profile from their schoolteachers.

The areas where the abused children and those who failed to

thrive were similar to each other were: lower scores than their comparison groups on the verbal scale of the WISC-R; lower reading age; lower language development; and an increased number of personality abnormalities on the behavior questionnaire.

REFERENCES

1. Cattell, R.B., Eber, H.W., & Tatsuoka, M.M. (1970). *Handbook for the 16PF.* Champaign, IL: Institute for Personality and Ability Testing.
2. *Administrator's Manual for the 16PF (1972).* Champaign, IL: Institute for Personality and Ability Testing.
3. Porter, R.B., & Cattell, R.B. (1979). *Handbook for the Children's Personality Questionnaire.* Champaign, IL: Institute for Personality and Ability Testing.
4. Cattell, R.B., & Cattell, M.D.L. (1975). *Handbook for the High School Personality Questionnaire (HSPQ).* Champaign, IL: Institute for Personality and Ability Testing.
5. Piers, E.V. (1976). *The Piers-Harris Children's Self-Concept Scale.* Nashville, TN: Counselor Recordings and Tests.
6. Wechsler, D. (1974). *Wechsler Intelligence Scale for Children—Revised.* New York: The Psychological Corporation.
7. Hufton, I.W., & Oates, R.K. (1977). Nonorganic failure to thrive: A long-term follow-up. *Pediatrics, 59,* 73–77.
8. Schonell, A.J., & Schonell, F.E. (1952). *Diagnostic and Attainment Testing* (2nd ed.). Edinburgh: Oliver and Boyd.
9. Doll, E.A. (1965). *Vineland Social Maturity Scale.* Circle Pines, MN: American Guidance Service, Inc.
10. Rutter, M. (1967). A child's behavior questionnaire for completion by teachers. *Journal of Child Psychology and Psychiatry, 8,* 1–11.

11

Discussion and Implications of Findings

Most studies of abused children and children who have failed to thrive have not been controlled and, as the majority of detected cases come from the lower socioeconomic groups, it is possible that some of the factors that have been ascribed to these families may in fact be characteristics of social class rather than of child abuse and deprivation. As families in this study have been matched as closely as possible, including matching for social class, the significant differences that have been observed are more likely to be related to the subject under consideration.

A valid criticism of any long-term study where there is a loss to follow-up is that the lost cases might have been different than those cases reviewed. This criticism has been partly answered in the present study by showing that the families found and those lost to follow-up since the previous review were not significantly different on several variables where information was available for both groups.

A further criticism of a study relying on maternal recall for some of its information is that recall may not be accurate. The question of reliability of maternal recall may be less important than the maternal perception of events, as it is the perception of the child that is likely to color the mother's attitude toward him. Even so, in this study it was shown that where information was available to compare mater-

180   CHILD ABUSE AND NEGLECT

nal recall with objective birth data, there was not a significant difference.

CHILDREN WHO HAVE BEEN ABUSED

Although the same proportion of abused and comparison children describe themselves as being friendlier than other children, further questioning showed that the abused children actually had fewer friends and played with their friends less frequently than comparison children. This suggests that the apathetic, withdrawn behavior of these children at the time of presentation (1, 2) and their inability to develop basic trust (3) persist long after the initial incident.

The lower job ambitions held by the abused children are likely to reflect their lower self-esteem, resulting from their inability to meet the high expectations of their parents. The high expectations the parents have for their children become counterproductive, with the children becoming failure-oriented and lacking in self-esteem and ambition. This is supported by the low scores of abused children on factor F of the Children's Personality Questionnaire, suggesting that they are more serious and cautious. This may reflect the high parental expectations and may also result from the role-reversal situation, where the parents may look to the child in a quite unrealistic way to have their own emotional needs met (4). The lower scores on the second-order factor of the CPQ, related to extraversion, also support the interview findings that abused children tend to be shyer, more inhibited, and find difficulty in interpersonal relationships.

The results of the Piers-Harris Children's Self-Concept Scale, while falling at either end of the fairly wide normal range of this test, were significantly lower in the abused than in the comparison children. This is different from Elmer's (5) study where no differences were found using this scale but do agree with Kinard's (6) findings of low self-concept in abused children.

Abused children scored lower than the comparison children on the three scales of the WISC-R. This finding of low intelligence had been reported by Elmer and Gregg (7) and by Morse and colleagues (8) in uncontrolled studies. In Elmer's controlled study (5), an analysis of

DISCUSSION AND IMPLICATIONS OF FINDINGS 181

school performance data showed that while all children performed below average, no significant difference was found between the study and control groups. However, in that study school reports were analyzed by psychologists but no formal tests of intellectual function were performed. The lower performances of the abused children on the verbal language development scale and reading age are likely to be due to a lack of appropriate verbal stimulation at home. As one might expect, the study and comparison children who come from predominantly low socioeconomic groups are below average for reading age, although the abused children are significantly further behind.

Even though intelligence was lower in the abused children, there was no difference between them and the comparison children in social maturity. This was not surprising as in many of the interviews with the mothers and children it became apparent that the abused children had to, of necessity, develop certain social skills, being often left to fend for themselves so that they developed some of the skills that the social maturity scale tested.

The highly significant difference found between the study and comparison children on Rutter's Children's Behavior Questionnaire means that the way these children present themselves and behave at school is likely to partly counteract whatever beneficial features schooling may have for them. The even higher proportion of abnormalities seen by the mothers may reflect the structure of the test, which was initially designed for teachers. However, it may also suggest that these mothers see more abnormalities in their children than others see. This may be related to the high expectations for behavior that they hold for their children.

CHILDREN WHO FAILED TO THRIVE FOR NO ORGANIC REASON

Although none of the failure-to-thrive children were below the third percentile for weight and only one was below the third percentile for height, a significantly greater number had a height age or weight age one or more years below their actual age. Other follow-up studies are conflicting on this issue. Elmer and colleagues (9) found that seven of 15 children followed for between three and 11

182   CHILD ABUSE AND NEGLECT

years were below the third percentile for height and weight, while Mitchell and co-workers (10) found that failure-to-thrive children were significantly lighter but not shorter than comparison children after five years. However, what is far more important than catch-up growth is the psychological functioning of the child.

The failure-to-thrive children in this study had lower ambitions than the comparison children for the job they thought they would be able to obtain, even though their parents had been matched for social class. This finding is particularly relevant as, at an average of 13.8 years, these children are approaching the age when within a few years they will be seeking employment. The finding that the children who failed to thrive were more likely to enjoy school than the comparison children is difficult to explain, although it is tempting to speculate that school was seen by them as a good place to be, in contrast with their unsatisfactory home environment.

The High School Personality Questionnaire results, which showed that the children who had failed to thrive were significantly lower than the comparison children on ego strength, should be interpreted with caution, for when the norms for this test are considered it is the study group that fell within the normal range and the comparison children who were above average on ego strength. As the norms for these tests are based on American children, it may not be valid to compare the Australian children in this study on the basis of American norms, although it is acceptable to compare the performance of the study children with a comparison group, using the American norms only as a guide to the normal range.

In contrast to the marked differences in self-concept found between the abused and comparison children, no difference was found between the failure-to-thrive children and their comparison group. The absence of high and unrealistic parent expectations for the failure-to-thrive children, which is a common feature in abusive families and may lead to a deterioration in the child's self-esteem, may be the reason for this difference.

The lack of a significant difference in the full-scale IQ between the failure-to-thrive and comparison children is in contrast with the findings of earlier uncontrolled studies (9, 11), which found low IQ scores in children who had suffered from nonorganic failure to

DISCUSSION AND IMPLICATIONS OF FINDINGS

thrive. However, Elmer et al.'s study (9) did not do psychological testing, the intelligence of children being based on clinical impressions. Although formal testing was done in Glaser and colleagues' study (11), analysis of the results shows that the distribution of the intelligence scores approximated a normal distribution with a slight skew to the left. Calculations from the data supplied in one of the figures in Glaser et al.'s paper shows that the average IQ of the children was 98, although six of the 40 children had an IQ below 85.

The effect of inadequate intellectual stimulation leading to delay in verbal abilities has been shown in early studies of English gypsy children (12) and from isolated American families living in the Tennessee mountains (13). Deutsch (14) suggested that children's verbal intellectual development is impaired in homes where there is a predominance of meaningless noise over meaningful communication. Friedlander (15) found that the presence of children leads to a tumultuous clamor in which several people speak at once on different topics. Perhaps in large, but more particularly in disorganized families, it is this linguistic chaos that impairs the development of verbal skills in children. These concepts would explain the discrepancy in reading age in the failure-to-thrive children, where over half had a reading age of three years or more behind their chronological age and where they were significantly lower than the comparison children on the verbal language development scale.

The high proportion of children receiving an abnormal score on the Behavior Questionnaire confirms the results when these children were previously reviewed (16), but is in contrast to the controlled studies of Pollitt and Eichler (17) and Mitchell et al. (10) where no major behavioral differences were found in children who had nonorganic failure to thrive. However, these studies used interviews rather than formal tests and the children were much younger, with an average age of three years for Pollitt and Eichler's study and a range of three to six years for the study by Mitchell's group.

Rutter (18) claims that parental discord, disharmony, and quarreling are associated with antisocial behavior in children. However, in the present study the high level of antisocial behavior in the children who failed to thrive did not correlate with any significant differences being found between the failure-to-thrive and comparison mothers

184 CHILD ABUSE AND NEGLECT

for marital stress and disharmony. This may be because the mothers did not admit to stress, but is more likely to be due to these children being subjected to high levels of family stress in their early years as shown by the significantly higher numbers of broken homes in the failure-to-thrive group. The antisocial behavior and perhaps the increased amount of cognitive problems now being seen is likely to be a result of these earlier family stresses.

SIMILARITIES BETWEEN ABUSED CHILDREN AND CHILDREN WHO FAILED TO THRIVE

While both the failure-to-thrive and the abused children showed more abnormalities than their comparison groups, the children who were abused showed a greater number of abnormalities. Those who failed to thrive were no different than their comparison group in the number of friends they had compared with the abused children, who had fewer friends and were more inhibited in their interpersonal relationships.

Both groups of children performed less well than their comparison groups on the cognitive tests, but the differences between the abused children and their comparison group were more marked. The abused children were lower than their comparison group on all three scales of the WISC-R, while the failure-to-thrive group only showed a difference on the verbal scale. This deficiency in verbal abilities in both groups was reinforced by their lower scores on the verbal language development scale and their lower reading ages.

The failure-to-thrive children had a lower social maturity quotient than their comparison group, whereas this difference was not found in the abused children, whose social maturity may have been elevated as a result of the pseudomaturity that was forced on them.

Both the abused and failure-to-thrive groups were seen by their teachers, completing a behavior questionnaire, as having more abnormalities, particularly antisocial behavior, than the comparison groups. While the mothers of the failure-to-thrive group did not perceive more abnormalities than the comparison mothers who completed this questionnaire, the abusive mothers saw significantly more

DISCUSSION AND IMPLICATIONS OF FINDINGS

abnormalities in their children than comparison mothers, reflecting the high expectations and abnormal perceptions held by this group.

These differences between the abused and the failure-to-thrive children may be explainable by the different sort of family pathology in the two groups, but may also be explained on the basis of the age difference between the two groups with the possibility that the degree of abnormality in the failure-to-thrive group may have become less with the passage of time. What does seem important is the clear message that comes through from this study. This is that both child abuse and nonorganic failure to thrive and the family conditions that lead to them have long-term adverse sequelae. It would be wrong not to mention the role of the child in both of these conditions. Children are not passive recipients of influences from their parents. They elicit responses from others (19) and their characteristics determine how their parents respond to them (20, 21). This may explain why in some cases just one child in the family suffers from nonorganic failure to thrive or child abuse while others do not.

PARENTS WHOSE CHILDREN HAVE BEEN ABUSED

The lower proportion of abusive mothers compared with comparison mothers who had voluntarily spoken to their child's teacher in the last 12 months supports the notion of these mothers being less able to make contact with authority figures and perhaps being less interested in their child's education. Although the incidence of preschool attendance was equal in both groups, many of the abused children had their preschool arranged for them by authorities when it was felt that this would be helpful for both the child and the mother. Preschool placement is usually recommended as part of the treatment for abused children and is one of the few resources that can be readily made available for these families. However, the adverse findings found in the children in this study suggests that preschool placement by itself is not enough if the adverse sequelae are to be avoided. A much more active, therapeutic program for the child is required.

The high and often quite unrealistic expectations that have been described for abused infants appear to persist as the children grow

186   CHILD ABUSE AND NEGLECT

older. This is shown in the way the abuse-group mothers were more likely than the comparison mothers to feel their child was not performing up to their expectations at school. These high expectations are often coupled with a lack of supervision. This puts the child in the difficult position of his parents having high expectations for him but providing him with minimal supervision—a situation where the child is more likely to fail through lack of supervision and teaching. This may precipitate abusive incidents when the parents' expectations for the child are not met and is also likely to impair the development of the child's self-esteem as he becomes oriented toward failure.

The greater number of abuse-group mothers not brought up by their own parents and the higher incidence of negative feelings they held toward their fathers confirm the impression noted by other authors (22–25) that some of these mothers tend to be deprived and possibly abused in their own childhood. The higher proportion of negative feelings toward the fathers held by the study-group mothers is of interest as there was no difference between the two groups in negative feelings toward their fathers. A history of sexual abuse in the mothers' own childhood was not specifically sought in this study. However, it is tempting to speculate, since the family psychopathology in sexual abuse and physical abuse is often similar, that in some cases it may have been past sexual abuse within the family that influenced the mothers' negative feelings toward their fathers.

No difference between the study and comparison mothers was found in factor B on the 16PF, a factor which gives some indication of intelligence. The literature is not clear on the intellectual level of abusive mothers with some authors finding low intelligence (26, 27) and others finding intelligence within the normal range (28, 29). The probable reason for these differences is that there is no clearly defined pattern of abusive parents. They may come from a wide intellectual range and the differing results of studies, particularly uncontrolled studies, probably represents sampling bias.

The number of families who did not have the telephone connected may be explainable on the basis of these families moving more frequently and having fewer friends and fewer family supports so that they felt less need for a telephone. However, the high proportion

DISCUSSION AND IMPLICATIONS OF FINDINGS

(almost 50%) of abuse group families who had a telephone connected but whose number was unlisted was surprising. The usual reason given for this was that they wished to avoid harassment either from separated husbands and other aquaintances but sometimes just from the world in general. This finding strengthens the earlier concepts about the social isolation of these families and the difficulty helping agencies have in assisting them. Some of these families seem to prefer to isolate themselves from the rest of society, to feel vulnerable, and to be wary of outside contacts.

PARENTS WHOSE CHILDREN HAD NONORGANIC FAILURE TO THRIVE

Although difficulties around the time of birth and during the perinatal period have been described as being more common in failure-to-thrive children (30), there was no increased incidence in this review. The comparison and study groups both had a relatively high incidence of problems, with 26% of the comparison group finding the pregnancy difficult and the birth unpleasant. This high incidence of problems in both groups illustrates why, in uncontrolled studies, problems in the pregnancy and perinatal period could be cited as being a common feature of these mothers.

The finding that significantly fewer failure-to-thrive mothers knew the name of the child's teacher or had spoken to the teacher in the last 12 months confirms the clinical impression that these mothers are often overwhelmed by just trying to cope with day-to-day activities and do not have time to develop an interest in their child's education or to have the motivation to discuss progress with the teacher. In contrast with the abusive parents, who felt that their children were not performing as well at school as they would like, these parents seemed fairly out of touch with what was going on at school.

Very little has been written about the formal intellectual testing of these mothers. Elmer (31) noted that the mothers did not plan well and seemed to be of limited intelligence, but no formal measurements were made in her study. Polansky and colleagues (32) did intellectual testing on a group of mothers of Appalachian children and found a mean IQ of 79 with no differences between verbal and performance subtests. The small study by Hess et al. (33) showed

188   CHILD ABUSE AND NEGLECT

lower intellectual levels in mothers whose children had nonorganic failure to thrive compared with those infants who had an organic cause for their growth failure. These findings are supported by the present study which shows that the failure-to-thrive mothers were lower than the comparison group on factor B of the 16PF, a factor relating to intelligence. A low score on factor B also indicates a tendency to concrete thinking, supporting the conclusion of Fischoff and co-workers (34), who felt that an active, practical, and supportive program would be more suitable for these mothers than a problem-solving psychotherapeutic approach.

SIMILARITIES BETWEEN PARENTS WHO ABUSED THEIR CHILDREN AND PARENTS WHOSE CHILDREN FAILED TO THRIVE

While there were some similarities between the abusive and failure-to-thrive parents, such as the higher incidence of single-parent families than in comparison groups, a higher dependence on social security payments, and the fact that the children in both groups were functioning less effectively than the comparison children, there were many more differences. The families where the children failed to thrive had mothers who were duller than the comparison mothers, had evidence of little verbal stimulation, and had less interest shown by the parents in how the child develops and performs at school. In contrast, the abused children were handicapped by high and unrealistic parental expectations causing them to become failure-oriented and to have low self-esteem.

The mothers from the abuse group had a high incidence of recently requiring help for emotional disorders, had a history of deprivation in their own childhood, continued to have poor relationships with their fathers, and tended to prefer to be isolated from other people. These features were not found to be more frequent in the mothers whose children had failed to thrive. When contrasted with their respective groups of comparison families, there was a greater degree of disturbance in the mothers whose children had been abused than in the mothers whose children had failed to thrive.

DISCUSSION AND IMPLICATIONS OF FINDINGS

IMPLICATIONS FOR TREATMENT AND CONCLUSIONS

This study has shown that abused children and children who suffered from nonorganic failure to thrive have more problems in personality development, intellectual ability, and school adjustment than comparison children. The abused children have a greater number of problems and are probably more disturbed than the children who failed to thrive but because the two age groups are dissimilar, it is not certain whether this has accentuated or minimized the differences.

Although child abuse and failure to thrive are not identical in the characteristics shown in the families and in the children, there are several areas of overlap so that it is likely that within the failure-to-thrive group some cases of physical abuse will also occur. What is clear from this study is that child abuse and nonorganic failure to thrive have long-term adverse sequelae. It is highly unlikely that these findings are a direct result of the injury or malnutrition that first brought these children to medical attention. Rather, it is likely to be the disturbed family environment in which these children remain that has continued to impair their development. What is of concern is that the long-term adverse effects of these conditions are likely to interfere with the capacity of these children to be effective parents themselves.

It is also clear that the methods of treatment and follow-up provided for these children when they initially presented were not adequate to prevent these adverse effects. Treatment for the failure to thrive, when little was known about this condition, consisted merely of nutritional rehabilitation in hospital with an outpatient follow-up appointment which was infrequently kept. Treatment for the abuse group consisted of family assessment (although a full assessment of the child's strengths and weaknesses was, in retrospect, less thorough than it should have been), outpatient follow-up appointments, home visiting by a hospital social worker in some selected cases, and a referral to the already overburdened state child welfare services for continuation of follow-up.

In the midst of these pessimistic data it is important not to lose

190 CHILD ABUSE AND NEGLECT

sight of the fact that not all of the children have done badly. Although the overall features of the two groups of children were less satisfactory than the comparison groups, some families and children within both study groups are very well adjusted and are performing at least as well as the comparison families on all measures. Three of the nonorganic failure-to-thrive families and six of the abuse families had no detectable problems on the measures used and their children showed no abnormalities. Although this is a small group, it is one worthy of further study to answer the question of why some families do well while others do not.

In some families the abusive incident may have been a "one-off" episode, with the family having sufficient strengths and supports to function effectively once the stresses that led to the incident had been resolved. The investigation of a family following an episode of abuse can also be a major stress. It is incumbent on those working in this area to avoid clumsiness and lack of sensitivity in investigating these families so that in those families that have strengths and where abuse is unlikely to reappear, the investigation and actions that follow do not do more harm than good. Those children with nonorganic failure to thrive who do well are more likely to come from the group of mothers who are basically capable, but temporarily overwhelmed by a series of events that have undermined their basically good mothering capacity (35) rather than from the groups of mothers who have significant psychological disorder, who see their baby negatively, or who show extreme anger and hostility (35–37).

Management of families where there had been nonorganic failure to thrive or child abuse should include a thorough assessment of the family, a long-term treatment plan, and an increased focus on the child. Pringle (38) has described the needs of children as: the need for love and security; the need for new experiences; the need for praise and recognition; the need for responsibility. These are basic needs which should be considered in any treatment program of abused children or neglected children.

The prerequisite for any treatment program is the assessment of the family and child. There is no such thing as a simple assessment. Assessments take time and skill. It may be relatively easy to determine whether the problem is one of physical abuse or of neglect.

DISCUSSION AND IMPLICATIONS OF FINDINGS 191

However, far more important than an assessment of the type of injury is a careful assessment of the family's strengths and weaknesses. A relatively minor injury may be a far more serious problem in a family with very few strengths and no social supports than a more serious "one-off" injury which occurs in a family where there is the potential for coping effectively.

While in the past much attention has been paid to the assessment of the family, in many instances inadequate attention has been paid to assessing the needs of the child. Assessment of the child should include an assessment of the child's developmental level, personality, and emotional needs. Assessment of the siblings is also desirable. A single evaluation of the child can be misleading. Clinicians who work closely with abused children have observed that the residual effects of the abuse or neglect, especially a "hypermonitoring" of adults, may prevent the child from giving full attention to a test. This may result in the child being more concerned with the tester than the test—a situation that would depress intelligence scores (39).

Any child abuse service that overlooks the treatment needs of the abused child is failing to do an adequate job. This is particularly relevant in view of the evidence from this and other studies that abused children do have long-term emotional and physical damage, including a high risk of damage to the central nervous system and maldevelopment of ego function (40–42).

It is likely that increasing use of videotaping of interviews with the parents, of reactions between the parent and the child, and of the behavior of the child will be used as part of the assessment process. While it is important that confidentiality should not be breached by the indiscriminate use of videotaping, this tool is likely to become extremely valuable in the evaluation of the assessment process, in presenting segments of interviews in court, and in monitoring progress in the child and in the relationship between the parent and child. The use of videotaped assessments of the interaction between mother and infant in nonorganic failure to thrive has been found to be of value in deciding which infants were able to be returned to their mothers and which required foster care (43).

When assessing the parents it is important to remember that not long ago many were themselves abused children and that they will show the characteristics of lack of trust, hostility, low self-esteem, and poor verbal skills that are typically found in abused children. Because their basic need to be seen as real persons in their own right has never been met, it is important not to focus exclusively on their parenting abilities, particularly in treatment, but also to concentrate on their own needs as individuals.

It is also essential in assessment to consider the way the parents perceive the abused or neglected child. That parents generally have a poor perception of these children has been demonstrated in this study. However, a generalization such as this is inadequate. As more is learned about parental behavior in child abuse and nonorganic failure to thrive, it has become clear that there are a number of different patterns of parent behavior, each of which may require a different form of management. It is also true that some of these behavior patterns may be more amenable to help than others. Haynes and colleagues from Denver have recently shown that in nonorganic failure to thrive, quite distinct patterns of interaction between mother and child can be demonstrated and that these patterns have implications for the type of treatment offered (44). These authors also demonstrated the severity of the disturbance in the mother-child relationship and the need for more intensive intervention than had previously been made available.

It should be remembered that many of these families are difficult to work with and as a result many treatment programs break down. Typical problems are: failure of the parents to take children to preschool programs; failure to keep appointments; and failure to be at home when the visiting worker calls. Some of these problems can be interpreted as the parents' difficulty in forming a trusting relationship so that workers in this field need to be both understanding and persistent. Parents sometimes become jealous of the amount of attention and care their child is receiving in treatment programs and this has to be anticipated and dealt with. The message is that we cannot set up a treatment program and assume that our responsibility ends there.

The treatment program for the child and parents should be flexible and must be reviewed regularly. To believe the responsibility toward the family ends once a management plan is made is a serious error. The responsibilities to the family start with the creation of a manage-

DISCUSSION AND IMPLICATIONS OF FINDINGS 193

ment plan. Because a number of people representing a number of different disciplines and agencies may be involved in the care of the family, it is important that they should work cooperatively and communicate frequently.

Day care is one of the readily available and valuable ways of providing help for abused and neglected children. It has the advantage of allowing the child to mix and develop with other children as well as providing the parent with some relief from the constant strains of childrearing. However, careful consideration should be given to deciding on *appropriate* day care. Simply "rescuing" an abused child from further abuse may not be sufficient to break the cycle of child abuse, which really represents a problem in relationships. In day care programs the staff need to be shown how to pay special attention to the child's social relationships and development. Day care workers should know they may be greeted with rejection and avoidance (45). However, they must respond with steady affection, rather than with diminished interest in the child. It is unreasonable to expect the day care workers to innately have these skills. Teaching and training are required. As mandatory reporting legislation often requires day care workers to notify suspected cases of child abuse, they require some education in recognizing the problem. Equally important, they require more sophisticated training in helping to care for and successfully cope with abused and neglected children placed in day care as part of a management program. Ideally, day care staff given some training in child abuse recognition and management will also become involved in preventive activities such as parent education and parent counseling, as recently demonstrated in a survey of day care centers in Pennsylvania (46).

In developing treatment plans for children who remain with their family, one must be aware of the problems likely to occur if the child is changed by the treatment and stripped of some adaptive behaviors that are valuable in a dangerous environment. For example, exploration, questioning, and initiative may not be encouraged in an abusive home. It follows that any treatment plan for the child must be offered in the context of a carefully devised treatment plan for the whole family.

When assessing the child, one should remember the links between the acute center where the child presents and where the assessment is usually done and the community agencies that are usually involved in the long-term follow-up. These community agencies should be involved in the initial assessment of the child and consulted about treatment programs. It could be regarded as unreasonable to ask agencies to follow up cases in which they have had no involvement in the initial assessment nor any input into the development of the treatment program, particularly if they already know the family. Acute assessment centers are usually not burdened with the very difficult problem of long-term follow-up. Staff working in these centers need to have realistic expectations of the community services which become involved in the more arduous task of providing continuous care for these children and their families. Professionals working with abusive and depriving families should ideally have a long-term commitment to the work and to the families they see.

The prevention and management of child abuse is a concept that should pervade the entire health and welfare system, not only in terms of specific programs (which are also essential), but also in terms of society's attitudes to children and to providing emotional and practical support to families facing stress. Pawl (47) has argued that the pediatric setting should be the natural place for the integration of preventive services, as this may be the first and perhaps only contact the parents have with professionals. He argues that in addition to wider acceptance of the rights of children, the services provided should include emotional and practical support, education, interpretation for the parents of their current problems using a psychotherapeutic model, and specific intervention programs.

The extent of child abuse is such that there will probably never be enough professionals to provide the services to help these families. This means that voluntary agencies and the use of trained volunteers have to be considered as additional resources. A number of successful programs have been documented (48–51). In addition to the use of volunteers, families need to be put in contact with community agencies so that they can be integrated into their local community support systems. The drawback to relying solely on one professional doing casework is that there is a high turnover of professionals in this area; once the social worker or therapist involved is transferred

DISCUSSION AND IMPLICATIONS OF FINDINGS

to a new position or leaves, the family is likely to become "lost in the system" or overlooked unless they have been integrated with community facilities that can continue to help them, often on a practical level, and can continue to support them until a new caseworker is available.

With an increasing trend to early retirement and increased leisure in our society, consideration could also be given to enlisting the support of the retired age group to assist in supporting families with parenting problems.

Most of those who work in the area of child abuse and neglect would agree that certain children are far better off removed from their families. However, the question has to be asked, "What sort of environment is available for the child following removal?" Alternative care offered must be not only safer, but also therapeutic in that it should heal the emotional, social, intellectual, and physical damage that the child has suffered. A poor placement may harm the child more than the original injury. Child abuse cases are notorious for being moved from one foster situation to another, often with disastrous effects for the child. There is no guarantee for the child that foster placement is better. Evidence from studies in the United States and the United Kingdom consistently show that 15% of long-term foster placements break down. There is also evidence of disturbed behavior in children in foster placements. Thorpe (52) showed that 39% of children in foster care were disturbed compared with 23% of a socially similar population. Bolton and colleagues (53) in a study in Arizona showed that 7% of the child population in foster care had suffered from abuse and neglect compared with 2% of the normal population of children living with their parents. While it is likely that multiple foster placements will have a detrimental effect on the child's psychosocial development, a recent analysis of 4,288 children in foster care throughout the United States showed that fostering arrangements were more likely to break down, requiring re-placement for children who had behavioral and emotional problems (54). Obviously it cannot be assumed that foster care will automatically solve the problems, particularly when the abused child is likely to be disturbed as a result of experiences with his natural family.

It has long been known that some of the side effects of medical treatment given without proper care and planning may be more serious than the disease itself (55). This concept also needs to be kept in mind when planning foster care placements in order to ensure that foster families are carefully selected and given continuing support. Decisions about placing the child are often clouded by legal problems. In cases where parental rights are not severed, the courts sometimes make a decision that puts the child in a limbo situation. The child may be put in the custody of the state or moved among several foster parents; but the child will never be available for adoption or any meaningful commitment from foster parents who, despite their good intentions for the child, always have hanging over them the concern that if they become too attached to the child, the parting may be too difficult should the state deem that the child be returned to his family.

When children lose their parents through illness or an accident, we are aware of the adverse psychological effects on the child and appropriate treatment and counseling are provided. In child abuse and neglect cases where we may be *recommending* the loss of a parent as part of the child's treatment, we should be even more concerned about providing ongoing support and treatment to a child who may already be disturbed.

The principles of management in nonorganic failure to thrive are similar. While at one extreme the family may be so disturbed that termination of parental rights may be necessary so that the child may be placed in foster care before deprivation starts to have long-term effects, the majority of children are likely to stay with their parents. The simple approach of making these children gain weight in hospital and discharging them without adequate follow-up and support is not good enough. As for the abused children, there is a need for a much more intensive program of support than has been offered in the past.

Fraiberg and colleagues (56, 57) have described a successful approach for nonorganic failure to thrive which combines frequent home visiting and the development of a nurturing relationship between a skilled therapist and the mother. However, this model of treatment requires skilled resources and is extremely labor-intensive, so that it cannot easily be duplicated. What is probably more realistic

DISCUSSION AND IMPLICATIONS OF FINDINGS 197

is a program of practical help from community agencies and regular home visiting by a social worker or community nurse. The needs of the child should not be overlooked in the effort to help the mothers. As for abused children, placement in a stimulating, appropriate pre-school program may provide much needed relief for the mother and will also assist the child in language development and interpersonal relationships. This should be followed up by individual work with the child, depending on the needs of the child found at the initial assessment.

The cautionary note that fostering does not provide a simple answer in cases of child abuse should also be sounded in nonorganic failure to thrive. The Denver group (58) has shown that for eight infants placed in foster care, compared with eight infants returned to their parents, there was no difference between the two groups at the end of six months. The weight and developmental status of the infants in either group did not improve as expected, suggesting that early deprivation may have long-term effects on intellectual functioning. These authors stress the need to be aware of early indications that may suggest the development of a poor mother-infant relationship. They point out that these indicators may be detected as early as the neonatal period, recommending that treatment and services need to be provided when these early warnings appear.

Some would see the solution to many of these problems as being the provision of increased funds to develop assessment and treatment services. While this is a worthy desire, it should be remembered that the health and welfare dollar is limited and that children in need of protection tend to be a politically powerless group. In times of cutbacks in health and welfare, there will be no winners, unless being a winner means losing less. While these should not be reasons for not fighting to provide better services for these children (indeed, they should be reasons for trying even harder), there is also a need to demonstrate the cost effectiveness of programs. Hard decisions may have to be made about abandoning some, perhaps cherished, programs that have not been demonstrated to be effective. Innovative programs need to be tried, but those using new ideas will have to have the courage to evaluate them so that in the battle for funds, accusations about inefficiencies and ineffectiveness will not be able to be justified.

One new, exciting way of funding prevention programs is the setting up of a legislated trust fund that generates money from marriage license fees (59). These Children's Trust Funds, whose aims are at child abuse prevention and which are administered by a board of private citizens and state administrators, have now been set up in at least 16 states in the United States (60) and provide some hope for creating effective, independent, and well-funded prevention programs. It is hoped that other countries will take up this initiative.

Because of the very real pressures on child abuse workers, there is a tendency on the part of many of us to want to get out of the front line. This can be done by giving supervision to the front line workers rather than working in the front line personally, by teaching and lecturing on child abuse and neglect, and by doing research. All of these areas are necessary, but there is the danger of too many people making a commitment to these, often more satisfying areas, and not enough people actually working with the families. There may also be a temptation to become involved in needless research and information gathering.

Although the management of child abuse and nonorganic failure to thrive has a long way to go before we can be confident of a good outcome for the majority of children, people working in this area should be optimistic. Since these conditions first gained professional and public awareness less than 25 years ago, there has been an explosion of professional interest and knowledge with the development of many successful treatment programs. However, our optimism must be based on reality and on a careful analysis of the available data. Increased emphasis in the future must be on making a firm commitment to the treatment of these children—a commitment that goes far beyond simple child protection. Each child needs to be provided with a program that takes into account his own strengths and needs along with those of his family so that the child can develop effective coping mechanisms, even if the environment cannot be substantially improved. In this way perhaps these children will eventually be able to provide a more effective level of parenting than they themselves received.

DISCUSSION AND IMPLICATIONS OF FINDINGS 199

REFERENCES

1. Galdston, R. (1965). Observations on children who have been physically abused and their parents. *American Journal of Psychiatry, 122,* 440-443.
2. Ounsted, C.V., & Lindsay, J. (1974). Aspects of bonding failure. *Developmental Medicine and Child Neurology, 16,* 447-456.
3. Green, A.H. (1978). Psychopathology of abused children. *Journal of the American Academy of Child Psychiatry, 17,* 92-103.
4. Helfer, R.E. (1980). Developmental deficits which limit interpersonal skills. In C.H. Kempe & R.E. Helfer (Eds.), *The battered child* (3rd ed.). Chicago: The University of Chicago Press.
5. Elmer, E. (1977). A follow-up study of traumatized children. *Pediatrics, 59,* 273-279.
6. Kinard, E.M. (1980). Emotional development in physically abused children. *American Journal of Orthopsychiatry, 50,* 686-696.
7. Elmer, E., & Gregg, G. (1967). Developmental characteristics of abused children. *Pediatrics, 40,* 596-602.
8. Morse, C.W., Sahler, O.J., & Friedman, S.B. (1970). A three-year follow-up of abused and neglected children. *American Journal of Diseases of Children, 120,* 439-446.
9. Elmer, E., Gregg, G., & Ellison, P. (1969). Late results of the failure to thrive syndrome. *Clinical Pediatrics, 8,* 584-588.
10. Mitchell, W.G., Gorrell, R.W., & Greenberg, R.A. (1980). Failure to thrive: A study in family care setting, epidemiology and follow-up. *Pediatrics, 65,* 971-977.
11. Glaser, H.H., Heagarty, M.C., Bullard, D.M., & Pivchik, E.C. (1968). Physical and psychological development of children with early failure to thrive. *Journal of Pediatrics, 73,* 690-698.
12. Gow, F. (1925). A study of performance tests. *British Journal of Psychology, 15,* 374-392.
13. Wheeler, L.R. (1942). A comparative study of the intelligence of East Tennessee mountain children. *Journal of Educational Psychology, 33,* 321-324.
14. Deutsch, C.P. (1964). Auditory discrimination and learning: Social factors. *Merrill-Palmer Quarterly, 10,* 277-296.
15. Friedlander, B.Z. (1971). Listening, language and the auditory environment: Automated evaluation and intervention. In J. Hellmuth (Ed.), *The exceptional infant: II. Studies in abnormalities.* New York: Brunner/Mazel.
16. Hufton, I.W., & Oates, R.K. (1977). Non-organic failure to thrive: A long-term follow-up. *Pediatrics, 59,* 73-77.
17. Pollitt, E., & Eichler, A. (1975). Behavioral disturbances amongst failure to thrive children. *American Journal of Diseases of Children, 130,* 24-29.
18. Rutter, M. (1972). *Maternal deprivation reassessed.* Harmondsworth, England: Penguin Books.
19. Bell, R.Q. (1971). Stimulus control of parent or caretaker behavior by offspring. *Developmental Psychology, 4,* 63-72.
20. Yarrow, L.J. (1963). Research in dimensions of early maternal care. *Merrill-Palmer Quarterly, 9,* 101-114.
21. Cummings, S.T., Bayley, M.C. & Rie, H.E. (1966). Effects of the child's deficiency

on the mother: A study of mothers of mentally retarded, chronically ill and neurotic children. *American Journal of Orthopsychiatry, 36,* 595-608.
22. Kempe, C.H., Silverman, F.N., Steele, B.F., Droegmueller, W., & Silver, H.K. (1962). The battered child syndrome. *Journal of the American Medical Association, 181,* 17-24.
23. Skinner, A.E., & Castle, R.L. (1969). Seventy-eight battered children: A retrospective study. London: National Society for the Prevention of Cruelty to Children.
24. Kempe, C.H., & Helfer, R.E. (1972). *Helping the battered child and his family.* Philadelphia: J.B. Lippincott.
25. Smith, S.M., & Hanson, R. (1974). One hundred and thirty-four battered children: A medical and psychological study. *British Medical Journal, 3,* 666-670.
26. Smith, S.M., Hanson, R., & Noble, S. (1973). Parents of battered children: A controlled study. *British Medical Journal, 4,* 388-391.
27. Baldwin, J.A., & Oliver, J.E. (1975). Epidemiology and family characteristics of severely abused children. *British Journal of Preventive Social Medicine, 29,* 205-221.
28. Steele, B.F., & Pollock, C.B. (1974). A psychiatric study of parents who abuse infants and small children. In R.E. Helfer & C.H. Kempe (Eds.), *The battered child* (2nd ed.). Chicago: The University of Chicago Press.
29. Hyman, C.A. (1977). A report on the psychological test results of battering parents. *British Journal of Social and Clinical Psychology, 16,* 221-224.
30. Fanaroff, A.A., Kennell, J.H., & Klaus, M.H. (1972). Follow-up of low birthweight infants—The predictive value of maternal visiting patterns. *Pediatrics, 49,* 287-290.
31. Elmer, E. (1960). Failure to thrive, role of the mother. *Pediatrics, 25,* 717-725.
32. Polansky, N.A., Borgnan, R.D., & de Saix, C. (1972). *Roots of futility.* San Francisco: Jossey-Bass.
33. Hess, A.K., Hess, K.A., & Hard, H.E. (1977). Intellectual characteristics of mothers of failure to thrive syndrome children. *Child Care Health Development, 3,* 377-387.
34. Fischoff, J., Whitten, C.F., & Pettit, M.G. (1971). A psychiatric study of mothers of infants with growth failure secondary to maternal deprivation. *Journal of Pediatrics, 79,* 209-215.
35. Kempe, R.S., Cutler, C., & Dean, J. (1980). The infant with failure to thrive. In C.H. Kempe & R.E. Helfer (Eds.), *The battered child* (3rd ed.). Chicago: The University of Chicago Press.
36. Jacobs, R.A., & Kent, J.T. (1977). Psychosocial profiles of families of failure to thrive infants—a preliminary report. *Child Abuse and Neglect, 1,* 469-477.
37. Evans, S.L., Reinhart, J.B., & Succop, R.A. (1972). Failure to thrive: A study of 45 children and their families. *Journal of the American Academy of Child Psychiatry, 11,* 440-457.
38. Pringle, M.K. (1975). *The needs of children.* London: Hutchinson.
39. Rodeheffer, M., & Martin, H.P. (1977). Special problems in the development and assessment of abused children. In H.P. Martin (Ed.), *The abused child.* Cambridge, MA: Ballinger.

DISCUSSION AND IMPLICATIONS OF FINDINGS

40. Martin, H.P., Beezley, P., Conway, E.S., & Kempe, C.H. (1974). The development of abused children, I—A review of the literature, II—Physical, neurological and intellectual outcomes. *Advances in Paediatrics, 21,* 25-73.
41. Lynch, M. (1975). the prognosis of child abuse. *Journal of Child Psychology and Psychiatry, 19,* 175-179.
42. Jones, C. (1977). The fate of abused children. In A.W. Franklin (Ed.), *The challenge of child abuse.* London: Academic Press.
43. Haynes, C.F., Cutler, C., Gray, J., O'Keefe, K., & Kempe, R.S. (1983). Nonorganic failure to thrive: Decision for placement and videotaped evaluations. *Child Abuse and Neglect, 7,* 309-319.
44. Haynes, C.F., Cutler, C., Gray, J., & Kempe, R.S. (1984). Hospitalized cases of nonorganic failure to thrive: The scope of the problem and short-term lay health visitor intervention. *Child Abuse and Neglect, 8,* 229-242.
45. George, C., & Main, M. (1979). Social interactions of young abused children, approach, avoidance, aggression. In N. Frude (Ed.), *Psychological approaches to child abuse.* London: Batsford Academic.
46. Barber-Madden, R. (1983). Training day care program personnel in handling child abuse cases: Intervention and prevention outcomes. *Child Abuse and Neglect, 7,* 25-32.
47. Pawl, J.H. (1984). Strategies of intervention. *Child Abuse and Neglect, 8,* 261-270.
48. Oates, R.K. (1978). The use of non-professional workers. *Proceedings of the First National Conference on the Battered Child.* Western Australia Department of Community Welfare.
49. Gray, J., & Kaplan, B. (1980). The lay health visitor program an eighteen month experience. In C.H. Kempe & R.E. Helfer (Eds.), *The battered child,* (3rd ed.). Chicago: University of Chicago Press.
50. Hinson, J. (1981). Parent aides—Crisis workers. *Proceedings of the Second Australasian Conference on Child Abuse.* Queensland: Government Printer.
51. Barbour, P.J. (1983). Adopt a family—dial a granny. *Child Abuse and Neglect, 7,* 477-478.
52. Thorpe, R. (1980). The experiences of children and parents living apart, implication and guidelines for practice. In J. Triseliotis (Ed.), *New developments in foster care and adoption.* London: Routledge and Kegan Paul.
53. Bolton, F.J., Laner, R.H., & Gai, D.S. (1981). For better or worse? Foster parents and foster children in an officially reported child maltreatment population. *Children and Youth Services Review, 3,* 37.
54. Pardeck, J.T. (1983). An empirical analysis of behavioral and emotional problems of foster children as related to re-placement in care. *Child Abuse and Neglect, 7,* 75-78
55. Illich, I. (1975). *Medical nemesis: The expropriation of health.* London: Lothian.
56. Fraiberg, S., Adelson, E., & Shapiro, V. (1975). Ghosts in the nursery: A psychoanalytic approach to the problems of impaired infant-mother relationships. *Journal of the American Academy of Child Psychiatry, 14,* 387-421.
57. Fraiberg, S., & Adelson E. (1976). Infant-parent psychotherapy on behalf of a child in a critical nutritional state. *Psychoanalytical Study of Children, 31,* 461-491.
58. Haynes, C.F., Cutler, C., Gray, J., O'Keefe, K., & Kempe, R.S. (1983). Non-

organic failure to thrive: Implications of placement through analysis of video-taped interactions. *Child Abuse and Neglect, 7,* 321-328.
59. Martin, M., Scott, J., Pierron, J., & Bauerle, B. (1984). The Kansas Family and Childrens Trust Fund: Funding Prevention Programmes in the Eighties. *Child Abuse and Neglect, 8,* 303-309.
60. Helfer, R.E. (1984). Editorial comment. *Child Abuse and Neglect, 8,* 301.

Index

NOTE: Page numbers in *italic* refer to author citations contained in Tables

Aggression, in abused children, 82–83, 102
Alberman, E., 77–78, *78*
Altemeier, W. A., et al., 91–92
Ambitions
  of abused children, 154–155, 156, 157,
    180, 182
  of parents for children, 143–144
American Psychiatric Association, 4
Anderson, S. C., 71, 72
Apley, J., et al., *12, 13*
Approach-withdrawal scale, 9–10
Aragona, J. A., 73, 74
Assessment
  developmental, 8–9
  family, 60, 189, 190–192
  method of, in follow-up study, 121–124
  videotaping, 191
Assessment centers, acute, 194. *See also*
  Casualty department
Astley, R., 44
Attachment, mother-infant, 25, 27–28, 76–80
Ayoub, C., et al., 33, 34, *35*

Bakwin, H., 5–6
Baldwin, J. A., 48, 72, 74–75
Barbero, G. J., 32
Battered child. *See* Children, abused
Battered child syndrome, 44–45, 46, 48
Bayley Scales of Infant Development, 37
Becker, D. J., *12, 13,* 21
Beezley, P., 93, 100, *101*
Behavior, of abused children, 81, 82–83, 84,
    173–177, 181, 183, 184
Behavior disorders, 25, 28, 37–38
Besharov, D. J., 45, 47
Bias, 116, 117, 128

Bishop, F. I., 81, 93, 95
Blizzard, R. M., 16
Bolton, F. J., et al., 195
Bonding, mother-infant, 76, 79–80. *See also*
  Attachment
Bone scan, 60
Boriskin, J. A., 84
Brandon, S., 49
Bruises, 43, 55, 59–60, 110
Brunnquell, D., 91
Bullard, D. M., et al., 8
Burgess, R. L., 73, 74
Burns, 56–57

Caffey, J., 43–44
Carter, J., 95
Castells, S., et al., *12, 13*
Castle, R. C., 103–104
Castle, R. L., 69
Casualty department, 48, 61, 99
Catch-up growth, 34–35
Cater, J. I., 78, *78*
Cattell, R. B. and M. D. L., 123
Cattell, R. B., et al., 122
Cattell's Children's Personality
  Questionnaire, 163, 164, 180
Cattell's High School Personality
  Questionnaire (HSPQ), 123, 163,
    164–165, 182
Cattell's 16 Personality Factor Questionnaire,
    122–123, 158–163, 186
Chapin, H. D., 4–5
Character disorder, in mother, 32, 72–73
Chase, H. P., 33–34, *35*
Child abuse. *See also* Children, abused
  case findings, 48, 61

203

204 CHILD ABUSE AND NEGLECT

Child abuse (*continued*)
  causes, 68–84
  clinical features, 54–58
  cross-cultural aspects, 51–53
  defined, 45–46, 114–115
  diagnosis, 58–61
  history, 41–44
  incidence, 46–48
  legal aspects, 53–54
  long-term effects, 99–104
  management, 194–196
  medical features, 43
  "one-off" episode, 190
  overreporting, 47
  prediction/prevention, 89–93, 193, 194,
    198
  treatment, 93–96, 189–198
Child Abuse and Neglect (journal), 44
Childbirth, mother's recollection of,
  139–140, 187
Child labor reform, 42
Child protection agencies, 43, 47, 53
Childrearing attitudes, of abused children,
  155–156
Children. *See also* Infants
  abused (*see* Children, abused)
  failure-to-thrive, 25–28, 36, 106–107,
    108–109, 127–128, 132, 150–157 *passim*,
    164–178 *passim*, 181–185
  interviews with, 150–157
  parental expectations of, 143–147, 180,
    181, 185–186, 188
  psychological testing of, 163–178
Children, abused, 80–84, 106–107, 109–111,
  127, 180–181, 184–185
  behavior, 81, 82–83, 84, 173–177, 181, 183
  contribution to abuse, 84, 185
  development of, 99–104
  follow-up study of, 99–104, 150–157
    passim, 164–178 *passim*
  handicapped, 82
  health of, 82
  needs of, 81, 104, 190, 191
  parents' perception of, 81–82, 192
  psychological testing of, 163–178
  treatment of, 94–96
Children, neglected, 46, 103
Children's Trust Funds, 198
Coagulation studies, 60
Coleman, R. W., 6
Collingwood, J., 77–78, *78*
Community resources, 32, 194
Conger, R. D., 73, *74*

Criminal background, of abusive parents,
  70–71
Custody, 196

Daniel, J. H., et al., 93
Day care, therapeutic, 95, 96, 185, 197. *See
  also* Preschool
Denial of abuse, by doctors, 58–59
Denver Developmental Screening Test, 102
Deprivation
  emotional/nutritional, 3, 4, 14–17
  maternal, 14, 15, 16, 24
  in mother's childhood, 21
  parental, 24
Deutsch, C. P., 183
Doctors, child abuse and, 48, 58–59, 61
Drash, A. L., *12*
Drowning, 56
Dwarfism, deprivation, 11–14

Earp, J. A., *70*
Easton, P. M., 78, *78*
Education, mother's attitude toward,
  141–143, 185–186, 187. *See also* School
Egeland, B., 80, 91
Egeland, B., et al., 103
Eichler, A., *26, 27, 27, 28*, 183
Elmer, E., 6, 59, *70*, 99, 100–101, *101, 102*,
  180–181, 187
Elmer, E., et al., *26, 33, 35, 36, 37, 38*,
  181–182, 183
Emergency room. *See* Casualty department
Emotional development, of abused children,
  37–39, 102
Emotional problems, 131–132
Employment, in abusive families, 134
English, P. C., 4, 7
Environment, home, 31, 36, 189
Ethical issues, in prediction, 92–93
Evans, A. L., 24, 71, *72*
Evans, S. L., et al., 23, *24*
Evans, W. A., 44
Expectations, parental, 143–147, 180, 181,
  185–186, 188
Eyberg, S. M., 73, *74*
Eye injuries, 56

Factory Act (1802), 42
Failure to thrive (nonorganic), 107, 108–109,
  150–157 *passim*, 164–178 *passim*. *See also*
  Children, failure-to-thrive; Infants,
  failure-to-thrive
  and child abuse, 9

INDEX

205

Failure to thrive (nonorganic) (*continued*)
  clinical features, 7–11
  defined, 3–4, 113
  diagnosis, 4, 7, 8, 9–10
  family studies, 20–28
  historical aspects, 4–6
  incidence, 6–7
  management, 196–197
  outcome, 33–39
  predicting, 24
  treating, 23–24, 31–33, 189
Families, tracing (in follow-up study),
  118–120
Family advocacy programs, 96
Family practitioners, 48, 61. *See also* Doctors
Family problems, 135–136
Family relationships, 136–137, 151
Family structure, 132–134
Fanaroff, A. A., et al., 24
Fathers, 5. *See also* Parents
  abusive, 70–71, 74
  of failure-to-thrive infants, 21–24, 26
  psychological testing of, 158–159, 160
Feeding behavior, 25, 28
Feinstein, A. R., 113
Feshback, N. D., 68–69
Finkelstein, M., *12*
Fischoff, J., et al., 32, 188
Follow-up, 15
  loss to, 116–117, 179
Follow-up study, 106–198
  assessment method, 121–124
  baseline data, 107–112, 115–116
  comparison groups, 114, 120–121
  definitions used, 113–114, 115
  findings, 179–198
  instruments of measurement, 115
  limitations, 115–117
  methodology, 113–115
  psychological testing in, 158–178
  statistical analysis, 114
  tracing families, 118–120
Fontana, V. J., 42, 55
Foster care, 5, 35, 94–95, 195–196, 197
Fotheringham, B. J., 54
Fourth International Congress on Child
  Abuse and Neglect, 50
Fractures, 8–9, 43–44
  skull, 55, 61, 110, 168
Fraiberg, S., 196
Friedlander, B. Z., 183
Friedman, S. B., 48
Friedrich, W. N., 84

Friends, abused children and, 152–153, 156,
  180, 184
Frodi, A. M., 73, *74*
Frude, N., 49–50
Funding, 197

Gaensbauer, T. J., 84
Gagan, R. J., et al., 24
Galdston, R., 80
Gardner, L. I., 6, 33, 34, 106
Geddes, D. C., et al., 91
Gelles, R. J., 49
George, C., 83, *83*
Gil, D. G., 46, 47, 50
Glaser, H. H., et al., 7, 11, 21, 25, *35*, 36, 37,
  38, 183
Gordon, A. H., *26*, *27*, 27–28
Goss, A., 49–50
Graham, H., 49
Green, A. H., 80–81, 82
Green, A. H., et al., 73
Gregg, G. S., 59, 77, 99, 100, *101*
Groothuis, J. R., et al., 82
Growth pattern, 33–35

Hannaway, P., 7
Hanson, R., 56–57
Harris, J. C., 13–14
Hawthorne effect, 116
Haynes, C. F., et al., 192
Head circumference, 10
Head injury, 43, 55, 61, 110, 168
Health
  of abusive parents, 71
  of family, 131–132
Height, 33–35, 121, 150, 156, 181–182
  midparent, 34
Height age, 150, 156–157, 181–182
Helfer, R. E., 46, 47, 48
Helfer, R. E., et al., 59
Hensey, O. J., et al., 95
Herrenkohl, E. C. and R. Y., 82
Hess, A. K., et al., 22, 187–188
History, 8, 10
  developmental, 8
  of pregnancy, labor and birth, 6
  role in diagnosis, 59–60
Holter, J. C., 48
Home, violence in, 49
Home visits, 32, 33, 189, 196, 197
Hopwood, N. J., *12*, 13, 21
Hospitalization, 4–6. *See also* Institutions
  "cachexia" of, 4–5

Hospitalization (*continued*)
role of mother in, 6, 31–32
Housing, 132
Hufton, I. W., *35, 38*
Hunter, R. S., et al., 77, *78*
Hurley, J. R., 73, *74*
Hyman, C. A., 75
Hyman, L. A., 72
"Hypermonitoring, " 191
Hypopituitarism, 11, 13
Hypotonia, 25

Illness, factitious, 57–58
Infancy, mother's recollection of child's, 140–141
Infanticide, 41–42
Infants. *See also* Children
abused, 80–81
early contact and, 79–80
failure-to-thrive, 3, 4–6, 9–10, 15–16, 25–28, 36
hospitalized, 4–6, 31–32
maternal-infant attachment, 25, 27–28, 76–80
premature/low birthweight, 77–79
Ingraham, F. D., 55
Injury (-ies)
bruises, 43, 55, 59–60
burns, 56–57
eye, 56
fractures, 43–44, 55, 61, 110, 168
head, 55, 61, 110, 168
shaking, 55–56
unusual, 57
Institutions, failure to thrive in, 4–6, 15. *See also* Hospitalization
Intellectual development, 35–37, 38–39
Intelligence
of abusive parents, 22, 74–75, 162, 186, 187
of children, 36, 100, 166–169, 180–181, 182–183, 184
head injury and, 168
International Society for the Prevention of Child Abuse and Neglect, 44
Interpersonal relations
of abused children, 83, 151–154
of abusive parents, 73–74, 137–139
Interviews, in follow-up study, 121–122, 127–130
child, 150–157
parent, 130–150

Jacobs, R. A., 22–23, *24,* 33
Jacobson, R. S., 83, *83*
Jameson, J. C., *26, 27,* 27–28
Jeffcoate, J. A., et al., 77, *78*
Juntz, J. M., *70*

Kadushin, A., 69
Kempe, C. H., 46, 47, 48, 52, 59
Kempe, C. H., et al., 41, 44, 53, 54–55
Kempe, R. S., 95
Kempe, R. S., et al., 4, 23, *24*
Kennell, J. H., et al., 76
Kent, J. T., 22–23, *24,* 33
Kinard, E. M., 70, 102, *102,* 180
Klaus, M. H., 76, 79
Klein, M., 77, *78*
Klerman, L. V., *70*
Koel, B. S., 106
Korbin, J., 45, 51–53
Krieger, I., 9, *12, 14*
Kumar, R., 76

Laboratory tests, 6, 10
Lamb, M. E., 73, *74*
Language development, 8, 102, 183
Lauderdale, M. L., 71, *72*
Lauer, B., et al., *70*
Lay health visitor, 33. *See also* Home visits
Leonard, M. F., et al., 8, 21, 25, 32
Leventhal, J. M., 27, 79
Linear growth, 3, 10. *See also* Height
Longstaffe, S. E., 81
Low birthweight, child abuse and, 77–79
Lynch, M. A., *70,* 71, *78,* 79, 81–82, 101, 102, *102,* 104
Lynch, M. A., et al., 89

McCarthy, D., 8, 11
McCarthy Scales of Children's Abilities, 36
McRae, K. N., 81
Main, M., 83, *83*
Malnutrition, 35–36
Maltreatment, patterns of, 103. *See also* Child abuse
Martin, H., 33–34, *35,* 100, *101*
Martin, H. P., 84, 100, *101*
Martin, H. P., et al., 99, *101*
Martin, J. A., 69
Matson, D. D., 55
Measurement, physical, 121
Mellinger, R. C., *12, 14*
Melnick, B., 73, *74*

INDEX

207

Michigan Screening Profile of Parenting, 75
Minnesota Multiphasic Personality Inventory (MMPI), 75
Mitchell, W. G., et al., *26, 27, 27,* 28, 34, *35, 36,* 38, *38,* 182, 183
Moore, B. G., 81, 93, 95
Morse, A. E., et al., 96
Morse, C. W., et al., 100, *101,* 180
Mother(s), 6, 130–150 *passim. See also* Parents
  abusive (*see* Mothers, abusive)
  of failure-to-thrive infants, 21–24, 31–33, 109, 160–163, 187–188, 190
  high-risk, 90, 91–93
  of newborns, 49
  role during hospitalization, 6, 31–32
Mothers, abusive, 32, 72–73, 111–112, 158–160, 162, 163
  age of, 69, 111, 130–131
  own childhood, 21, 68–69, 112, 147–150, 186
  self-esteem of, 71–72
Mother-infant interaction, 24, 31, 33, 73, 191. *See also* Attachment; Bonding
Motor function, 8
Murphy, J. F., et al., 90
Mushin, A. S., 56

National Society for the Prevention of Cruelty to Children (N.S.P.C.C.), 100, *101*
Neglect, 46, 103
Neonatal separation, 79
Newson, J. and G., 45
Nixon, J., et al., 70
Notification, compulsory, 47, 53–54, 193
Nutrition, 3, 6, 14–17

Oates, R. K., *35, 38*
Oates, R. K., et al., *102*
O'Connor, S., 79
O'Connor, S., et al., 91
Oliver, J. E., 48, 72, 74–75
Ory, M. G., 70
Over-reporting, 47
Owen, Robert, 42

Parents, 130–150 *passim. See also* Fathers; Mothers; Parents, abusive
  of abused children (*see* Parents, abusive)
  expectations of, 143–147, 180, 181, 185–186, 188
  of failure-to-thrive children, 20–24, 109, 187–188

psychological testing of, 158–163, 173–177
social class of, 20–22, 61, 70, 89–90, 101, 109
Parents, abusive, 111–112, 185–187
  age of, 69, 111, 130–131
  characteristics, 68–76
  criminal background, 70–71
  health, 71
  intelligence, 74–75, 162, 186
  parental background, 68–69, 112, 147–150, 186
  perception of child, 81–82, 192
  personality testing of, 75–76
  psychiatric disorders in, 32, 72–73
  self-esteem and, 71–72
  social class, 61, 69, 70, 112
  support for, 94
  treatment of, 93–94, 95–96, 104
Parents Anonymous, 94
Patton, R. G., 6, 33, 34, 106
Paulson, M. J., et al., 75
Pawl, J. H., 194
Pearn, J. H., 56
Peel, Sir Robert, 42
Perinatal period, mother's recollection of, 140–141, 187
Personality tests, 75–76
Physical characteristics, 150–151
Physical examination, 8–9, 59–60
Physicians. *See* Doctors
Piers, E. V., 123
Piers-Harris Children's Self-Concept Scale, 123, 163, 165–166, 180
Pituitary insufficiency, 11–14
Poisoning, 57–58
Polansky, N. A., et al., 187
Pollitt, E., *26, 27, 27,* 28, 183
Pollitt, E., et al., 22
Pollock, C. B., 70, 71, 72, 74
Powell, G. F., et al., *12,* 13, 31
Prader, A., et al., 34
Pregnancy, 109
  mother's recollection of, 116, 139–141, 187
Prematurity, 77–79
Preschool, therapeutic, 185, 193, 197. *See also* Day care
Pringle, M. K., 190
Provence, S., 6
Psychiatric disorders, in abusive parents, 72–73
Psychological tests, 122–124, 158–178. *See also* names of tests
Punishment, vs. abuse, 45, 50

208   CHILD ABUSE AND NEGLECT

Radiology, 58, 60–61
Recall, maternal, 116, 139–141, 179–180, 187
Reidy, T. J., 82–83, *83*
Reinhardt, J. B., *12*
Reporting, mandatory, 47, 53–54, 193
Richardson, S. A., 36
Roberton, D. M., 60
Roberts, J., *70, 78*, 79, 101, 102, *102,* 104
Robertson, B. A., *70*
Robson, K. M., 76
Rooming-in, 79–80
Rosen, B., 71, *72,* 94
Rosenberg, N. M., et al., 92
Rosenn, D. W., et al., 9–10, 25
Rutter, M., 16, 25, 39, 104, 123, 183
Rutter's Children's Behavior Questionnaire,
      123, 164, 173–177, 181, 183

Sanders, R. W., 59
Sands, K., 84
Sargent, D. A., 9
Schmitt, B. D., 55, 93
Schonell, A. J. and F. E., 123, 169
Schonell Reading Age, 163, 169–171
Schonell Word Recognition Test, 123
School, child's attitude toward, 153, 157,
      182. *See also* Education
Self-esteem
   of abused children, 165–166, 177, 180,
      182, 186
   of abusive parents, 71–72
Sexual abuse, 186
Shaheen, E., 32
Shaheen, E., et al., 6–7, 26
Shaking injures, 55–56
Shorkey, C. T., 71, *72*
Siblings
   of abused children, 78–79, 82, 102, 104
   assessment of, 191
   of failure-to-thrive infants, 25–26, 37, 107,
      109
Siegel, E., et al., 80, 91
Sills, J., et al., 69
Sills, R. H., 7, 8
Silver, C. B., et al., 59
Silver, H. K., *12*
Silverman, F. N., 44, 55
Skinner, A. E., 69
Smith, S. M., 56–57
Smith, S. M., et al., *70,* 70–71, 72–73, 74, 75
Social ability, 8, 25. *See also* Social
   interaction

Social class
   child abuse and, 61, 89–90, 101, 179
   of parents, 20–22, 61, 69, 109, 112
Social interactions, 9–10
   of abused children, 83
   of abusive parents, 73–74, 137–139
Social isolation, 133, 187
Social maturity, 123, 163, 171–172, 181, 184
Society for the Prevention of Cruelty to
      Children, 43
Solomon, T., 69
Somatomedins, 14
Speedwell Society, 5
Speight, A. N. P., et al., 96
Spitz, R., 5, 14–15
Steele, B. F., 68, 70, 71, 72, 74
Stein, M. T., 71, *72,* 94
Stern, L., 77, *78*
Stone, N. N., et al., 57
Straker, G., 83, *83*
Straus, M. A., 45, 47, 49
Stress, and child abuse, 50–51
Subdural hematomas, 43, 55, 110, 168
Sudden infant death syndrome, 58
Supervision, parental, 144–145, 146,
      171–172, 186

Taitz, L. S., 104
Talbot, N. B., et al., 11
Tanner, J. M., et al., 121
Tardieu, A., 43
Teacher, child's, 123, 173–174, 177, 184, 187.
      See also Education
   mother's contact with, 141–143, 185–186,
      187
Telephone in home, 133–134, 186–187
Thompson, R. G., 16
Thorpe, R., 195
Togut, M. R., et al., 3–4, 21
Treatment
   of abused child, 94–96
   of abusive parents, 93–94, 95–96
   joint program, 95–96
Trowell, J., 103–104
Twins, abuse of, 82

Ultrasound, 60

Vaughan, B., 80
Verbal Language Development Scale, 123,
      164, 172–173
Videotaping, 191

INDEX

Vineland Social Maturity Scale, 123, 163, 171–172
Violence, in society, 49–51
Volunteers, 33, 94, 194. *See also* Home visits

Wechsler, D., 123
Wechsler Adult Intelligence Scale (WAIS), 74
Wechsler Intelligence Scale for Children—Revised (WISC-R), 123, 163, 166–169, 180–181
Wechsler Preschool and Primary Scale of Intelligence (WPPSI), 123, 163, 166

Weight, 10, 33–34, 121, 150, 156, 181
Weight age, 150–151, 156–157, 181–182
Weight gain, 3, 10–11, 31
West, S., 43
Whiten, A., 76
Whitten, C. F., et al., 15, 16
Widowson, E. M., 15
Williams, H. E., 6
Winick, M., et al., 36
Woolley, P. V., 44

Yates, A., 81